Whose Boy Be You?

Published by Ben Thacher 2007
East Dennis, Massachusetts
Copyright © 2007

TABLE OF CONTENTS

CHAPTER ONE

If You Care For Sand Dunes

The "quaint little villages" are now mostly · cluster housing, condominiums, motels and usually unoccupied trophy homes (read summer palaces) which mask most of the ocean view. A good many of the sand dunes are parking lots. Don't look for lobster stew, those birds are far too dear to stick in chowder, and our salt sea air, the environmental people say, is some of the most polluted in the country. It has something to do with particulates that blow over from main land industrial areas, local traffic and our own filthy Canal Electric plant. The roads, which used to wind have been straightened, curbed, and lead to shopping centers, and you're more likely to see the sun SET over Cape Cod Bay, which body of water lies to the north and west of much of the Cape.

I miss the Cape Cod where most houses had an attic containing remnants of seafaring days, and big old barns had old sleighs and wagons tucked in their walk-in cellars, and harness hung by the recently used stalls, and a mow perhaps still full of soft old hay for kids to jump in, and burrow under. That Cape was a great place to be a kid. You could take a short cut across a neighbor's lawn without fear of a scolding, more apt to get a cookie and a kind remark. You could wander most anywhere without alarming the parents because every one knew whose child you were, and turned you away from any dangerous enterprise. ("You, boy, stand away from that horse, he bites!")

I miss the home folks with just off-mainland New England accents, laced with phrases of sometimes-odd construction: "Whose boy be you?"…."He's a caution!", "If you get into them cookies, you'll know it!" and "Yes Yes" for affirmative, "No No" for negative (some say this last is a reflection of the nautical "Ay Ay," what with the long tradition of sending huge numbers of Cape men folk off on the oceans of the world).

Dad once described a stout woman as being "six ax handles across the arse" and an overly flirty girl was "No better than she should be" and would "Get her come-up-ance!" Sister Nancy reminded me of a bit of typically Cape Cod speech: "If you go down to the post office, I want you should bring me back a stamp."

When Uncle Fredson married a girl named "Edith", to identify her instead of his sister Edith, the new wife became "Edith Fredson", and thus was she known for all the years I knew her.

I miss hanging for a bit, often the only kid amongst a group of local men, near the post office stove while Mr. Bayles sorted the mail into the various boxes. Unwritten rule, NOBODY opened their box until the postmaster said "That's all, boys," (like not picking up your cards until the dealer is finished) then a movement to take out their flat box keys, get their mail, casual good byes, and off we'd all go. Used to be you could get some prime remarks down to (not "at") the post office, to the fire station or at the recess held at the midway mark during Town Meeting nights. Many of the most interesting comments tended to be a bit salty, but the ladies put in their two bits. An elderly woman who lived beside one of my brother's cranberry bogs called out to him as he worked on the vines, "You, Boy, you don't drink nor swear nor smoke none, do ya?" "No, Ma'am," sez he, tongue firmly in cheek. "Well then you're a good boy, come in and have a cookie!" An older lady began a phone conversation with me recently by stating, "I'll tell you who this is so you'll know!" Describing one of the salty talkers, "He don't talk fit to eat!", if some boy was talking when he should have been listening, "Hark you head, boy!", and one who "strayed" would "Come to no good end."

I miss the easyness of the Cape when many front "lawns" were not cut until the grass was long enough to be used for hay and then mowed with a long bladed, rhythmically swinging hand scythe. When many of the roads were still unpaved, and even some of the better traveled were of cinders, seashells, or sand (sand was easier on bare feet). When a panting steam train shifted cars at the lumberyard siding near our house, and took the mail and passengers back and forth to Boston, Hyannis and Provincetown morning and afternoon. You could take the train to Hyannis for shopping, and the Hyannis main street like most village centers on the Cape was bordered with Great Elms that arched over the street and during the summer in many areas, their leafy tops came together over the road to form a cool, green cave.

I miss the quiet Cape when motor noises were rare, almost no powerboats on the river and no incessant grind of highway traffic to mask the sounds of nature and living. You could hear wood being chopped back in the woods, children playing two houses down and my Mother's cowbell could summon us to supper from half a mile away. Automobile traffic was almost unheard of at night, and widely spaced even in the day.

Linwood Robins (left) driving around neighborhood kids.

The advent of a car on our street could make you look as it had been quite a while since the last one. Each spring, some time after the pink winks had begun their pond chorus, and again in the fall before it chilled, as the gold, red and brown leaves began to pepper the still green grasses, Linwood Robins' Model 'A' Ford would make an appearance on our street. It was an event not to be missed. Linwood had cows, usually a dozen or more, and he summered them on the open meadows of the north side of the Cape. Their winter home was in Dennisport, on the south side, a trip of about 10 miles.

Linwood would tie his lead cow to the back of the Ford, and very slowly persuade her, with the rest of the herd following, to make the trek across the Cape. He set his Ford to proceed at a cow's pace, and rode along with the door open stopping often to dissuade the herd from denuding bushes and front lawns as they passed. The animals seemed to take it in their stride, waddling along chewing their cud, with an occasional pause to collect a new mouth full. Just another cattle drive accomplished with little or no disruption of traffic, and no noise louder than the whisper of the autumn wind, and the laughter of excited children to scare the cows.

ON MEMORY

I deal with memories more these days.
Not living in the past,
More like enjoying little plays,
With my own all-star cast.

Some reminiscence, vague and frail,
Of folks I used to know.
Grows like a half remembered tale,
Or television show.

I think on friends and happy parts,
On things that make me smile,
If thoughts of time less pleasant starts,
I promptly switch the dial.

Each fragment needs a gentle touch,
I join them, row on row,
And fill out times and scenes and such
The deeper down I go.

The mind files every dream and ghost,
Age teaches us to use it,
Then, just when we enjoy it most,
Why, we commence to lose it.

CHAPTER TWO

Cape Cod Boys They Have No Sleds

Cape Cod boys kept their blood lines from getting too pure by marrying out-landers. Nearly every imported young girl teacher needed replacing by the end of the school year as the locals snapped them up for brides: sometimes they didn't make it through till spring. Mother got here on another route. A dark haired beauty, (once Miss Salem, Mass., with a cup to prove it) she had natural curls, a wonderful complexion and rosy cheeks which won her a job selling cosmetics in a Salem Department store. The boss wouldn't believe she didn't use rouge (which she didn't) and thought she would be a good ad for the product.

She became a hairdresser, worked in Salem and Boston, and was offered a job on the Cape in Hyannis. Her housing was arranged at a small inn here in South Dennis, just a stone's throw from the Post Office, run by-Guess who?? Yep, Pappy!! A combination of her own short hair, and her proficiency at the latest cut, the "Boyish Bob" earned her the nickname of "Bobby". Skirts just a tad shorter then the local style, stockings rolled down below the knee, I'll warrant; a real flapper, a Jazz baby! Word was, several fellows were "hangin'" at the P.O. when father first waited on this new city girl, and after she left, asked his opinion.

"She," goes the story of Dad's reply, "Can park her shoes under my bed anytime!"

Mother would have won Mrs. World in a motherhood contest. She not only fed, nursed us, bathed and dressed us and kept up the house around us in that age of prim-itive house keeping aids, (no microwave!) but found time to read to us extensively each night. Her love gave us a head start in the 'getting along in the world' department and laid a foundation for friendship between us kids which has seldom faltered during the seventy plus years since Nancy and I were the only two.

A very forthright and moral woman, it was none the less she who told me of the "Corset Checking" which took place at dances in her heyday. Grandma, (we called her Nana) as with other mothers of the times, insisted that daughters wear their corsets, with their metal or whalebone stays, when dressing to go out. Problem was, dances, like the Charleston, the Turkey Trot, the Camel, the Bunny Hug, etc. were very active, and just couldn't be danced in a "suit of armor;" besides, if you wore your corset, boys called you things like "Old Iron Sides". SO, ladies room, corset off, and in a brown paper bag, and CHECKED in the coatroom until after the last dance!

Father, the postmaster (for a short while), was country. He had been around a bit, traveled selling shoes, cut meat for S.S. Pierce in Boston, and spent some years building booths and such for exhibition halls in several cities from Chicago east. For all his travels, he never became overly sophisticated, and Nana in Salem used to warn him on each visit to turn the gas lights off, not blow them out as we did the kerosene lights on the Cape. Of course he knew better, but she liked to "rag" him in a good humored manner, as he did her. They were good friends.

Dad was pretty well educated for the Cape in his day; wrote a fine hand, and graduated from High School with excellent marks in spite of having missed lots of school for work. During cranberry harvests each fall, his family moved to temporary quarters around Onset and Wareham for a few weeks picking which extended into the school year, and sometimes he drove team for his Father, wagon or sleigh depending on season. It was his adventures as driver which, as much as anything else, kept me from ever having a horse.

The sleigh thing confused me; there were a couple down under the big barn at my grandfather's house. Brought up on the Cape when some winters didn't bring enough snow before February for a good sledding party, I wondered, why a working sleigh? Well, seems when they had early

snow in Dad's youth they didn't try to remove it from the road, but rolled it down hard and traveled over it by sleigh. A huge heavy roller, pulled by oxen did the job, and as subsequent storms added more snow, that was also rolled to make a good base, which stayed until spring thaw. Apparently it even became hard and slick enough to skate on.

As I was walking to South Yarmouth one day when I was about 12, an elderly man with a cane stopped me. "Oy, whose boy be you?"

"Freeman Thacher's boy, from over in South Dennis," I replied.

"Freeman, now, he was Charlie' boy, warn't he?" I had never heard my grandfather, Charles referred to as 'Charlie', but I replied in the affirmative.

"Oh yes, I remember seeing Charlie Thacher skating down to the post office on his acorn skates!" said the old fellow as he ambled off.

I thought it was funny, and later told mother. She went to the attic and brought down the acorn skates! They had a wooden foot shaped center, a short screw on the back part, which twisted into the heel of your boot, leather straps to secure them and a long runner of steel which extended back beyond the boot heel and curled up in front like the toe on an elf's shoe. It was capped with a small brass acorn!

But, I digress, as I often do. It's true; some winters were colder back in my youth, as well as in Dad's. In fact, I just lately heard a man on the weather station concede that weather in the 1930's was more given to extremes than recently. I know that during the winter of '33/'34 the sea froze clear from the Cape to Nantucket. They said someone walked across from Falmouth to the Vineyard, and they cut ice most winters on the various lakes and large ponds. Anson Howes had an ice house at Scargo Lake and as a boy I remember Dad taking me over there to buy some rock salt. I guess the ice cutters used salt in large quantities on walk ways to keep them safe to work on (along with ice crampons on their shoes when they were out on the lake). Men cut the ice into large rectangular pieces with long ice saws, hooked the cakes with giant Tongs attached to the harness of an ox or mule, and dragged them to the ice house. The ice was stacked high and insulated with sawdust (or I seem to remember, sometimes shredded newspaper, like the insulated ice cream bags). With layers of ice, and insulation up to the eves, the building was closed until warm weather and the ice was sold to fishing boats to keep their catch fresh. This went on even after the establishment of ice plants which manufactured ice year 'round.

Another digression, though a slight one. An ox, they said, was better than a mule for this work as the mule was too smart, and objected to working out on the ice. Linwood Robins told me of a blind mule that his father owned, who didn't seem to care where he was. Linwood, as a boy, was working the ice, when his father had to leave for a bit. His parting words, "Boy, watch that mule," were too soon forgotten, and as Lin's mind and eyes wandered, the mule also wandered; to the edge of the ice and over into the frigid water. That caught Lin's attention, and he yelled for help. The men got ropes on the mule, and managed to get him back up on the ice. They blanketed him, poured brandy down his throat, and led him coughing and wheezing up to the barn. Lin's father called him over near the ice-edge, and promptly, "Kicked me right in arse," said Lin; right into that icy lake. He was promptly pulled out, and blanketed, but not brandied.

"Now," said his father, "When I tell you to watch an animal, you do it!" And, Linwood did.

Freeman Thacher's graduation class

Even into his old age, he kept horses, gently, often buying some old nags at auction (headed for the glue factory, as they used to say,) and letting them live out their lives on his Dennisport farm.

Linwood, with horses and then later a tractor, used to plow and harrow Dad's garden most springs (which is by way of getting back to my family). Dad was quite a farmer. Stand him on a patch of black ground with a hoe and some seed, and by golly you'd have veggies. He also kept chickens, and harvested the produce of the Crow Pasture, Bass River, and the tidal flats on Cape Cod Bay. Mother canned and cooked, and their combined efforts kept us eating - well - thru all of the depression and WW II. "All" came to mean six young'uns before they got through, and then, when I should have been old enough to know better, I brought them home my first born, and he and I stayed for some years, just so they wouldn't think they were getting off too easily.

Dad's idea of relaxation after a hard day of whatever, (he was a jack of most all trades, and after his stint as postmaster, pounded nails, painted, wall papered, managed an experimental hen farm, was town tree warden, shucked oysters, and briefly, ran a potato chip business) was to dig a mess of quahogs, and usher in the darkness working in his garden. Sundays, he delivered the *Boston Sunday Post*, house to house, went to the dump, worked around home, cut wood for the winter and during the heat of summer, found some excessively hot area in a field or meadow, and picked blueberries. Sometimes with me, or all of us in tow. I found the picking arduous, but the "blueberry grunt" delicious.

CAPE CLIME

If you delight
In perfect skies,
A sun that daily
Seems to rise,
Sweet days
Of seasonal delights,
Sparkling, cloudless,
Star-lit nights,
If such a clime
Excites you, dear,
Then why on earth
Did you move here?

CHAPTER THREE

Sonny Boy

I be a Cape Codder, by birth and inclination. My roots in this sand go back to 1639 on my father's side. The first Thacher on the Cape was delegated, along with two other men, to trek down to what are now known as the towns of Yarmouth and Dennis with a King's warrant to dispense parcels of land to would-be settlers -provided they worshiped in the proper manner. It comes to about 10 generations of Thachers on Cape Cod, down to me, and what with children and grand children, it looks like our family's stay here is more than just an overnighter.

I was born at home, with Father as CEO, and Mother as the labor force. Pop, I'm told cut the ribbon, tied the knot, and had every thing ship shape before the doctor arrived. Typical Cape Cod medicine of the time, what few doctors there were made their way from house to house, between holding office hours in the front rooms of their homes. "Horse and buggy" doctors in Fords. The doctor congratulated the new parents, made note that every one seemed in good health took his medical bag, and split. I was their only, (at the time) as they had lost a previous child. Dad always said my arrival saved Mother's life. Fair enough, I guess I drove her nuts often enough, but that was later.

April 1928, the year Shirley Temple was born, and they elected Herbert Hoover. I missed April Fools by five days and I have been late ever since. 1928, 14 years after they first let the water flow through the Cape Cod Canal, cutting the last ties to the main land. It was the year they began using the "100" stocks to figure the Dow Jones average (in case you wondered) and Walt Disney introduced Mickey in a cartoon called 'Steamboat Willie'. Al Jolson was warbling "Sonny Boy" in a very early "Talkie". About a year and a half later, the stock market went all to pieces. Variety said the 'Wall Street laid an egg' and the world came down with the worst case of postpartum blues in history.

Our house sat on a small triangle of land in South Dennis bordered by Upper County Road, the Great Western Road and a seldom-used dirt track, Duck Pond Road, on the third side. Don't look for it, later construction of a four-lane road, Route 134, wiped the whole place out. I was born just about under one of the overhead traffic lights. The triangle was commodious enough to hold a barn with a oyster shucking shed attached to the back, a hen yard, Dad's large garden, the house and outhouse. There were a few scrub pines (one of which held a raggedy tree hut, complete with climbing steps nailed to the tree) and a large grove of lilac bushes. A few of the lilacs remain beside the road, the only thing left of my birthplace.

The house had a hand pump (no other plumbing), an ice box and was heated by a wood fire. Washing, of clothes and, on Saturday evening, of small bodies, required that hand pumped water, heated over the wood stove, then placed in a round galvanized washtub, and the subjects, or objects as 'twere, be dunked and scrubbed by hand. Scads of newspaper surrounded the tub in an effort to control spillage. On cold nights, the wood stove would be well stocked and roaring before the kid dunking began, and the oven door swung open. Two soapstone bed warmers with handles were put in the oven to heat, or when we grew more numerous than the available soapstones, bricks and sad irons were added. The hot objects were wrapped in flannel, and put in the beds, down around where your feet land. On the oven door, Mother hung towels and p.j... so you could pop out of the tub and into something warm on the way to bed.

The oven cooked unevenly, but it was great for warming stuff. Mom even tried making her own soap, once, out of grease drippings and wood ashes (potash). It was a tad harsh for little hides, but I guess did all right for laundry. In time, we acquired a used electric washing machine with a hand-cranked wringer that had to be pulled up to the sink to drain. It handled the clothes, but not the tots. One-step forward.

Dad's Store and Post Office

Mother cooked on the wood burning stove and did wonderful things with pies, cakes, peanut butter straws and bread in a portable oven, which sat over the main firebox. Her bread was out of this world, and she often left some dough to rise over night and fried it in the morning. When we smelled and heard that kettle of lard sputtering we wasted no time in getting to the breakfast table. Mother also knocked out a fine stew, and did appetizing things with what Dad raised and with his various seafood harvests. She was a general good cook and household keeper under what even then in other parts of the country were considered primitive conditions. Because of our parents' hard work, we kids never knew we had lived through a depression until we read about it in High School.

The depression, which clobbered the country and the world during the thirties, had a peculiar effect on Cape Cod. Before, and slightly after the Civil War, the Cape's prosperity had depended largely on the ocean, and sail. The development of steam ships and the railroad put a big crimp in the sail business. Steam engines moved products with great speed. Small local factories gave way to the large operations, which could sell their products for much less, and now could deliver them with ease. Even the salt making business, which involved the slow distillation of salt from seawater, faded as salt mines were opened in up state New York.

Owners of sailing vessels could not compete, and they began to sell their ships, and 'come ashore'. This meant less work for the Cape's young men, and they drifted away to the cities to seek their fortunes. By the late twenties, the Town of Dennis had only about 1200 citizens (current population, in excess of 15,000- triple that in the summer), there was little work, the Cape was financially depressed before the 1929 crash and stayed that way in the bad years which followed. What work was available was seasonal and part time. Cranberries, tending them in the spring/summer, picking the berries in the fall, manning alewife weirs for a few short weeks in the spring when the alewife/herring came from the sea into the local ponds to spawn, fishing (when the weather permitted), and a small but growing visitor trade. Most of the "summer people" were house owners, or rented from absentee owners. The visitors generally came for the season, rather than just a weekend, and by train. The summer places did need care and up keep, and the visitors needed local services so there was apt to be some work in the summer. Winters were a disaster. There might be ice to cut, or wood to chop, and that was about it. Stores and other businesses that did some winter trade had to wait until spring for payment.

Father rented space for a small store, and kept the village Post Office. When the bills (unpaid) piled up past a certain level, the postmaster's wages became less than adequate, and Father had to sell the store, cease posting letters, and join the chase after what few jobs there were.

When the Roosevelt work projects began to employ people in depressed areas, the Cape towns received money for several municipal projects, many local men including Dad benefited from the grants. Dennis repaired roads, built some sidewalks, and did a large amount of tree work. Courtesy of a WPA paycheck, local workers cut many of the diseased Elms along the roads, and started a Town forest of white pine. Father was tree warden for a while, and had a job dispensing the Government surplus food that F.D.R.'s 'New Deal' gave out. Cape kids had grapefruit and oranges that had never been part of their diet before. Mother used to say that it was the first time in years that Cape men had work and pay checks in the winter.

As kids, we had chores to do around the house as soon as we were big enough. There were hens to feed, gardens which grew a fine crop of weeds along with the vegetables, stove wood needed to be brought in, and Mom's chores could always use another hand. Dishwashing, setting tables and keeping house, generally. When I was about six, Dad let me take some excess vegetables in my cart to see if the neighbors could use them. I do not believe he thought of payment, but I came back with a tidy sum. After that, I went out daily, widened my field, and came up with cash enough to buy some of my school clothes for first grade. Dad never took any of the proceeds, although he performed the harvest, on top of the growing. He usually did have a small table of "Garden Fresh" out in front of the house . . . sold a lot, too. One gentleman, (here summers only) owner of a boy's camp, Camp Bonny Doone on the Yarmouth side of Bass River, used to do his own picking. He arranged with Dad to let him come into the garden just after daylight for cucumbers. Said he preferred them "with the dew on them." Always left a quarter, Dad was happy.

THE POND

I don't think I've been by the pond since she froze,
Been staying to home keeping warm, heavens knows,
But missing a lot I so used to enjoy,
Of the chill wint'ry world that I knew as a boy.

The woods were right quiet and standing, alone,
I felt an old urging to heave out a stone,
And watch it go skittering over the slick
To splash where the spring-hole feeds into the crick.

I dare say the young ones are skating here still,
Complete with the bonfire under the hill.
How pleasant to sit there enjoying the heat,
While strapping the runners on tight to our feet.

The pond has grown smaller, the winds a bit colder,
Or maybe I'm taller, and just
a mite older.

CHAPTER FOUR

How Dry I Am

In one of the villages on the lower Cape there are bumper stickers describing the area as "A Quiet Drinking Village with a Fishing Problem". Pretty much right, on both counts. Due to a shortage of fish, and subsequent government regulations the fishing industry, already in trouble, has diminished even further. Cape Cod is short of codfish. As to drinking, the bent elbow and open mouth has been with us as long as the fish. There was no Cranberry sauce at the first Thanksgiving, but there was beer, brandy, wine and gin! Some Sauce! As one who gently partakes of fermented beverage on occasion, (only on days which end with the letter "Y", and then paying careful attention to the sun's position relative to the yardarm) I have for years been interested in the higher than average imbibing which seems to take place here on Ye Old Peninsular. This interest is natural, after all, I note that ancestor 'One' of the Cape Cod Thachers, Parson Anthony, was appointed not only the Local 'marrying Sam', dispenser of land and long time town treasurer, but also inspector of anchors, bullets and booze, which give him plenty to inspect. (I am sure the shape of the Cape has nothing to do with anything, but note that Cape Cod does resemble an arm with bent elbow.)

A psychology teacher who taught evenings at Cape Cod Community College some years back (she was a full professor at, I think, Emanuel College and an assistant Professor at Harvard, a difficult position for a women to attain in those days) told us she had researched the subject of our local consumption of alcohol, which is more than the national average. She thought one reason was the "easy" life style. People here seemed to be less apt to involve themselves in their neighbors' activities, acceptant, I think she said, busy enough with what went on in their own homes; let the person next door do what he will, as long as he does it over there. Any way, people who had habits or lifestyles which did not always jive with their old neighborhoods (like maybe sipping too much or working too little) could move to Cape Cod and slide by with fewer or no problems. You could see it, years back, by driving through a village. An extremely neat, well-kept area might contain one or several old, or somewhat run down homes, less carefully tended, littered with the owners possessions and perhaps an unregistered, undriveable hulk of a car in the back yard. There did not seem to be much concern about the condition of your house diminishing the re-sale value of my house. Of course, back then, most folks were not much interested in selling, anyway.

The unusual working conditions probably contributed to both the acceptant attitude, and the alcohol consumption. In the days of sailing ships (which employed a huge portion of the Cape's able-bodied males), men returned from a voyage and, as the saying went, "added a room to the house, got their wife pregnant, and went back to sea." In between times, the need for male companionship, and the dry nature of the months - sometimes years at sea, certainly called for raising a mug with other sailors at the neighborhood groggery, or tipping a jug with friends around the hearth.

From the early days, fishing has been a Cape mainstay, and as it depends on reasonable weather, many a foul day or dense fog bank has led men away from their boats toward the local pub. Then, due to the seasonal nature of the Cape, being out of work or between jobs was not a remarkable condition. Reason enough, said the Professor, for some who were dissatisfied with their own more restrictive communities to migrate to Cape Cod and bring their drinking habits with them.

The U.S. went 'dry' in 1920, (I had nothing to do with it.) Of course, the prohibition against manufacture and consumption of alcohol was not a new thing to Cape Cod. Even with the generally more acceptant life style abstinence, temperance and prohibition church groups were here in abundance, but so was booze. A main cross roads on the north-south track across the Cape from the north side Packet Landing at Corporation Wharf to West Dennis was (and still is to old timers) known as Rum Crossing. During the days when coast-wise sailing packets docked and did business at the Corporation Docks in the north of Dennis, money was handed, clandestinely, to the morning northbound stage driver, and the evening stage would halt briefly at the dark corner to roll down a barrel of spiritus frumenti to waiting hands.

In the hay day of salt production along the Dennis shores, ox and horse teams carried the salt from the various salt works to the packet landing in Dennis village. It became customary for the packet Captain to leave a jar of water, a jar of sugar, and a jar of rum near the main mast of the ship which was being loaded for the refreshment of the ox team drivers and often while the salt wagons were being un-loaded, the drivers were taking a load on. This custom when discovered horrified and was halted by reform groups.

The town fathers posted rules at an early town meeting requesting that no liquor be sold near the hall during the noon recess, as it was too difficult to gather a quorum for the afternoon session.

During one of the "dry" periods, a leading citizen of the town was suspected of storing liquor at home, but an investigation found nothing but some empty liquor bottles in his

cellar. Asked how they got there, he answered, "I can't say, I never bought an empty liquor bottle in my life."

My brother in law prizes a bottle he discovered out on a sand flat while pursuing the wily sea clam just a few years ago, but most of the prohibition alkey has been drunk, or vanished. One of the last caches of prohibition liquor from the National, (Constitutional) dry years was discovered by accident a few years back when a group of workmen started to clean out a dry cistern which had in earlier days caught and held water for use watering crops, or for household use in dry times. On removing the cover (certainly, for the first time since the early thirty's) the men discovered a large quantity of full bottles bearing labels in French. There and then, a grave mistake was made. One conscientious workman proudly showed a bottle to the Boss, and described the find. He forgot that this boss was a dedicated teetotaler. On his direction, the crew (no "drys", they) had to stand mournfully watching as the company bulldozer crushed the bottles of what was probably fine French Brandy, and filled in the cistern with sand.

Dad tried his hand at making home brew at least once. He expected a group of friends to visit from Salem, Mother's childhood home, so knowing the visitors liked to raise a convivial glass; he pulled out the washtub, brewed, and carefully following the directions which came with the hops (these by the way you could buy openly.)

Directions read, "Warning, don't do this and that, you may end up with illegal beer!" He mixed, aged, bottled (used Mom's root beer bottles and caps) and stored the brew. When the guests came, Father proudly presented the beer, which, I fear was a bit

...ed to give ...ome bot- ...had put ...ice all but ...urple liq- ...chen ... ...nd bottle. ...le guest, ...his beer, ...hat grape ...it, or the ...ry big in ... in those prohibition years. Although the friendly bootlegger on the corner was a folksy character in many communities, big, bad organized crime was back there making large dollars on the illegal Alkey, with gang wars over territory, killings and for the unwary drinker, the possibility of sickness or even death from bad booze. In spite of, or maybe because of, the ills of Prohibition, liquor figured in much of the entertainment of the times...not just drinking, but also in jokes, funny post cards, movies and songs. Bert Williams, who was the only Afro-American to make it as a Broadway star of that day (in the Ziegfeld Follies) made big hits with songs such as "Everybody Wants The Key To My Cellar", and dozens of phonograph records featured liquor oriented numbers-pro or con. "I Never Knew I had a Wonderful Wife, Until The Town Went Dry", "Alcoholic Blues", "How Are You Going To Wet Your Whistle (When the whole darn world goes dry)". On the negative side, "Jakey Ginger Blues" which told of drinking Ginger when you could not get rye (it could destroy your nervous system and was about as deadly as the poisonous 'rot-gut' wood alcohol). Temperance songs, "The Drunkard's Daughter", "The Brewer's Big Horses", "Don't Drink, My Boy, Tonight" were unfunny, but popular in their own right.

Mother said the most hilarious skit she had seen in a review at Liberty Hall had several 'hobos' (one of which was my father) gathered around a fake bonfire, telling stories, and passing around a jug, which rumor had it was NOT filled with water. As the jug passed, things got funnier and funnier, wandering far from the show's script. It culminated in this locally composed ditty:

Oh, the moonshine in North Harwich,

Is awful stuff to drink,

And every time I bring it home,

My wife dumps it down the sink,

If I drink it all tomorrow,

Then the next day after that,

Doane and Beal will get me,

In their Big Black Cadillac

Doane and Beal, of course, local undertakers. 'Nough said.

On the radio, former baseball star now preacher Billy Sunday was having his own war against Satan and Demon Rum. He was against the whiskey kings, the German warlords and suffragists. ("You can't pray 'Thy Kingdom Come' and then sit down at some bridge-whist party and look at God through the bottom of a beer mug") but the demon rum flowed on. There were several stills on the Cape, and the gentlemen with black bags were around to make intoxicants available. All over America police and Coast Guard tried (sometimes only half-heartedly) to stem the incoming tide of forbidden alcohol, but on the Cape as well as other coastal areas with multiple rivers, beaches and small bays, the booze just kept sailing in.

Jay Crowell of Dennis Village told of a shipment of liquor washed ashore on the north side beach, most likely thrown over board to avoid a Coast Guard inspection. The Coast Guard was trucking it away while a group of "locals" watched. As the Guardsmen tossed the last of the cases, some complete, some open, into their truck the watchers began to wander off.

One neighbor noted another, clad in an over coat, standing motionless on the beach. "Well, might as well go home." he said. The friend stood still. "I think," he said, being careful not to rattle the bottles stuffed into his boots, shirt and pants concealed beneath the over coat, "I shall wait until the Coast Guard are out of hearing distance, in case I clink."

Dad had a healthy respect for the Law, but when asked by his mother in law to bring her a bottle of whisky on a visit, (for medicinal purposes only) he obliged, and fretted about it all of the long three and a half hour trip from Dennis to Salem. Our car was old, a Willis-Knight Touring Car, with bald tires, a faulty engine, loose snap-in windows, (with isinglass, just like the "Surrey With The Fringe On Top") and weak brakes, which ceased to be effective at a traffic light in Quincy. At a red light on a corner beside the main police station (a police station from which a large number of uniformed officers were then emerging), Dad nearly wrecked the car. He was sure they were on to him for crashing thru the red light and smuggling liquor. They were not, and he did not, but I do not believe any other liquor was transported in that car.

Almost, though. A late night knock at the door one evening turned out to be a neighbor, the Fire Chief. "Freeman," sez he, "Some cases of 'shine' have floated in to West Dennis Beach. Come on, we'll get a couple of bottles for emergencies." They were off, but came back empty handed.

"No luck?" Asked Mom

"No," said Dad, "The Police Chief got there first."

ALCOHOLIC'S ALMANAC

On Cape Cod there's a tendency,
That borders on dependency,
When January's boring
You start right in pouring drinks.
Then as February's drab it
Seems to reinforce the habit,
March titillates more tippling
Than anybody thinks.

April? Cold begins to splinter
Drain a dram for dregs of winter,
All through May you may
Toast hopefully each sunny day ahead.
Often June is wet and mucky
Dry martinis may be lucky
As July is hot and dry, why,
Try a lager beer instead.

August, when the heat is chronic
Wash it down with gin and tonic.
For the harvest month, September
You might well remember wine.
In October, ale is super,
And can cause a lovely stupor.
While November winds are nipping
Sipping brandy will be fine.

As the year begins to wind up,
Have a lot of liquids lined up,
Greet December celebrations
With some strong libations near.
Though each drink may send a shiver
Gently coursing through your liver,
Knowing months of dissipating
Are awaiting you next year

CHAPTER FIVE

Two of Our Pullets Are Missing

It was cold the day the hens disappeared. We heard Dad break the ice from the drinking pail, then stamp through the back room into the kitchen to fill it at the pump.

"Dog or some-damn-thing got two of the pullets."

"Did you check the barn and trees?" As Mother knew, several of our hens were "flyers," given to sleeping elsewhere then on the roosts in the hen house.

"No, there's lots of feathers around, some-damn-thing got them." Father had a fine vocabulary, but there were several working words of the "damn" variety, which got over used when he was provoked. He went off to work, fuming. Jobs were as scarce as hens' teeth, so you did not miss any workdays.

For a small family farm, hens were ideal. The eggs were a food of many uses, from breakfast to Dad's favorite desert custard. Roosters and hens past their prime were meat for the table, and their manure was as fine a fertilizer as ever nurtured a honeydew melon. Table scraps and waste from our abundant summer vegetable garden supplemented by grain nourished them nicely. Hens were cheap to keep, and an important adjunct to our depression diet. These particular hens were special. Normally, we let setting hens from the flock hatch chicks in the spring. We raised the young to fill in for the older birds when they had become a Sunday main dish. This flock was getting older, and in-bred, and Father felt some new blood would perk up the flock. He had heard that the Barred Plymouth Rocks were better producers than our old Rhode Island Reds, so he ordered a box of chicks by mail. We picked them up at the train station on an icy early spring day, and installed them in the back room on layers of newspaper. A low wire fence surrounded them, and a borrowed "brooder" which resembled a large inverted pan cover on legs assured their comfort. It was heated by a 60-watt bulb. Here, while we kids watched their yellow fluff change to black and white striped feathers, they received mash and TLC until their age and more clement spring weather made it practical to shift them out to the hen yard. Now, as pullets, still under a year old, they were just starting to produce a substantial amount of eggs. Losing two was bad news.

When Father got home after work, he was still fuming over the lost hens.

"Ol' Frank's dog. He was around here a couple of times. Frank forgets to tie him. I think I'll go speak to him."

I didn't ask if I could go, just grabbed a coat, and was out, across the porch and into the passenger seat of the Willis-Knight before he noticed. It wasn't far, but a cold walk across the river bridge to Ol' Frank's shanty. The building, which resembled a series of mismatched flat boxes, perched on what is now extremely valuable water front property. Frank was a drinking man who spent a good part of his time making various kinds of intoxicants, and sitting around the shack with his cronies testing their potency. He was an acrimonious old curmudgeon, and we kids would have avoided him entirely, except for his rowboat. The boat, a flat-bottomed skiff, floated out from Frank's dock and made an irresistible deck for diving out into the current. Frank watched the skiff like a hawk, and the first kid to climb on it received a severe tongue-lashing and threats of a caning or an attack by the dog. I never saw Frank use the boat, but he protected it from all boarders with the zeal of a buccaneer. The younger children stayed across the river by the public dock, well away from the main current and deeper water. The older boys, however, could no more stay away from that skiff than they could fly. They would swim across, or start from above the bridge and float through with the tide until they could grasp the side of the boat, which faced away from Ol' Frank's shack. A quick hike up into the boat, and a one swift leap into the water was usually all they could manage before Frank burst out the door waving his stick and mumbling semi-coherent curses.

The dog in question was tied outside the shack and making loud angry sounds as we drove up. I was tight behind my father when the door gapped, slightly, in response to his knock. Ol' Frank's scruffy face appeared in the crack, blinking out at the dark while he controlled the size of the door opening with one hand.

"What-Oh, hello, Freeman, what you want?"

"Frank, was that damn dog of yours home all night? I'm missing a couple of hens."

"Why, tied tight, like you see him. I don't let him off the rope, he'll run, you know."

"He'll also raid a hen house, if you don't watch him. Well, if you're sure." As father started to leave, Ol' Frank underwent a change. His face lit up with a crooked but neighborly smile.

"Two hens, well, that's too damn bad now, these days they come too dear to lose."

As he spoke, the hand that had been holding the door in its semi-closed position strayed up to scratch at his tousled white hair. The door swung open into the room, revealing an intriguing tableau. Deep in the room stood a scarred wooden table, illuminated by a smoking kerosene lamp. Three men sat around the table, which held several bottles, glasses and a large stew pot. One of the men was tipping back a bottle, another stared blankly at the opened door. The third was gnawing on what, even from our position on the step, plainly resembled a chicken leg.

Nobody spoke. There was nothing to say. We knew as we stood there that what was left of our two chickens was in that stew pot and that it had been a two legged dog that raided the hen yard, but proof? Short of an outright confession, there was none. After a good hard look at each of the silent men, Father turned on his heel and marched back toward the car. This time I preceded him. His hand was reaching for the door handle when Ol' Frank's raspy voice called out to him. "Freeman."

Father stopped, but did not turn.

"What?"

"You... You can use that boat there any time you'm a mind to..."

Father fished a lot during that winter, spearing flounder and eels, and raking quahogs and oysters. Our own skiff stayed in the barn, received some well-needed repairs, new caulking and a fresh coat of paint to ready it for the next fall's scallop season in another part of the river.

PROGRESS REPORT

That spot you'd love to see again,
Is not the way you knew it.
They've torn up every Lovers Lane,
And built a highway through it.

The skating pond, old dating pond,
That 'stay out late' fomenter?
They dug it up, and filled it in,
And built a shopping center.

Each parking place, each 'sparking' place
We used to know, is missing.
I wonder, is this progress' march?
Or plots to cancel kissing?

CHAPTER SIX
And The Living is Easy

Summers were mostly quiet on Cape Cod in the thirties; winters were even quieter. Summer visitors have always been with us but before WWII, they didn't stir things up too much. Most of the house owners came year after year, with substantial year round dwellings "back home" and second homes (cottages) on Cape Cod main streets or by the shore. But there were the inns, B & B's, cottage colonies and some camp meeting mini-villages; one as I remember in Eastham, and one in West Yarmouth. There was a grand hotel by Corporation Beach in Dennis Village called the Nobscussett, complete with its own golf course where wealthy city folks used to sail in by Packet Ship, later, by railroad to South Dennis, and across the Cape by carriage, or motor car for month long stays by the sea. It was, alas, closed by the Depression.

South Dennis had a cluster of family owned houses near the river, called Heirs Landing where some groups from New Jersey summered. I am sure there was more action up Cape, in Falmouth, Bourne, Barnstable and such, but by the time the traffic filtered down here to South Dennis, things stayed calm. As with other vacation centers and college towns, the arrival of these part time citizens caused mixed reaction amongst the Natives. Financially, the migration was a boon, outside money helped to catch up on winter bills and as most of the summer folks were repeaters, they were "on to" Cape ways. Lots of them didn't think of year-rounders as a bunch of web-footed-inbred-fishermen scuffing about on the sandbars in search of clams as we were pictured on many of the post cards they sent back home; lots did.

My friends and I were buying nails at our local lumberyard, in one of our hut building phases, and were as usual, light in the finance department, but still treated with friendly patience by the clerk. We were picking, almost nail by nail our small change purchases, and he dutifully pulled them from the various barrels. He was bagging them when a less than gracious wealthy woman who owned a large pillared house near the Church approached the counter. She was obviously expecting instant attention as befitted one who had arrived in a chauffeured limo. Clint W. continued to work with us, his earlier clients, debating the need for some of the bigger, more expensive nails, "Them 20 penny spikes is costly, maybe we ought to stick in a few more of these 8 penny..." and so forth. The woman coughed none too gently for attention, but got none. She asked for service, and was told politely, he'd be with her as soon as this current sale is completed. The nail count went on, and finally in high dudgeon the woman exclaimed, "Young man, I'll have you know I am Mrs. P.!" Clint removed his ever present and fragrant pipe from his mouth with his left hand, cordially grasped her right hand with his and shook it enthusiastically, "Well I'm Clint W., how do you do! Now, Boys, think you need some shingle nails in this order?" Mrs. P. - in higher dudgeon - marched back to her limo.

When there were disagreements between the city folk and the natives, they were quite apt to be about time. Cape clocks and calendars never ran to the same tempo as the visitors and "I'll be there to work next Wednesday." meant different things to the speaker, and the hearer. After one unsatisfactory discussion on this subject, the workman walked off, leaving his would-be employer fuming. He truculently remarked to a native bystander, "There sure are some peculiar people on Cape Cod!"

"Yep," agreed the native, "But they'll all be gone, come Labor Day!"

Let me tell you something about my little stories. Either I was present or heard them from someone whose veracity I honor.

I was among the buyers in the nail tale, for the other, well, it could have happened. Such like did go on, and I have no reason to mis-doubt the person from whom I heard it. A newspaper arti-cle following a talk I gave some years back referred to "Thacher's tall tales". I resent the inference, but not very much.

Carry Your Bags Sir?

may indicate they had deep roots on the Cape, were of the old school; genteel, rather Victorian in manner, wearing always lovely long, nearly ground-sweeping gowns, and large impressive hats. My Mother asked them one day where they bought their hats and they answered, "Oh, we don't buy them, we have them."

My Mother told me this, so we would all do well to accept it as gospel. A young tourist, lightly clad in extremely revealing halter top and short shorts, approached the postmistress (I was told it was in Osterville).

"I have been here almost a week, and I don't think I've seen any real Cape Codders. How would I know if I saw one?"

The somewhat tight-lipped postmistress did not smile. "It's easy," she said, "They'll be the ones wearing clothes."

It might have been the same post lady who responded to a nosey visitor who inquired, "What on earth do you do around here when the tourists leave?"

The Caper's answer was one snappy word, "Fumigate!"

My contact with the visitors was gener-ally friendly. I sold them vegetables from my little pull cart, played with their chil-dren, and grew to be possibly less of a country bumpkin because of contact with the summer people. In keeping with the easier ways of the times, our busy, often untidy, little patch of ground stood right next to a summer "cottage" called "208 in the field" by its owners. Two elderly sisters, Mrs. Brownell, and Mrs. Blashfield and Mr. Blashfield, a well-known painter, came with the sun each spring. The ladies, who had been the "Hall Girls", a name that

I took the sisters on a trek one day to a stream where I had seen a cardinal, and they trudged gamely after me up and down hill through fields of long grass, thoroughly soaking the hems of their gowns. We missed the bird but found some orange flowers. They gravely thanked me for the experience.

Edwin Blashfield was a noted American artist and muralist. His painting "The Three Graces" (and I suspect other of his works which featured stately women in long gowns) used the "Hall girls" as homegrown models. We were fascinated during one of their summers there when he had built on to the back of the house a studio with great slanting overhead glass panels, "to catch the North Light." Blashfield's works hang in many art museums, adorned the walls of public buildings and New York mansions and a collection of copies of his works, along with a huge original mural, grace the walls of the South Dennis Congregational Church, given by Mrs. Blashfield.

The "girls" stopped at the house during their almost nightly sunset tours down to the Bass River Bridge and my sister and I often accompanied them. They sometimes brought us gifts; I remember specifically an English children's book called "the Chatterbox," a fat volume of stories, and I seem to remember some Pooh things... A sometimes-visiting friend at the "cottage" who joined in on our sunset walks was an instrumentalist with the Philadelphia Symphony, surely one of the few women to achieve such a position in those years.

The Rands, mother and daughter, Mrs. and Miss, were another altogether pleasant experience for my sister and me. I do not remember how we met; they summered in Harwich, the next town. Probably Dad did some work for them, or sold them oysters (he was always making friends that way). They became friendly with Mom, and asked sister Nancy and I to come to their winter home for a short stay. Mom must have thought very highly of them as she said yes. We had a strange lovely week with the Rands; visited an exhibit of exquisite miniature rooms at the Boston Museum of Fine Arts, stayed in their large Newton Center home and enjoyed a Gilbert and Sullivan operetta, "Iolanthe" performed by the Newton Women's Club. The programs for the operetta were around the house for years, and Nancy received a book of G & S musical numbers from Katherine Rand, which she

Nancy and Ben as 'First Commers'

practiced with diligence on our old upright. ("We are happy little fairies and we're singing and we're dancing...")

In general, we had exposure to more "worldly" people than would be possible in most rural areas. The poet Conrad Aiken rented the house

across from our church for a winter. Ethel Barrymore, one of the many stars who appeared at the Dennis Playhouse, attended an 'Old Folks Concert' at the church that Nancy and I appeared in, sang "Rubin, Rubin, I've Been Thinking", or (maybe it was the one about early days of the town, I disremember). She did not rush any of us off to Broadway or Hollywood, but 'twas said she enjoyed the performance.

Gertrude Lawrence, the famous English actress, lived on the Cape for a time while she and her husband ran the Playhouse and Fred Allen, at that time a top radio star, summered one town over. Later in my capacity of bellboy (at the Lighthouse Inn at 16) I met, served and learned from such people as the then owner of the St. Regis Hotel in New York, the family of a Supreme Court Justice and practiced my high school Spanish with the wife of the Columbian Ambassador.

They were wonderful people to have around and certainly put us country kids in touch with the rest of the world. I still won't forget, however, the lady who thought a dime was proper payment for a painful couple of hours on my bare knees pulling weeds by hand from her sharp pointed oyster shell driveway ("Don't break them off, you'll leave the roots!").

BUS TOUR

Went to Cape Cod,
And the gift shops were grand,
Brought home a bottle of real Cape Cod Sand
Side roads pass quaint little towns, I expect,
Our driver said highways
Were much more direct.

Went to Cape Cod,
And we sure saw it all!
Lovely motel, and a marvelous mall,
Loaded with dear little places to shop,
And I think there's a beach,
But the bus couldn't stop.

Our supper, Italian,
Was all one could wish,
Every one voted against trying fish.
A movie that evening just topped off our stay.
Went to Cape Cod,
But it took us all day!

CHAPTER SEVEN

Take Me Out Of The Ball Game

I never did take to baseball. Likely part of the reason was that I was abysmally bad at it, and during cow-pasture scrub games I injured more parts of me than I knew I had. Sprained thumbs (several), bat over the head (not intentional, but bloody), knee ripped open on a broken glass something hiding in the grass near first base. Oh, it was dreadful. Not that I usually cared so much for blood and bruises, most of our early play caused plenty of those.

Climbing trees, digging underground huts and running full tilt through the woods were not passive activities. They all worked in conjunction, some how. See, to have a well protected underground hut, you had to have a guard up a nearby tree to slide down a wire or rope, and give the alarm in case of intruders. We didn't seem to want to defend the hut, as I remember, but took the warning to crawl out the tunnel at flank speed, and scatter through the woods ASAP.

Our largest underground effort was about eight feet across, a hole about six feet deep, with a twenty-five foot approach tunnel. After we had it dug, displacing enough sand to accommodate several funerals, boards, mostly misappropriated from our various father's lumber or woodpiles, were placed over the holes and trenches, and covered with sand. Then the whole was masqueraded with pine needles, grasses and bushes to conceal our work. You entered the tunnel via a hole under a bush, and crawled to the main meeting room. As a precaution against winter damp, we had installed a small wood stove in the main room with a piece of stovepipe projecting upwards through the roof. It worked, and the fire took the chill off but dragging wood and paper in through the tunnel was rather labor intensive. The stovepipe, of course, was not such that you could conceal it and when one of the group left a meeting in anger, his means of retribution was close at hand.

Avoiding discovery by the guard, he stuffed enough leaves and pine needles into the stove pipe to deny the thick pine smoke its usual avenue of escape. The smoke belched out through every crack and crevasse of the old rickety old stove into the subterranean room, dimming the kerosene lantern glow, and causing a mass exodus via the tunnel at knee-breaking crawling gallop. It was the passengers fleeing a leaky vessel, miners struggling upwards from a mine explosion, rats leaving as leaking vessel. Once out safely, we hunkered in the bushes and watched the smoke drift up from cracks in the sand covered roof, and billow out of the tunnel mouth. It took a long while for the smoke smell to leave the hut, and I think our enthusiasm for underground living flagged. Besides, we had other quests to pursue.

When I was younger, before the mole project, there were the Indians. We never saw any, but Norma, who was older and knew things, told us they were there, armed and dangerous. This required forts and hidden huts where we could run to avoid a massacre. Then, in the early 1930's, after the crime had been solved, we had to look for the missing Lindberg baby, all the while, of course, avoiding the kidnapers. Our one clue was that the newspapers and radio news, which we heard the grown ups discussing, had told of a note received by the police stating that the baby was safe, and aboard a boat somewhere between Horse Neck Beach, and the Elizabeth Islands. The note proved false, the location given was at sea, and 50 miles from our area, but no matter, we searched.

Oh, yes, and our great hunt for Public Enemy #1, John Dillinger. I think Harold got us started on that one. He knew even more than Norma did. My, that was a hunt! There were all kinds of other nasties whooping and stomping around out there, Baby

Face Nelson, Pretty Boy Floyd, Machinegun Somebody, but Dillinger was the chief baddy. After due consideration, we brought out the big guns. My father had a fine collection of local Indian arrowheads, which dated back to when there had been original people here on the Cape. We tied them not very securely to semi straight sticks with chicken feathers on the other end, took bow in hand, and went hunting. Success? Zero. The G-men had shot ol' John some time ago while coming out of a movie house in Michigan. Don't know if he enjoyed the picture, but he did not get an after show snack. We did not find any of the boys, not Big Al, or anyone, but we almost made my father into a criminal. He wanted to strangle me for losing all those arrowheads.

There was lots of baseball around when I was a kid. Dad used to turn on the Boston Braves, or the Red Sox of an afternoon, while he was painting, if he could work it. No portables early on, but he had a small paint-spotted plug-in affair he used to take with him. Many times, the customers were happy to leave him to his work, and on went the radio.

When I was quite young, he listened on Sunday afternoon but only to away games, there was no baseball in the Bay State on Sunday, or dancing. Also, for a long while after the wets voted out Prohibition, you could not tip a legal glass in many towns. Ye Old Blue Laws. I think they also had one on the books about not kissing your wife on the Sabbath, but nobody paid much attention to that one.

Vannevar Bush

Just after WWII, our fire chief bought a surplus set of field lights from the government, and local ball aficionados could watch the Dennis Clippers whack the ball around in the early evening. Dad and our across the street summer neighbor were addicts. The man across-the-street-but-south-a-bit (Neighbor #2) who was given to dropping by to chat just about any old time, ambled over. He was one who, though retired, never got out of the habit of wearing a business shirt and necktie at all times. He seemed intent on setting on our outdoor swinging sofa for a good talk. Dad 'loud as how Neighbor #1 was due, and they were headed for the ball game. N. #2, who had opposite opinions about most everything, snorted!

"Cripes, Free, damn waste of time watching those amateurs, nobody with half a mind could stand that game, any way, even with good teams playing! Watching this bunch is a pass time for the simple minded."

N. #1 interrupted his tirade by appearing from around the house.

"Already, Free, want to get started?"

Dad's friend and "simple minded" frequent company for the Game was Dr. Vannevar Bush, Former Dean of the School of Engineering at Mass. Institute of Technology, President of Carnegie Institute of Washington, inventor of some of the earliest computers, author and head of the Government Wartime Science Research Bureau who played a major part in organizing the Manhattan Project, sometimes called one of the fathers of the Atomic Bomb. Neighbor #2 sidled off.

DIAMONDS ARE - FOREVER?

Late in the fall,
Early in spring,
'The Boys of Summer,'
Do their thing.

For wives who yearn,
For the season's end,
The diamond is NOT,
A girl's best friend!

CHAPTER EIGHT

One, Two, Three Strikes You're Out

In spite of my ineptitude for all phases of baseball, I seemed to be involved in a lot of it, the scrub-in-the-cow-pasture kind. Scrub, as the kids today do not seem to know, was played with any number of guys - over two, but less than a number that could be divided up into two teams. A batter, pitcher and catcher are pretty essential, a couple of men in the field helped, and sometimes a first baseman. That is one of each, revolving in turn. Strike out, you go to the outfield, pitcher moves to catcher, catcher bats, and every one moves into a new position. If you hit, and make it to first and back home, you are up at bat again. Some guys, like Eddie Crowell, batted so well you had to impose a limit, like five hits (he always argued to be allowed just one more) before being sent out into the field. When I moved toward the plate, everybody started in toward his next position. They knew it would only be three swings until a new batter replaced me.

Nobody wanted to use my glove while I walked to the plate, and swung three times. It was a real leather glove, but one my Dad got somewhere at a bargain. The fingers stuck out at strange angles, and I never could get it to develop a "pocket". I prized it, knowing Dad had spent money he could not really afford to get me the thing. Lots of kids with hard working families did not have gloves and swapped off when they came up to bat. Mine, they called the 'Octopus', and when I went from the field straight to the plate for my brief attempt at batting (bypassing the pitcher and catcher positions, because I threw and caught so inadequately I slowed the game down), it lay there, fingers extended, just where I dropped it in my outfield position, until I returned. Sometimes I just stayed in the outfield, and let the game go on. I had some thinking to do, anyway, like where I would hide if the F.B.I. was on my tail, or how Friar Tuck clobbered Robin Hood with his staff.

The location of our games varied, depending in part, on where Thoph Smith had staked his cows that day. There was a field next to Thoph's barn which was ideal, after he and the herd (usually three) had begun to use another location. You let it cool down and dry out for a few days, (or, as the old joke went, you might get in a real mess sliding into what you thought was first base). The cows spent part of their grazing days there, but we never knew if Thoph owned the field. In those days, if there was not someone actually living on a piece of ground, folks were apt to make free use of it. We did know he didn't own the green fenced in around Liberty Hall, but the cows kept that grass short and fertilized too; I suppose somewhat in the nature of Boston Common in its early days. They did try to keep the cows out, and get the flaps raked up before any event was to be held on the green, like an outdoor fair, or a clambake.

You could tell when a bake was coming up without reading the posters because of the hole they dug in the park, the pile of rocks, and firewood collected. On the night before, the fire was started in the hole, the rocks put in to heat to a fiery red and Nate Eldridge was in attendance to keep us kids out of the immediate vicinity. Nate Eldridge seemed to be the Master for all the bakes. Most of us kids knew him, his wife was a Sunday school teacher, Nate was a fireman, and they lived just by the post office. What I don't think most people remember of Nate, is that at one time he and my Father kept all the South Dennis fire fighting equipment in Dad's garage. It consisted of brooms and buckets- that was it!

The piles of wet seaweed, which supplied steam and flavor, arrived on the morning of the bake, along with the burlap bags of clams, and the rest of the food.

The outdoor tables were brought out, and stands pounded in to the ground to support them. I well remember the bakes, corn ears baked in their husks, potatoes in their skins, and  up with one hell of a mess and some sweetish swampy tasting water that we actually tried on a pancake. It just didn't make it, but it was a good try. I guess Harold should have read further, or maybe they were not clams in their shells. Great dunking containers of melted butter, and clam broth. Funny, though, I do not remember lobsters, maybe clams was as fancy as Cape folks got in those days.

The hall that the little green belonged to was named Liberty Hall first, then re-named Totten Hall after benefactors who gave it to the village of South Dennis. Later, during WWII and after, it was again called by its old name of Liberty, and was the scene of many childhood activities. We played kick the can there, tag, used it for an alternate ball field (small, but useable), at one time had a croquet set up, did a few field days (sack races, and things) and there were summer time fairs on the little green triangle. Behind the hall in one corner sat the "his and hers" two seaters, no plumbing until much, much later. By the way, this outhouse suffered the indignity of being up-ended on many Halloween nights.

Harold and I got in a little trouble for attempting to tap the maples in the little park. We got some sap before they stopped us. Harold read up on it, and knew just how to drill, and arrange the taps and buckets, but the fire chief caught us and made us remove the taps for fear we would kill the trees. I remember we covered the holes with clothe or tape or something to slow the flow of tree sap. They lived. We boiled the fluid for hours on his mother's kitchen range, and ended that kind of maple.

The hall itself hosted dances on the second floor (until some early teen jitterbugs broke a support beam, which had held up under quadrilles, waltzes, and maybe even a Charleston, for about a century). It had a small stage, scene of a variety of entertainments. Medicine shows, traveling puppeteers, magicians and at least one W.P.A. two-person vaudeville presentation. The upstairs was also a meeting place for men's clubs and such, many a local minstrel show, old folk's concert, and Four-Square-League play was executed on its stage. It was also used from time to time for church services. The hall had been a school for a while, and in its beginning, I believe a furniture store. Down stairs was a serving kitchen with stoves and a sink, (hand pump) and in the main room, tables for church suppers and such.

I myself strode the boards of said stage in my role of Master Magician. Sister Nancy (who was awfully good about it) and yours truly presented a full evening of magic which lasted, I seem to recall, about one hour and twenty minutes including intermission. At fifteen, I imagine my expertise was suspect, but I had a fine audience, if a tad short of a full house, and amazed them, I'm sure, with such feats as removing the shirt from a willing gentleman without opening his jacket.

I also magically broke a pane of window glass suspended behind my sister (with a skeet-shooting rifle), the idea being that the projectile had to pass harmlessly "through" her body to reach the glass. She also held a selected playing card in front of herself, and subsequently showed it to have been punctured by the blast, which shattered the glass! Luckily, the only harm that came from this Marvelous Death Defying Display of Mystic Marksmanship was a small red spot on Nancy's neck where the wadding from the gun nicked her, and a sweater full of glass shards a schoolmate received when he peeked through the backstage curtain at the moment of the glass' demolition. For a wonder, the flying glass completely missed his face and eyes! The "take" was meager, but the response was warm, and I continued to perform magic for the next fifty plus years-sans the glass trick.

Ironically, noting my lack of enthusiasm for the game, (I have still never seen a professional team play) in my later guise as a clown magician, I met and entertained the Boston Red Sox team, their wives and children at several Cape Cod Day celebrations presented on local beaches by the Cape Chamber of Commerce. They were fine people, a delightful audience and cared not a wit that I was a total loss with ball, bat and glove.

SPRING HOPES ETERNAL

Beneath a sky of layered grays
There hangs a sullen fog.
We haven't seen the sun for days.
The world feels like a bog.
The air is chill, but by mistake,
Some buds seem just about to break,
My weather knee begins to ache.
- I think it might be spring.

The oak trees show some sense, at least.
They know it isn't nice.
The wind blows from the north by east
Right off a field of ice.
One silly jonquil is in view.
My sinuses are aching too.
Hay fever, or the asian Flu?
- I think it might be spring.

CHAPTER NINE

Back For More Rocks

So, it all started like this. A great old glacier, the last one of the last ice age (so far) formed in the area of the Laurentian Mountains in Canada about 25,000 years ago, give or take, and commenced to move southward like a giant bulldozer, pushing all manner of sand and rocks ahead of it. They say it was a mile high wall of ice, but I do not believe anyone saw it. It pushed down, through southern Canada, some of New York State, New Hampshire, Vermont, upper Mass. and such, and ran out of juice in the Atlantic Ocean, southern edge stopping right about where Nantucket and Martha's Vineyard sit. There was a lot of coming and going, with the ice turning back to water and the seas rising, then falling, and the land actually rising, the huge weight of the ice mass lightened as the glacier melted. It left things pretty much as they are today, the Islands, a rather shallow sandbar-cluttered sound, then Cape Cod. The south side of the Cape is soft and sandy, reason why we could make those underground huts so easily. The Cape is higher in the middle, and then from the high point north down to the Cape Cod Bay, it is like the Rocky Coast of Maine!

There are some pretty huge rocks here and there, glacial erratics, they call them, like the Doane Rock in Eastham, and the Hokum Rock in Dennis named after an old Indian who lived there years ago and shouted "Who Come?" to passersby, or so the story goes. You will find stonewalls all over the north side of the Cape; rocks dug from the fields as the farmers plowed and cultivated. They were used to make safe pasture-fields for stock, (mostly sheep, in the early days). They made decorative walls in the front of the homes along the roads, sometimes for the walls of the whole house, or mill, stone foundations for the homes and barns, siding for wells, cellars and silos. Later, builders of big things got so fond of rocks they even brought them in by train, kind of carrying on where the glacier left off. They used them for piers and break-waters, to wall in the Cape Cod Canal and for fence posts around cemeteries. One tower (of local rock) perched on top of Scargo Hill, is now just an attraction, but in the past, was a valuable tool in watching for fires during dry seasons, and in WW II it was used to watch for possible enemy planes.

Many of the Dennis stonewalls are incomplete. When they built what is now called Route 134, East West Dennis Road, they bought stonewalls, or parts of them, and trucked the rocks to a "crusher," probably steam operated, broke them up and used them for a base for the road. My Grandfather with his horse and team (probably several horses - those rocks are heavy) was employed as a trucker. A few years back, when my wife and I built along Route 134 we asked the electric contactor, an old school friend, to bring the cable under the road instead of above it on poles. He tried. Said it was the toughest digging he had ever encountered, thank you very much, next time call the competition. We live on the side of a hill, mostly rocks. When they dug the cellar, they came up with several rocks that were half the size of my pickup. Half way down they met the champ, one they could not move with the bulldozer.

"No problem," said the boss excavator, "we'll get someone to blast it out."

Wife is a rock nut. "No," She said, "we'll keep it!"

It is there in our cellar, over four feet high and big enough so we'll never have a Ping Pong table down there. They put one of the house-holding columns right in the middle of it, so I guess the house will not go anywhere soon.

The sand on the south side? Well, they used a lot of it filling in holes. There are tons of holes on the Cape, left by the receding glacier. Huge chunks of the ice stayed when the great ice sheet receded and melted more slowly than the rest. They had been on the bottom of the glacier, coated with tons of sand and dirt, which acted as insulation.

Where they sat they compressed the ground into hollows, or holes in the ground surface, which filled with water from the subsequent melting and rains, and peppered Cape Cod with the 350 plus lovely ponds and lakes we still enjoy today. Other holes were just that, gaps in the ground often situated just where humans desired roads and railroad beds. Fill them with sand. Sand also mixed with cement to make concrete, and with oil into tar to surface the roads. There were lots of well used roads during my boyhood, which were still unpaved, and piles of sand and smelly oily tar were a part of the 30's scenery. Surprisingly, the sandy soil down Cape formed an excellent base for turnip growing, and Eastham devoted considerable acreage to growing the sweetest turnips found anywhere. As kids, we used to make the trip every fall when Dad fetched home a bushel or more to store in our Cape Cod round, rock walled root cellar for the winter. The Wife and I still like to drive down there just after the first frost for turnips to use as a vegetable or mix into a zesty beef stew.

Then there were the Cranberries. Early comers to the Cape took a cue from the natives, and picked and used the small sour berries for cooking. They kept well and helped supply nutrition during the winter months. As time went by, farmers lucky enough to have a small bog helped things along by ditching along the edge of the bog to let water into the vines. One Dennis farmer came out to view his bog after a heavy storm and found the wind had piled several inches of sand over the vines, apparently smothering the berries. He thought his crop was doomed, but found in the fall he had a bumper crop! Some experimenting proved that judiciously applied sand, which would grow very little else, (except turnips) did wonders for cranberries. So, berry growers began to dig more holes in the Cape, to get sand.

Many years later, my brother became heavily involved in the cranberry business. He is a bog owner, and grower for Ocean Spray.

He fertilizes the bogs, regulates the water flow, fights insects, cleans ditches, clips and extracts unwanted weeds, chases the geese away, (they ruin large portions of the bog), irrigates during frost-filled fall nights to save the vines, harvests, some times profitable, some times not, then floods the bog. During the winter, when all the bogs dotting Cape Cod are frozen, he and his crew drive small trucks out on the ice, and spread sand.

The sand needs to be rock free, so growers set up sand pits where they have screening apparatus, and a machine for digging the sand, putting it through the screening process, loading it on trucks, and moving the screened-out stones to a pile out of the way. The stones are later sold to landscapers and such for driveways and such. Driving by his pit one Sunday, my brother saw an unknown woman moving a substantial part of his rock pile into the trunk of her car. He stopped, and courteously asked if he could help. Yes, said she, they are heavy. They put more of the small rocks into her trunk, and thank you, she said, that will do.

"That will be five dollars for the rocks," said my brother.

"Five Dollars?"

"Yes, ma'am, five dollars, you see, these are my rocks."

"Why," said she, "You can't own these rocks, these are wild rocks!"

They say a visitor stood watching as a Caper dug deep in his field, prying out rock after rock, and adding a layer to his wall. The day was stifling, the work was hard, and the worker paid no never mind to the watcher.

Scargo Tower

"My, there sure are a lot of rocks around, how did they get here?"

"Glacier brung 'em." The Caper strained another great stone up on to the wall, straightened his back, and wiped sweat from his flushed face.

"Oh? Where did the glacier go?"

"Back," said the worker bitterly, "For more rocks!"

PLEISTOCENE SCENES

inspired by an article by Malcolm Wells

We need a Glacial Video,
To help fill in the gaps,
By showing us the truth about
Those lovely polar caps.
Advance praise for the camera crew,
They'll take an awful risk,
But the ice age was a nice age,
If you like your weather brisk

The scenery? some monotony,
As plants and trees had died,
And people teaching botany,
Would not be satisfied.
Except when snow was blowing,
That ol' sun was rather bright,
But the ice age was a nice age,
If you're really into white

The scenes that showed the building
Of the Cape would be first rate,
Complete with junk-lined, tarred moraine
We'd call Route 28,
Now, since the ice retreated,
And the gentle ocean swells,
The ice age left a nice age,
For the men who build motels.

Historically significant,
But subject, not ideal,
The record of a great event,
With little "pop" appeal.
I perhaps, would steal some naps,
(One viewing would suffice)
For the ice age was a nice age,
Only if you're hooked on ice.

CHAPTER TEN
Get Out And Get Under

In 1902, or 03, depending to who's telling the story, C.L. Ayling of Centerville, decided to try out his Stanley Steamer on a pleasant trip down Cape. It took him a whole day, in spite of no traffic tie-ups. You see, there were no other cars, also no hard roads, just heavily rutted sand trails, use-able by horse and team (which usually weren't going very far anyway), but totally unsuitable for a motorcar, or horseless carriage, as they called them there early metal monsters. He must have been glad for the many ponds and lakes along the way, from which to replenish his water supply, for from what I hear, the early steamers used more water than fuel. Besides, it must have been pleasant to stop shaking for a few minutes and stretch out the kinks.

The people in P'town looked kind of sideways at the Infernal Machine; first they'd seen, and to a man refused him garage space in their barns, certain the thing would set things afire during the night. In fact, they 'llowed as how she might blow up, and burn the whole village, so could he please leave it out in a field some distance from anything. He did, and no midnight fires occurred. Trouble the next morning however, P'Town was plumb out of filling stations! Word was, though that those early steamers could burn most anything, so Mr. A. was able to borrow or buy some kerosene- lamp oil or brush cleaner from a painter, waited the half hour it took to get up a head of steam, and to the relief of the locals, bumped his way out of town and back up Cape. Mr. Ayling was later instrumental in establishing the Cape Cod Hospital, the Cape Playhouse in Dennis, and the Centerville Fire District and was involved in other philanthropic projects around the Cape. Quite a man!

Dad's first non-four legged transport was a belt-drive Indian motorcycle. Well, he had 'the wheel' for a brief time, but never said he used it. Those rutted trails that passed for roads in his day did not make for very smooth riding, particularly when you were doing the pedaling. His next vehicle was a model "T". His father would "have no truck with it." Scare the horses (I suspect he also thought of a fire in the haymow). Dad kept it in his Grandfather's barn, just up the street.

My Grandfather, as my Dad did after him, augmented his income by delivering the Sunday newspaper. He did it winter and summer, traveling by horse and wagon. One dreadful winter day, snow, wind, and I suspect a bit of rheumatism, made the task of digging his way out to the barn, harnessing the horse and starting out on the route seem to be more than Grandpa was up for. He poked around the house, grumbling under his breath, his moustache bristling and puttering with inconsequential tasks, obviously putting off the decisive moment when he must don his storm gear and get going. Grandmother, sensing the situation, took Dad aside.

"Freeman, why don't you offer to take him around his route in your motor?"

Dad offered, Grandfather grumped somewhat of an affirmative, and Dad brought the car around, and helped Grandpa load his papers into the vehicle. It certainly beat the wagon, no heat, but the canvas curtains at least kept out most of the snow and wind. At the first stop, Grandpa took over direction of the voyage.

"Now, Freeman, one goes over there to Eldridge's, just throw it on the porch, they don't mind. Take 2, the other goes across the street at Hall's; knock, they want it in the house. Then, we go down to...."

So it went for the whole trip. Dad drove, and did the legwork, Grandpa "sot" to the passenger seat in comparative comfort and gave orders. When they got home, Grandpa marched into the house like a Captain on his bridge, no "thank you's," but as he passed Grandmother, he said, "Alice, tell the boy he can keep that motor in the barn if he wants to."

From then on, each Sunday, it was "Come Freeman, time to do our papers".

As soon as they got some of the main roads paved, (they were still working on that in the thirty's) the auto seemed to be just what the doctor ordered. Things on the Cape were so far apart, and horses walked so slowly. Many of the early cars were Ford Model "T's".

The "Tin Lizzie" of joke and story. (When one Model "T" passes another Model "T", what time is it? Tin past Tin......F.O.R.D.= Found On Road Dead, or, I named my Ford after my wife...After I got her, I couldn't do a thing with her!). They were sometimes funny, finicky machines that Henry Ford said you could order in any color you liked....as long as it was black.

The "T's" had a "planetary" transmission, no clutching and shifting gears, just stop, step on the other pedal, and start off in the other direction. One cute trick of the "T", in cold weather, heavy grease kept the gears from disengaging, so start it at your peril. If you cranked, and the motor caught, your Lizzie might just knock you down, run you over, and proceed until she came up against a large tree. To forelay against that, one had to jack up one of the rear wheels, then start 'er up, and wait until the jacked up wheel stopped spinning, lower the wheel, pack up your jack, climb in, and drive off. Even with the precaution of a jacked up wheel, starting the "T" was quite a chore. There were spark and fuel settings, ether to put into cups by the plugs, then, around in

front to crank and turn engine over. Re-set the spark and fuel, and crank for effect. If you didn't flood the engine, it might fire off, (be careful she doesn't kick, those cranks have broken many an arm). If it fires, you run around to the steering side, re-set the spark and fuel intake, around front again to remove the crank and put it away, get aboard, and, if you stepped on the correct pedal, fine, you backed out of the barn, stopped, pressed the forward pedal, and off you go!

Elnathan Fisk, who lived just up the street from Father's boyhood home, was in a hurry, as he often was, one morning and did every thing right, until it came to stepping on the pedal. He tromped on the forward pedal, and instead of backing out of the barn, he crashed out through the back of the barn. Elnathan did not stop, (he was late, remember?) but drove around the barn out to the road, and off to work. About noon, two workmen drove up in a wagon and commenced to work on the wreckage where the Ford had slammed through. Not just common repairs, though, they constructed a second pair of doors on the back of the barn. From then on, late or not, Elnathan opened both sets of doors before he started up his Ford.

The old cars were difficult, in some ways, but they were just what rural people needed.

The "T", for instance, could be, and was, used as a tractor, as a power plant for sawing wood and many other farm chores. You raised one rear wheel on a jack, and ran a drive belt from the wheel to what ever equipment you choose to operate. Only the elevated wheel would turn. Sears, Roebuck or Montgomery Ward carried the adapter parts, and many a small farm became a better producer due to the Ford's versatility.

There were lots of things besides Fords that needed cranking. Mom's sea clam grinder, a vital part of making chowder, or sea clam pie, was a crank job, as was the potato slicer Dad and Uncle Ray used in their

intense, but rather short life in the potato chip business. The wringer on Mother's first washing machine also required manual cranking. This machine was a hose-out-the-door affair, still required water heated on the stove, and you had to take the hot clothes out of the machine with a stick and put them through the wringer by hand, but saved a lot of scrubbing. There were still a few old wells, which needed a crank apparatus to carry the "Old Oaken Bucket' of water and of course earlier on, seamen cranked a windlass to raise anchor, trim sails, and load cargo. I remember watching Dad crank his big round grindstone by pushing his foot up and down on a bar while he held the ax blade firmly against the rough surface. It was fun watching the sparks it made. Oh, yes, the phonograph also had to be cranked, and a spring wound tightly, before you could stick a disk under the needle, and dance to a new big band record, or hear an old favorite. For my birthday last year, my wife gave me a short wave AM/FM radio with a re-chargeable flash light on it and a crank for charging the batteries, in case of a power shortage. Progress.

Dad's cars were usually pretty old when he got them, but they sure did yeoman service. He used them not only to go to work, but, as we burned wood for heat, the wood, which we cut in various woodlots was trucked home in the back of the car, after the rear seat was removed. Likewise, oysters, big wet burlap bags of them that he got in Cotuit, shucked, and sold, loads for the dump on Sunday, egg deliveries, and once, I even managed to take home a full-grown, and well horned, billy goat my uncle gave me. His cars were usually still in the "fix them with a little piece of bailing

wire" category, tires with tubes which you could patch, a carburetor which could be adjusted and a fuel pump which could be cleaned and regulated, not like today's computerized models.

I got my first car at 16 sharp 16, (I remember, for $25) it was very little younger than I; it was a 1932 Ford, a model "B". The "B" was an adaptation of the Model A, but with a longer front end, and a big V-8 motor. It didn't do all those jobs the old "T" could do, but it sure helped me get around. The car had been named "Cassie" by her former owner, and following the tradition about changing the name of a ship being bad luck, I left the name of my Ford alone. She was a fast little thing, gave me very little trouble and I kept it until I went into the service, used it for work, school, and play. Henry F. apparently did right smart job of souping up the little four cylinder model "A", and he kept the price down, around $500.00: good thing, too, what with the depression. Side note, it was the same model Ford, according to Robert Lacy, ('FORD: The Men and the Machine') that gangsters Bonny and Clyde Barrows apparently preferred, (they were killed while driving one, but earlier wrote Ford attesting to the quality of the Model "B" V-8) and it was called "A wonderful car," by Public Enemy number one, John Dillinger in a letter sent to Henry Ford in 1934!

How, someone astute might well ask, could you go many places on the War Time Ration Quota, which was for a nonessential worker, or a kid, only three (3) gallons per week? Burned kerosene, my friend, just like the Stanley Steamer! Gas motors really don't like it, and today's cars probably would cough and quit, but that old Model "B", put some gas in the carburetor, pour kerosene into the tank, start her up, and keep her going. It belched smoke like the Canal Electric Plant on a very bad day, but what did we know about Pollution back then . . . Oh My, My!

ON MOCKING BIRD'S TRILLS

The trilling of the mocking bird,
So thrilling, and enthralling,
Might discompose his spouse, I 'spose
She never knows who's calling

I wonder, is he feather-brained?
Or slightly addle-witted?
One mating-call, I'm sure, is all
A wise bird is permitted.

For even though he tries so hard,
To fly the straight and narrow,
From Mrs. Bird he'll hear, she heard
Him calling to a sparrow.

CHAPTER ELEVEN

Un-Pasteurized Cape Cod

I miss the Cape when the percentage of genuine "Characters" amongst the population was much higher. People who thought little about the norm, wore their individuality with not a hint of self-consciousness, and walked their own path. Linwood was one. Thoph (Theophilus Smith) was another. Thoph was for many years the custodian of the town disposal area; the dump keeper. His father was a seafaring man, but Thoph decided not to go to sea. Instead, he settled in for a farmer's life on family land on the corner of Main Street, and Upper County Road in South Dennis. He raised vegetables, hens and geese and cows. We used a lot of his milk. Thoph came by most every day with a tin milk can, and poured milk into Mother's bottles, the ones she kept in the ice box in the summer and a cooling box outside of the window during the cold months. I always thought Thoph had a kind of platonic crush on Mother. He called her "Bobby" after the fashion, came around daily, with sometimes still warm unpasteurized milk, and was always good for a little conversation. Once when Mother purchased a second hand piano from people in Dennisport, she prevailed upon Thoph, who had a horse and wagon at the time, to hire a man, and move the piano to our home. A walking horse will do well to make the trip to Dennisport and back in a forenoon; plus the hired man. Mom asked the price, and Thoph, after some calculating said,

"God damn it, Bobby, fifty cents will do."

Nor would he take more.

Thoph kept his animals until they drifted away due to natural causes, had a yard dotted with tired, past laying age hens, and molting muscovy ducks, which he fed well, but which never fed him. I think we switched to pasteurized milk from a regular milk company one winter when Thoph's cows went dry. We kids liked Thoph, and would often swing past his barn at milking time. Thoph sputtered a lot, and was given to the regular use of expletives, but meant no harm by it. I doubt he even was conscious of the fact that he interjected curse words about twice to a sentence, and invoked the name of the deity with some regularity, although not a church going man. It rolled out of him with no self-consciousness, no attempt at vulgarity, and after we kids had our first giggle at the use of words we weren't allowed, ("God damn Boys, Don't ...here, now, don't step on that God damn hay, damn cows wount eat it. Cow's smarter than a horse; God damn horse'll eat any God damn thing. Look-a-here, boy, apple pie'll make you cry, blue berry pie'll make you die ... Too bad, ain't it ... Jesus Christ, ... By God"). If he was milking, he would line us up, and squirt milk straight from the cow's teat into our mouths. I never knew him to miss.

When he was keeper of the dump, he kept about two dozen cats there, which probably kept the pest population under control, and perhaps kept the mice and rats from migrating into the village when cold weather cut down the food supply. Thoph felt the mostly feral cats needed a jag of good wholesome milk with their wild dinners, and took several two quart cans of milk up with him each day. His trip to the dump, less than a mile from his barn was slow. Thoph never got onto autos, and bicycled both ways, winter and summer.

No one could ride a "Wheel", as Thoph and my Father called them, more slowly than Thoph. We kids used to follow along with him sometimes as he creaked through the village, stopping to walk over the railroad track, and then remounting with sighs and cusses. He rode so slowly you couldn't believe he could keep his balance. In order to stay and talk with him, we had to walk slowly BACKWARDS, and then stop and wait.

"Look out there God damn it, boy, you'll upset this God damn wheel."

Some older boys got into the dump enclosure one night, and set a fire which caused quite a bit of damage to the surrounding woodland. Thoph was called as a witness in the case, before Judge Hall, a well known local jurist (called "Judgie" by the girls who worked in his Harwich office). As testimony and motions, and court procedure went along, Thoph's obvious discomfort disturbed the proceedings. He sighed, mumbled beneath his breath, and squirmed until the judge directed his attention directly to him.

"Mr. Smith, is there something wrong with you?"

"No, But God damn it, Judge, I got to get back to that God damn dump!"

Every one laughed except Thoph. And the Judge.

"Very well, Mr. Smith, you may proceed."

Thoph thanked him, and went outside to where a police car waited to whisk him back to his official place of duty; the Dennis dump.

Thoph's sister Lizzie kept house for him for years. The house was made up of tiny rooms, poorly insulated, and heated by a wood stove. The storm windows and Thoph's red flannels went on with the first chill of fall, and stayed tight until spring was well established. As to the flannels, he seemed to abide by the old adage, 'Stick to your long underwear until your long underwear sticks to you'. Between the smoking stove, the lack of ventilation and Thoph's barn work, the air in the house was apt to get a mite 'high' by Christmas. Lizzie used to put some apple peelings or a touch of cinnamon on the range to flavor things up a bit. Thoph said she was

addicted to the headache remedy Bromo Seltzer and asked Dad when he ran the store/post office not to sell her any. In fact both he and their Mother, when she was still alive, used to call Dad at the store to warn him that Lizzie was on her way, so please hide the Bromo! She apparently got jittery without it, and at one time, became so distraught that Thoph phoned Dad, "For God sake, Freeman, damn it, give her what she wants, I can't stand it!!" After she died Thoph hired a woman to clean up and cook. She became well known and liked in the neighborhood, and when she wasn't seen out and around for a spell Mother asked Thoph if she was ill. No, B'god she had been fired. Seems Thoph had come in from cleaning up after the cows, and gone straight to her newly cleaned living room, set down, and put his boots up on a chair with a newly washed and pressed antimacassar on the seat. She told him to get his damn feet off the furniture.

"Have no God-damn woman swearing at me!" Thoph said.

When I picture Thoph in my mind, he is always wearing the brown working man's bib overalls, often with a metal bicycle clip on each leg, a brown canvas barn coat, and a checked cap. I'm sure he did without the coat in hot weather, but I can't visualize him without it. He was always clean shaven, and had a ruddy complexion, with deep groves around his eyes and forehead. I see him standing near the 'pile' near the edge of the bank, where you threw refuse with pitchfork in hand, tending the small fire he often kept burning to dispose of papers and other light materials which would otherwise blow around. Thoph kept a neat dump.

"Here," he'd say, "You, Freeman, that boy you got likes wheels. Well, look there, at that baby carriage, God damn, got four good ones. Take that along, now."

Dad would take the carriage, with a "Much obliged, Thoph," and there was another truck. My brother Link was a builder of trucks comprised of wheels, orange crates, a few old boards and lots of large nails. He used to line them up in the driveway. They took up the whole driveway, and most of the side yard.

On a fair day, when all the papers had been burned, and customers were scarce, Thoph would go to the porch in front of the small bad weather shed near the entrance to the dump, tilt an old chair back against the wall, and doze. He was there this day, snug in the arms of Morpheus and snoring slightly when a hearse came to the dump. The driver, one Mr. H. was, when on duty, generally a serious man, as befits one with such solemn duties but when not in the company of a 'dear departed,' was apt to be a joker. I knew him well from the Pharmacy where he made frequent stops to secure his favorite 'Black B.L. Plug' Chewing tobacco. I sold him many a plug, but never dared ask if he kept a 'chaw' in his cheek during funerals. (He might have, I knew a gentleman once who did that sort of thing, and as it requires some spitting, carried an olive bottle concealed in his inner jacket pocket, and became adept at turning, raising the bottle, spiting, and returning to his original stance in one smooth, almost invisible motion.) This day, as the funeral was over, I am sure Mr. H. had a satisfactory cud jammed between his cheek and teeth. The

hearse was filled with the remaining flowers, from an apparently well attended burying, which were being taken to the dump for disposal. The sight of Thoph, sitting leaned back against the building, and comfortably asleep was more than Mr. H. (the joker) could walk past. Gently, he and his partner took all the floral arrays from the hearse and piled them in a tasteful display around the sleeping figure. They pulled the black hearse up in front, stood there between Thoph and the vehicle, still dressed in their black working suits, and toned, "Mr. Smith, Mr. Smith, we have come for you!"

Thoph's chair came down onto all four legs, and his hand reached reflexively for the every present pitch fork. "God Damn, Boys, Don't take me now, I hain't dead yet!"

Afterwards, when the jokers finished laughing until they cried, he 'lowed as it was a purdy good joke, "But boys, Damn to Hell, don't do that again!"

It has been a good many years since kids have had the pleasure of walking backwards beside Thoph's 'wheel', delighting in his innocent blasphemy and homey philosophy or gulped warm milk squirted across the barn directly from his cow. If you look at a map of the Town of Dennis, you will find an approximately one mile long road which leads from Route 134 in South Dennis to our state-of-the-art Disposal Area (dump). It is named Theophilus F. Smith Road. It was dedicated to him just before he died in the late sixties. I hope he felt somewhere near the pleasure from the event which so many of us former kids get from remembering him.

THE TOOL

I lay in that hard sun with salt-wet eyes,
Despite the kerchief tight around my head.
The stone still quite unmoved, submerged in sand,
And there, the shovel, mis-used in the work,
Lay shattered on the ground.

"Boy, you break that handle, why, you'll know it!
A shovel's not for prying rocks,
Just moving sand.
You need to lift, or pry, then get a bar.
There's one up to the barn."

I heard it plain as though he stood there then;
Watched as I pushed the edge beneath the stone;
Saw my frustrated lunge against the handle;
Heard the sick loud cracking of the wood
That dropped me in the dirt.

I knew the need to clear and plant this land,
And understood his deep respect for tools.
My father's ways were as his life was, hard.
I'd broken both his shovel and his rules.
In fear I took the pieces to the barn.

"The shovel handle's broke, yes, I know, Boy,
I cracked it proper, prying out a rock,
I thought she'd give out.
There by the bench, I brought one out from town.
She'll soon be good as new."

And so, almost, was I.

CHAPTER TWELVE

Relative Ramblings

As I grew up, it became clear that the family lines of my Thacher grandparents connected me to most of the families in the mid Cape area. Bringing in schoolteachers and hairdressers through the years hadn't entirely broken the connection with the past. I realized before I escaped from grade school that I was at least a distant relative of about 75% of my 30-student class, (the largest ever to go through the Dennis school system up to that date). The connections were not so tight that Capies had pink eyes or webbed feet as on that post card, but many of us twigs could be traced back to branches of familiar trees. Sears, Thacher, (sometimes Thatcher), Crowell (sometimes Crowe, seems they were sometimes indifferent spellers in them days) Hall, Paddock, Nickerson, Baker, etc., etc., were transported by the long dangerous sea voyage from the fields and shores of England, via the Plymouth of Massachusetts Bay Colonies. These names are still to be found in the Cape phone directories, but the ranks are thinning. The first European (English) settlers began to trickle down through the woods and dunes just a few years after the Plymouth Colony was established in 1620. They followed Indian trails, with no transportation aids except their feet, or boated across the bay by sail and oar.

The three who first trekked to the area now named Dennis and Yarmouth appear to have gotten off on a decent footing with the Native Americans, made acceptable trades and agreements with the local chiefs, and then settled in to worship, farm, fish, hunt, whale, and build (churches, fort, then homes, in that order.) From the first time Anthony Thacher put his buckled shoes east of the swamps and streams, which later became the Cape Cod Canal, there have been Thachers on Cape Cod. The only one I knew first hand in the long line, which preceded my Dad, was Grandfather Charles. Charles had lost his first wife and had a daughter, Florence, when he wed Alice Hall and together they had two boys and three girls, Freeman, Fredson, Alice, Edith and Cynthia, who drowned at an early age. A visit to the Grands was quite an expedition, by the time I was two, a teeny weenie baby.

Nancy was with us, which meant Mom had to push the old wicker carriage while trying to curb a little wanderer and a large Airedale, Wow, over the course of the mile or so between our house and theirs. She had a harness and reins for me, but the dog ran free. No sidewalks, but then, there were hardly any cars and seldom any walkers. A big attraction at the Grands were Grandmother's sugar cookies; big thick crispy on the outside, topped with crystallized sugar, with a center unbelievably cake-like and delicious. Mother, who was a good cook, tried to get the exact recipe, but Grandmother was vague and said things like, "Put in a little of this, not too much of that," Mother came close, but never quite. Mother used to repeat an old joke after every sugar cookie attempt: an aspirant cook trying to get a cookie recipe from a famous chef was told several times to use her own judgment on amounts, "But," she asked, "If I don't have any judgment?" "Then," said the chef, "Don't make cookies."

Grandfather was a short stocky man with white hair and a king sized moustache. He sipped his tea from a 'moustache cup' with a special guard across the center of the cup to keep his upper lip shrubbery dry. He was not young when I knew him. He used to take me on his knee and call me 'Peck's Bad Boy', after the title of a popular children's book, but Grandmother used to counter with, "No, Charles, he's 'Peck's Good Boy'." I don't think it was settled to anyone's satisfaction, but as long as those cookies kept coming.... Grandfather had better than ordinary early education, attending a boy's prep school in Rhode Island. I do not know how he fared there, but he had a neat sterling silver napkin ring with his name on it. It was later given to me, as oldest grandson, and my first name is Charles, as on the ring, although I seldom use it. I gave it to my youngest son, C. Noah, who seldom uses his first name either, but then, we seldom used the napkin ring, either. Dad always said his father had peculiar ways. For instance, he decided smoked and cured meat was to be avoided at all costs. Once at our house, while Mother was feeding me, Grand-mother broke off a bit of bacon from my plate and popped it into her mouth.

"Don't eat that, Alice, it'll make you sick!"

"Oh Charles," answered Grandmother, "It's alright, Hattie feeds it to the baby!"

"Well, let her kill the baby, if she wants, don't mean you have to die too!"

One night when they came to supper, Mother forgetting the prohibition, served ham. Charles pronounced it good, and came back for seconds.

"That's good, Hattie what is it?"

"Ham," said Mother.

"Harump...lf I'd known that, I wouldn't have ett it." (He finished his second serving.)

When he and Dad worked on the road, building exhibits, Grandfather would always order clam chowder, and never liked what they brought him. He would grump all through the meal, remarking on

Alice Hall Thacher

Charles Thacher

the thinness, or the thickness, and lack of flavor.

"They must have just one clam on a string that they drag though the bowl!"

If they encountered a skating rink in their travels, Grandfather would rent a pair of runners.

"Watch me skate like a crab!" he'd say, and off he would go across the ice... Dad said he watched, but never did figure out what that meant.

When Dad graduated high school (one of a class of 12 in 1910), Grandfather gave him a watch. In those days, you couldn't get a Timex, or a cheap but dependable Wall-Mart special. A watch was a thing to prize. Dad seldom took it to work, saving it for best.

One day he came home to find his father in possession of one of those bicycles with the great four-foot tall front wheel. "Boy, watch me ride this wheel!" said Grandfather, and kicked off, mounting the bike in motion, and climbing up from the step at the rear to the seat, posed high above the wheel.

These bicycles had no brakes to speak of, just a squeeze affair that tried to stop the spinning front wheel. It was more likely to throw you and the back of the bike up and over the big front wheel. If you started down an incline, you either stuck with it until an up grade came along, or you fell over. The only real way you had of stopping was called a collision! Grandfather used this method about 2/3 of the way down the long slope behind the barn. The high-wheeled monster crashed into the bushes, and Grandfather sailed over the bushes. He picked up, and marched up the hill toward the house. As he passed Grandmother and Dad at their viewing spot he said, more or less to my Father, "Boy, that's your wheel" Father asked his Mother where the bicycle came from she said, "Well, Charles traded your watch for it."

Dad said he never touched the "wheel", and eventually his father sold it. In his youth, Grand-father had sailed on his father's (George Engs) ship, and became first mate. When Dad was growing up, his father had horses, wagons, the sleigh and an independent attitude. Dad said he would sit to home, and not go looking for jobs.

"If they want me, they'll come and get me!" said Charles.

I guess they did, he brought up five children, owned his home, didn't go hungry, and Grandmother could sit by the window in her old years, and surreptitiously suck on chocolates from the Candy Cupboard box she kept concealed under her apron.

STONE WALL

A graceful wall grown up with vines,
All heavy gray and serpentine,
It cleaves a meadow, climbs a hill,
A monument to human will.

300 years since it was made,
- I conjured up the builder's shade,
And, (dabbling now in the occult),
He 'lowed as how we might consult.

"Planned? Waal, no, I never planned,
Just framed the borders of my land,
Although one neighbor claims I strayed,
I piled them there and there they stayed.

"The glacier put 'em here, you know,
Where I envisioned corn should grow,
Three years I labored, sweat and pried,
To move them over to the side.

"Two hernias, a twisted back,
But there they stand, all in a stack,
Artistic? No, it's passing crude,
I just made room for growing food."

This lovely wall, then, had its start,
As something far removed from art.
And like much beauty that we see,
Commenced as 'Practicality'.

CHAPTER THIRTEEN

By The Beautiful Sea

There were a lot of people using our ocean before the Pilgrims sailed in to P'town, Provincetown. They landed there before they sailed across the bay to Plymouth, which has since taken all the credit as first landing place. I guess P'town didn't have any big rocks on which to carve 1620. There was boat action off the Cape even before the Figaway races between the Cape and Nantucket. It is said that Leif Erickson and his mighty band of Vikings moored their dragon-headed ships in the upper reaches of Bass River and historians say they've found a large rock where apparently Leif moored his boat. Both French and English explorers had staked out the area. The English fished for Cod and such off the Cape, and built racks on the beaches, (flakes, I think they were called,) to sun dry or smoke the fish for transport back to England. Little air pollution in them days to spoil the food. They also harvested trees; hard wood, and white cedar, to bring back to timber-poor old England. Irony, my great Grandfather carried boards and timber as ballast on the way home from trading in the West Indies and other of the Caribbean islands, and many Cape homes, (including several in South Dennis) were constructed from this imported lumber because we were about out of big native trees.

By the beginning of the nineteenth century, it seems that there were very few local boys who had not tried their hand at some work involving the sea. Many stuck to it, working the fishing industry, and with luck, eventually owning their own fishing boat. They fished in the bay to the north, the sound to the south, or far out on the "Banks" miles from shore; line fishing, trapping, tending weirs, dragging nets, or scratching the bottom of the ocean and rivers for shell fish. Whaling was a long term ocean going experience.

A single whaling voyage could last for several years, and Cape boys (both the "English", and some of the Native Americans) became very handy at catching the huge mammals. So good, in fact, that it was a local boy who taught the Nantucket sailors the fine craft of whaling.

The deep sea vessels which carried on the trade between the countries of the world also carried a heavy representation of Cape Cod men and boys in their officers and crews. Likely based in one of the cities with a deeper harbor than in a Cape port, the Tall Ships were often owned at least in part by captains who had come up through the ranks to mate, then master of their own vessel. My great grandfather owned and captained a ship which bore his name, the "George Engs Thacher." She was a three mast "hermaphrodite" schooner, (called so because she used both fore-and-aft and square sails) the schooner part, apparently a name given by the man who first made that kind of ship, a Captain Robinson of Gloucester, Mass in 1713. The word 'schooner' comes from a Scottish word 'schon', meaning to skip across the water as a flat stone does. George sailed her to Europe as well as to the Caribbean. We have a strange watercolor painted in Texel, Holland in 1890 showing the vessel sailing in two different positions in the same picture. What with the pressures of the steamship competition, and I suppose the hardships of the sea life, George "came ashore" in the nineties, and settled down to be a gentleman farmer. Trouble was, the weather is no gentleman and one year some severe winter storms pushed salt water over the dykes around his riverside cranberry bogs, ruining the crop, and the bogs, so he didn't prosper as he had expected.

Dad told of raiding his orchards, pears, apples and such, and he seemed to have had some greenhouses near his barn, grape vines, and large gardens, so at least he didn't have all his eggs in one basket, or berries in one bog, so to speak. Dad's uncle Pele , one of George's sons, didn't "swallow the anchor" but moved on to captain a steam vessel. I didn't get to know Captain Peleg. He owned the house across the street from his brother, Charles, but only summered there. He died when I was about six, leaving a wife and four children who never married, and the family continued to summer in the old homestead until the last son died, just a few years ago.

George had a reputation of being a hard man, as you might expect would be necessarily part of the equipment for a ship captain. Life on the bounding main was no picnic, the life was hard, the men were hard, and the master of the vessel had to keep things in line sometimes for months during a long voyage. When George injured an eye during a time at home, he walked to the station, rode the train to Boston and walked from South Station to the hospital. The doctor told him the eye had to come out and began to prepare a local anesthetic.

"What is that for? " asked George, pointing at the hypodermic.

"Why, to dull the pain."

"No, I don't want that horse piss in my blood, just take it out!"

The Doctor took it out, sewed it up, and George walked back to the station, and rode the train back to South Dennis.

Grandfather (Charles) sometimes shipped aboard as first mate and once while returning from a transatlantic voyage he was in charge of the deck when an unexpectedly violent storm arose.

Grandfather went below to the captain's cabin to suggest that they take in some of their sail to lessen the strain on the ship's masts. He found George involved in his favorite off duty pass time when at sea; he was playing his violin.

"Father, I think we might do well to shorten sail a might, she's blowing hard out there."

"No," says George, cranking away on his fiddle, "I believe we shall be all right."

Charles went back to the bridge, but when the winds grew stronger he felt impelled to return to the captain's cabin.

"Father, she's blowing a fair gale out there, I think we should take in some sail, we're straining those masts."

The Captain fiddled on, "No, boy. I told your mother we'd be home by the third Thursday in September, and I wish to be on time."

Charles took up his mate's position again, and as the storm strengthened, the

The George Engs Thacher

ship began to take on water. The call went to man the pumps. After more than an hour of backbreaking work on the pumps, it was obvious that they were not getting the water out as fast as it was rushing in. Back to the Captain's cabin, this time in desperation.

themselves from their fishing boat construction and for a while produced a line of tall, fast Clipper ships, known as the Greyhounds of the Sea. They worked out of little Sesuit Harbor in East Dennis, and their ships became record holders for their speed, crossing the Atlantic in as little as fourteen days.

"Father, carrying all this sail is making us nose down into the waves. There's flooding down below. We have to take in some of the sails. The men can't pump fast enough to get ahead of the water!"

George Engs applied a dab or two of rosin to his bow, and snuggled his violin in below his chin.

"If they don't pump," said George, sliding his bow over the strings, "they'll drown."

Although the big ocean going vessels general worked out of the deep water harbors, there was a going concern, called the Shiverick Ship Yards, which bestirred

Ocean going sailing ships also sometimes 'wintered in', as my father told me, in the bays and rivers on the Cape. His father told of seeing "30 sail of vessels" waiting out the cold season in Bass River, and I, swimming near the High Bank Bridge with some of the other kids and feeling around with our feet in the muddy bottom for quahogs (out of season) found several intact ship's lanterns stuck in the thick mud, stumbled on them, you might say, stubbing our toes on relics of Cape Cod's seafaring past.

POSTING FOR THE LAST FOREST

Walk, friend, but very gently by these trees,
Do not disturb the leaves, for they are king,
And should ride winds to settle where they please,
To rot and build the soil for the spring.

Step carefully, please crush no sleeping mouse
Or hibernating toad; this is their land.
We humans are intruders in their house,
And should not change its patterns out of hand.

Please, break no living branch. Don't take away
Seed bolls nor any acorns you may find.
Pull up no grass or flowers, but let them stay
Re-carpeting the forest with their kind.

Bring not, I beg you, guns with fear and pain,
To kill and cripple rabbits, birds and deer.
This is their haven, thus it should remain.
They have no other place to go, save here.

Preserve this forest, friend,
It is your duty,
For children of your child
Will need its beauty.

CHAPTER FOURTEEN

Suppertime

On an early thirties visit to our Salem Grandmother Hersey (Nana), the family medic, Doctor Hogan, who I think had delivered Mother, asked how we on Cape Cod were weathering the Depression.

"Fine," said Mother, "But we get kind of tired of eating oyster stew, roast chicken, fried scallops, and flounder."

"Goodness," said the Doctor, "I wish we could afford any one of them!"

Of course, those were not on the menu for every meal. Saturday night was unfailingly baked beans and homemade brown bread, the leavings of which, mashed with mayonnaise became sandwiches for school on Monday, unless we got lucky and had the leftover beans with codfish cakes for Sunday breakfast. Sunday dinner was apt to be a roast, often a chicken from the backyard or, if we could afford it, leg of lamb was a favorite. Leftovers were rehashed some time the first of the week. Dad was something of a 'meat'un'taters' kind of eater. He did not go much for 'fancy', but ate most anything. He had to have bread with every meal. His approach to food was deliberate, and though he was a big eater, he didn't get fat. After serving us, he would serve his own plate slowly, seemingly thinking about how much to take, and just where to put it, cut things up, or mix or mash them to his desired consistency, and chew every thing thoroughly. Result being, that us kids were ready for seconds before he had downed his first bite. Remarks like (Mother) "Wait until your father has something to eat," and (Father), "Yes, dammit, let me get in a couple of mouthfuls!" were common. Dad ate with great relish, but never was one to remark graciously about Mother's cooking. At one supper when she had tried a new recipe, she asked if he liked it. "Well, I ate it, didn't I?" was all she got from him. Having filled his tank, he would refuse an additional helping with "No, little does for me!" He really enjoyed eating, and obviously liked Mother's cooking, but compliments came hard. "I do like to eat meals on time," he said more than once, "If I wait too long, I get the guts ache."

Sunday night was usually kind of 'pickup', toasted peanut butter sandwiches, welsh rabbit. Sometimes, in season, of a Sunday evening we were forced to exist on nothing but a huge strawberry short cake with home made biscuits below, and mounds of hand whipped cream on top, and Dad's home grown sweet strawberries in between. All you could eat! That was hard. Dad particularly liked crackers broken up in milk and often got them for Sunday supper. Mother was big on vegetables, and what with the garden and preserves, we got our share. During the first part of WWII, Mom got on to something the Government recommended called "Antiscorbutic" Salad, which was certainly a healthy thing if you lived in the city, and were worried about scurvy.

A favorite dish which came down from Dad's family, and had been a mainstay at sea, was potato bargain, or slum gullion, (also called lobscouse, lob skow or potato son-of-a-bitch). Fat salt pork fried out in a spider, with onions, sliced potatoes, lots of them, and salt and pepper. A bit of water, cover, and let them smother. I could eat it until my sides ache! As long as there were plenty of onions, this might have been good for scurvy, I suppose, also. Mother was a big fan of onions, said her father bought them a bushel during the first war, about the time the Spanish Influenza was beginning to rampage through the world; it killed more people than the fighting. Anyway, Mom's family ate lots of onions that year, and their home was one of the few where the flu didn't strike. Whenever there was a rumor of flu in the neighborhood, or even a lot of local colds, Mom trotted out the onions. Luckily we never did have a problem with scurvy.

I will not even try to discuss the platters of fried scallops, on which we dined at least once a week from October first until cold suspended scalloping activities. A delicate creature, they would freeze if they were out in the frosty air too long before you got them home.

We ate a lot of stews and chowders, beef or lamb, oyster or scallop stew, clam or corn chowder. Kernel corn and beans (succotash) made a protein rich non-meat meal, as did scrambled eggs with corn, both good for the pocket book, and the war effort. If ever there was a meal we didn't quite finish, you could count on seeing it again as 'hishyhashy-hell-of-a-mess,' or 'eat it quick, before it spoils' leftovers. What tiny bits were left on plates, plus peelings, com husks and so forth, which had food value, were re-cycled by being fed to the hens or the pig when we had one.

A very friendly summer lady from across the street complained to Mother that, although she had a once every two weeks trash pickup, she hated to keep food scraps that long in the summer heat.

"Well," said Mother, "We feed ours to the pig".

The lady promptly bought a piglet, and as she had a cook, advised her to feed it all leftovers in addition to the special pig diet. She had to hire a man to build a sty, and secure considerable pig food, plus paying two dollars for the piglet, but during the summer allowed as how she was satisfied with the venture. In the fall, looking forward to returning to her city home, she called the pig man. The piglet was by now a huge, well-fed porker.

"Do you buy back your pigs?"

"Well, yes, sometimes," said the man

Sister Nancy and friend

cautiously, thinking price while looking at the fat and fancy pile of pork chops, "Just how much did you want for him?"

"Oh, well," said the lady, cool and business like, (she by habit usually braced one hand on her hip when standing around talking) "I'd like to get one dollar!"

"One - one dollar?" asked the pig merchant, seeing large hams, fresh shoulders and sides of bacon.

"Yes," said the lady, adjusting her pince-nez, "I paid two dollars for him, but after all, I used him all summer!"

The pig man/butcher shut up, paid up, and loaded up, leaving the lady thoroughly content with her summer disposal project.

Our first pig we named 'Warfie' after a pig in a movie, and he became a pet of the family, which made his eminent demise in the early winter an emotional experience. Dad arranged for the pig person to take him away while every one was in school, and when the meat was delivered, no one really noticed. It was cold enough that winter so that the bacon and a ham could be hung in the barn, the rest sent to a freezer locker. When the first pork dinner was set on the table, however- er, Lil' Brother Link noticed. "Is ... is that Warfie?"

Nana Hersey

56

Answer in the affirmative, and he stuck with potatoes while our heartless sisters and I ate away. After that, it wasn't mentioned, and during that winter, he joined us as we ate everything but the 'oink'. The next two pigs, (called 'Points' and 'Rations' in honor of the wartime food rationing,) were not so much a part of the family during their growing season. There was a calf, too, a combined effort of Dad and a friend. Come killin' time, to save money by not having the butcher come to the house, it was decided that two grown men could do the job, load the animal in our multi-service car, and deliver him to the butcher ready to be chopped into steaks. The beast and his co-owners marched down into the woods, taking along a rifle. There was a period of silence, then the beast and the two men with a gun marched OUT of the woods, and Father called the man to come and take care of things. There was something said about aiming the rifle, then looking into those trusting eyes.

We did get steaks eventually from the cow, however, which is more than we ever got from the turtle. He was a huge snapper. He was caught crossing the road and Dad probably would have let well enough alone, except for Ben Black, the southern gentleman who was cook and chauffeur for the man who also employed Dad. Ben noted that there should be plenty of meat in that Ol' critter for a fine turtle soup, which he would make at our house. The critter was given a stick to snap on, and landed upside down on Mother's kitchen table, to her disgust. The question of how to begin consumed some time; although Ben had prepared turtle soup, he had not started from scratch.

Ben and Harriet Hersey (my maternal grandparents) with a daughter who died in childhood

The turtle was understandably unwilling to assist in the process but lay there on the table clawing the air, mouth tightly holding the stick. A boyhood chum of Dad's dropped by, as he was wont to do, and tried to give advice, but the turtle wouldn't take it, and the would be cooks couldn't make any good use of it. We kids got a few glimpses of the procedure, but the language in the kitchen wasn't fit for our consumption.

Mother kept us in the other room and turned up the radio. Bedtime came and things in the kitchen were still in an uproar, and next morning the turtle was gone, but Mother's kitchen took some time to get back to normal... I do not think they ever got inside the shell, and turtles, like snakes can take a long time dying. I guess Thoph Smith's dump got the remains, and suffice to say we didn't have any turtle soup. To date I never have tried it, but frog legs, ah! That's another story.

Mother and Uncle Ben with their grandfather (Ben Hersey)

We didn't have much to do with 'store bought' snack food during the depression. No Fritos, Pringles or Cheezits for afternoon snacks. Mothers did pretty well with cookies, and our Mom rolled, hand cut and deep-fried a pile of crisp brown donuts most every week. She also made highly desirable peanut butter straws, (pie dough, folded over peanut butter sliced into thin strips and baked, delicious with the root beer she brewed each summer). Sometimes, though, a person gets an appetite attack while playing. When that happened out in the field or woods, you made do. There were often things you could pick to eat, checker berries in the winter, which tasted like Teaberry gum, wild black, blue and strawberries in the summer, and for more elaborate fare, puffball mushrooms and fried frog legs. Harding French knew about the frog legs; catching, dressing, and cooking. Harding (Frenchy) and his sister Eugenia, (who occasionally sat for us when Mom and Dad went out - she was really nice and always good for a few ghost stories). They lived with their mother in Mayfair, an area about a mile and a half north and west of the South Dennis Village, now a community of hundreds of homes, but back then a pretty lonely part of town. After his family moved from their solitary house down into the village, someone gave Frenchy a small building, which we took apart and moved, with the help of an old wagon, down, behind his new home.

Greatgrandmother, Pauline (Baxter) Hall

Greatgrandfather Hall

It was the clubhouse, and scene of some fine cook-ins. Frenchy was in charge of the frog leg department, while Harold Wilkey and I scavenged for puffballs, and any other goodies, which we could acquire without risking arrest. The puffballs (I'm sure they had a more proper name) were fungi of the mushroom family. They grew around pastures where cows were kept; 6 to 10 inches across and looking like somewhat misshapen spotted balloons. Harold knew about them. Sliced and fried, they tasted something like cheese. The frying of puff-balls and frog legs took place on the clubhouse on a wood burning stove, sanitation was nil, and we had no kind of assurance the mushrooms were fit for human fodder, but man, were those club snacks sumptuous.

The wagon we used to move the clubhouse supplied us with a fine tool to use in our food marauding expeditions. It was a discarded canoe with a rotten bow which we discovered near a local pond loaded on our wobbly buggy and pulled home. Harold's father's carpentry shop was enlisted, and we designed a tall dragonhead, which filled in the broken bow of the canoe, and stuck up about three and a half feet in front as in the old Viking boats. Strange but true, we hadn't heard at that time of the supposed Norsemen's adventures on Bass River, but there we were in a dragon headed boat, (which took in only a little water). With our 'green dragon,' we added courses to our clubhouse snacks by some clandestine shopping in a large commercial garden conveniently located on the bank of the river about a half mile below the bridge. Tomatoes, carrots, radishes, and just over the first rise, MELONS! Musk melons, cantaloupes, watermelons, what a feast!

We heard that Mr. Nickerson, who owned the farm had a rock salt loaded shotgun at the ready for garden thieves, but we were clever, and never once did he suspect us as the culprits in the Great Melon Raids in spite of the fact that of the six or eight young teens in the village, we were the only three who paddled the river in a green dragons-head canoe.

Rena, Raymond, Nana, Ben and Mother (Herseys)

CLAM CHOWDER

An old Cape Codder, on a trip.
Had packed some vittles in his grip.
He nibbled as the train rolled on,
By Buffalo, supplies were gone.

Although the train sold things to eat,
He stoically kept to his seat,
Till, in Chicago, feeling gaunt,
He spied the depot restaurant,

The menu didn't tempt him much,
He wasn't used to steaks and such.
About to give the beans a try,
Cape Cod Clam Chowder caught his eye!

His innards had commenced to roll,
As he addressed the steaming bowl,
But when he'd tried a spoon or two,
He stared, down-hearted at his stew.

Just then a waitress, passing by,
Observed his frown, and heard him sigh.
She sensed his somber attitude,
And asked him how he found his food.

"I found it looks alright," he said,
"New England white, not New York red,
It's hot the way it should be, Ma'am,
But tell me, where'd you hide the clam?"

CHAPTER FIFTEEN

Save It For A Rainy Day

Been said, (I believe erroneously) that parsimony is wide spread on Cape Cod. I misdoubt not the veracity of the accusers, but perhaps should endeavor to cast a rather clearer illumination on the situation. A blacksmith - well, farrier - of my acquaintance described a customer as a fellow with deep pockets and short arms in other words, a cheapskate. Well, I knew the fellow, and true, he was known to squeeze a nickel until Jefferson was INSIDE Monticello, but cheap? No, just holding on for the hard times.

Cape Codders are saving people. They have had to be. Through the years, there have been considerable more lean times than fat, and Cape Codders know it! Mother said you should always use every thing at least twice. Like, if you had to smoke cigars, at least save the ashes. They would keep moths out of the closet, and soaking the cigar butts in water made a good aphid killer for the roses. Old sayings such as "haste makes waste", and "take care of the pennies and the dollars will take care of themselves" found fertile soil here. See, it's a matter of taking care, being careful, and making do. A woman in West Dennis used to save her tea bags, dry them on a line, and reuse. Except for one, which she kept moist for sealing envelopes. Sound cheap? No, saving! Mother said she knew a woman who kept everything, even had a box marked 'pieces of string, too short to use', but I think she read that in the *Reader's Digest*.

Mother was not a Caper, but she knew. She was from Nova Scotia stock, (by way of her mother,) another piece of ground, which, like the Cape stuck out into the Atlantic, its people fishermen, and the like. Nana was among other things a time saver. She used to like to sit on our front porch when she made a summer visit and eat fresh cucumbers from Dad's garden. She never peeled them, nipped off the stem end,

salted, and munched away, skins and all. Saved time. Her breakfasts were interesting. She would put a shredded wheat biscuit in a bowl, drop a soft boiled or poached egg on top; and pour coffee over the mess, and EAT it! Saved time.

Charlie B. who lived up near the head of the ponds in Mayfair was a time saver, He realized what a waste of time it was to cut his fireplace wood into small pieces when it was just going to burn up anyway, so he utilized the old 'day log' method, (it was mentioned in 'Drums Along The Mohawk'). He stuck one end of a long log into the fire, and as it burned, he just shoved it in further. Saved quite a bit of time, too, 'til one day it set fire to his house.

Mother was not one for throwing things away. She grew up during WWI with meatless Tuesdays, heatless Wednesdays, save peach pits for gas mask filters, roll and save the tinfoil from your candy wrappers, easy on the sugar and "don't forget to take your fat can to the butcher". Then, later learning to make do on Ol' Cape C. with one, two, and eventually six young'uns called for recycling before the word was popular. An old Sears Roebuck Catalogue, for example, there is many a rainy day's activity in a catalogue. Paste a pictured model on some cardboard, you have a paper doll.... and on the next few pages, her wardrobe. Folding down each catalogue page in a triangular pattern can make a door stop. Then, too, you can always sit alone, quietly and leaf through the catalogue, decide on something you need and then go back up to the house and order it.

Mother was a prodigious re-user of newspapers. So much so, that if my Father had not delivered the *Boston Post* door to door on Sundays, we would have had to send out for more. Often left with extras, Dad dutifully brought them home. Mother lined everything with newspaper: trunks, drawers, closets and pantry shelves.

She spread newspapers on newly washed floors to give us a walking area while the floor dried. Stormy days found newspaper at the door as a boot and rubber catcher and as little tots our Saturday night dunk in the portable enamel or galvanized tub (depending on the year) took place in the kitchen with

Father (center) and friends, Bass River, c.1904

the tub on the floor, surrounded by pads of newspaper. She put newspaper under mattresses to keep the metal springs from staining, wrapped breakables such as Christmas ornaments and used it for padding in mailed packages. She used it as an absorbent surface for cleaning fish or vegetables, as a material to sop up spills, and as a lint free substance for cleaning windows.

The word was, NO holes in the newspaper until Father had read it, so many activities had to wait, but there were the funny papers: pre-comic book, pre-television, often really funny comic strips. So much a part of Sunday life, that during a newspaper strike, the mayor of New York City, Fiorillo LaGuardia, read the comics over the radio so children (and not a few adults) would not miss the activities of Dick Tracy and their favorite characters! In addition, particularly in the Sunday paper, there would be a children's activity page, dot-to-dot pictures, puzzles and conundrums, and some times an on-going children's story or sing-along lyrics for Christmas or Easter songs. After the reading was finished, cutting could begin. There were paper dolls, material for scrapbooks, recipes, household hints and a radio guide for the week. On a rainy afternoon after school, Mother's imagination helped us fold newspaper sheets into soldier or Napoleon hats, boats and, with a bit of cutting, rolled up papers became fir trees, ladders, or pagodas.

Flat, specially-folded squares could be cut into strings or circles of identical paper dolls, soldiers, hearts, or ship's wheels. The bright comics, cut and pasted into interlocking colorful loops, made chains for the Christmas tree, or cut into long triangles, rolled on a knitting needle and glued, became multi-hued beads to string and wear. Newspaper soaked in water, or in a flour and water paste made a splendid papier-mâché from which to model puppet heads. And that was just newspapers!

Mother sewed, knitted and darned, altering, making, and repairing our clothing, which were as often as not hand-me-downs from an older child in the family, or up the street. Some companies began to use printed cotton for bagging flour, and animal grain. The bags came in pretty patterns, and Mother's scissors and foot powered sewing machine, with the guidance of some Buttner's patterns, transformed them into dresses and aprons for her and the girls. Clothes no longer repairable found themselves cut into strips, and braided into a rug, so that that which you could no longer wear, you could walk on.

Dad recycled just about every thing. From oyster shells crushed up small for the hens, (gave them calcium for stronger shells) or used to resurface the driveway, to hen manure, seaweed and wood ashes plowed under in the garden to sweeten the earth (the ashes, some of which Mother used in making soap, also did a good job of providing traction on icy walkways). When hens quit laying, they found their way into the pot, and remember, everything's chicken but the bill. If you killed a pig, you used every part of it except the squeal. Dad saved old boards; partial cans of paint, previously used, and often bent nails. His workbench was always full of retreaded glass food jars of odd, but re-useable screws, bolts and assorted hardware; a repair project might be harder to do with used material, but who could afford new stuff. In fact, during WWII you couldn't buy new building supplies.

The best paying job I ever had to that date was in 1944, after the hurricane struck Cape Cod. This was war-time, and neither man power or materials were available to help put the ruins of the Dennis and Yarmouth south shore cottages back to useable condition. I was hired to pull the old nails from the broken boards and timber, stack the useable wood, straighten out the nails, and save them. Wages, a smacking seventy-five cents an hour! For saving things! Louis Kelly told of a small dairy farmer on the north side who knew how to make do. He supplied milk for a girl's camp, and while he was at the sink pumping water to wash some of his gear, the mistress of the camp came by.

"Mr. H.," she sez, "We will be needing milk for four more girls next week, I hope that won't put too much of a strain on your supplies."

"No Ma'am," sez Mr. H., "Not as long as that pump handle holds out!"

An old timer down the street smoked cigars. He kept the butts for chewing tobacco, dried out the cuds to smoke in his pipe, and used the ashes for snuff. Now, that isn't being cheap, That's fore laying! Putting it by for the bad times. Willful Waste Makes Woeful Want!

PROCRASTINATIN'

Day before Christmas and winter has landed.
Although there's no snow, and not too much ice,
Still, it's a mite chilly for working bare-handed
And it has froze up over-night once or twice.

I'll finish this pipe and get on with my chores,
There's various things to be done for the season,
Like, wood to be split and then carried indoors.
It's hard gettin' started this year for some reason.

I highly suspect that the wood is quite damp.
Last week there it rained for two days without stoppin'.
And that's when my elbow developed this cramp.
Be better tomorrow, and easier choppin'.

I 'spose I should first clear a place in the shed,
So when the wood's cut I'll have some place to stack it.
Then, maybe I'll wait for the cold days ahead,
When wood's good and froze, it's so easy to crack it.

It's not so much doing, as startin' the thing.
- I may let 'er set and go south until spring.

CHAPTER SIXTEEN

The Customer Is, Always

Stores, now, that was another side of things. Even with heavy recycling, you still have to do some buying. I mentioned that Dad ran the P.O./store in South Dennis for a spell when I was a baby, and just before I got here. Years before he ran the store, he worked there. Located across from an off and on skating area and swamp (used mostly in the winter), the store stocked general groceries, and had a large wood stove in the center for customers to gather around in cold weather. I never remember the store when Dad ran it, but in my youth, the next owner had kept the general decor, and the stove, of course was sacrosanct. Summer times, there were benches on the porch in front for the mail awaiters to slouch, smoke, spit and jaw while the mail was sorted. Clarence Baylis ran the shebang when I was a kid. He was fire chief, which meant the P.O. closed whenever there was a fire. Actually, most of the village closed, because just about every able-bodied man was on the all-volunteer force.

Clarence started the drive to clear a skating area in the front of the cedar swamp. He took up a collection and hired a bulldozer, and had the area cleared of the reeds and mud, which clogged the tiny natural pond, pushed up mud walls to frame a rink of sorts, and waited for the rain and cold weather to finish what he started. Many of the villagers laughed at the effort, called it 'Baylie's Folly', but it rained, it froze, and lots of kids enjoyed skating on the safe, shallow area over many a year. When they got cold, they could cross the street to the post office, and thaw out. Clarence was active in the first aid organization set up during the war, and was a prime mover in the boy scouts. A mighty fine citizen. Thanks, Clarence.

When Charlie Underwood owned the store in South Dennis (and hired Dad), it was back in the horse and buggy days, and the next nearest grocery store was West Dennis, or Dennisport, out of town, so to speak, and a long drive in a surrey. In Charlie's time, there were very few individually packaged items. Pickles came by the hogshead, crackers by the barrel, vegetables in picking baskets. Raisins and beans, corn meal, rice and sugar were scooped from a large container into a paper bag, weighed and tied with string. Fruits were counted into a bag or basket, cheese was cut off a large wheel wrapped in white paper, and tied with string. Bananas were sold by the bunch, if they had them (and they might well from time to time, since that down-Cape fella, Lorenzo Dow Baker, started United Fruit and began shipping them in from the islands). You might say that stores in those days were really full-service, because the clerk or owner had to stay with you every step of the way.

Flour came in large barrels, and a busy cook would buy it that way, by the barrel. Anyone who just wanted a little could have it in a brown paper bag (which bag was likely made on a machine invented by Luther Childs Crowell, of West Dennis). One local woman who enjoyed a fabulous reputation for her prize pies, cakes and cookies bought a barrel at a time. She insisted on King Arthur Flour, would have none other. One time when she came for her flour, there was a problem. The flour barrels came UNLABLED, the flour was all the same grade, and came from the same mill, and the company sent along several assorted labels, so the storekeeper could label a barrel with the brand the customer preferred. Except, Charlie Underwood was currently out of King Arthur labels. Charlie was up for the challenge. He was temporarily out of King A. he told her, but had some due in the first of the week.

"In the mean time, why, you just take this new stuff home, I'll put the barrel on the buckboard for you, and, say, maybe Tuesday, if you don't like this flour, why, bring it back, and exchange for a barrel of good King Arthur, and I shan't charge you for what you use!"

The lady knew a deal when she saw one, so she took the flour home, did a fine double bit of baking, even put up several loaves of bread and then on Tuesday, brought what remained of the flour back, Wouldn't do, she wanted her King Arthur. Charlie took the partly used barrel to the back room, refilled it from another barrel, put the top on tight, and affixed a King Arthur label. The woman left content, but returned two days later, madder than a wet hen. Seems she got part way down in the barrel, and she found her own flour sifter!

A woman came up to Dad when he was clerking, and asked for a quarter's worth of sugar. Dad weighed it and bagged it.

"Now, how much would that be," sez the lady.

"Twenty five cents," sez Dad.

"My," sez she, dipping into her change purse, "How things has gone up!"

Tell a store story, and you'll get a couple back. Storekeepers were right obliging in those days. Lady came into Goodspeed's store in Dennis village just as he was closing of a Saturday, said she was having guests and wanted some fancy very thinly sliced cheese for the party. The proprietors pulled a new big cheese wheel out, and taking special care, sliced a half pound of delicately thin pieces, wrapped them carefully, and gave them to the pleased customer. Monday morning, she returned the cheese. Said her guests didn't come.

Henry Kelly told me this one: running a

charge in the local stores was a way of life in the winter. As the spring work revived the customer's financial condition, he paid off his debt. One fellow had run up an uncomfortably large bill at Sears store down on Sesuit Neck, and Old Sears told him, regretfully, that they could extend him no additional credit. He didn't come in for a few weeks, and then appeared, with a smiling countenance at the counter. "I would like to pay my bill, thank you, and I will need a few items." The owner cheerfully bagged the 'few items', at which the customer said thank you, and started out with the bundle.

"Just a moment," said the owner, "I thought you said you were going to pay up your bill!"

The customer stopped, hand on the door. "No, I believe what I said was I would like to pay my bill, and I would, but that will take a little more time. Thank you!" And he slipped out.

When I was 14 and jerking sodas and selling nonprescription drugs in the West Dennis Pharmacy, a woman breezed in, went to the back of the store, grabbed something, and breezed out with a "Put this on the bill, thank you." I knew the lady, and she did have a reputation for being a tad vague, so I reported the incident to the owner.

"How can I charge her when I don't know what she took?"

The owner smiled, "She does that regularly; all you can do is charge her for what she might have taken." So I did. Some times proprietors are as interesting as their customers. An Eastham owner when asked for Wonder Bread said, "No, we don't carry it no more, we was always out of it."

CHAPTER SEVENTEEN
Who's Minding the Store?

I spoke earlier of the stores in Hyannis, and Dennisport. There were as mentioned three 5 & 10's in Hyannis during the thirties: Grant's, Woolworth's, and McLellan's, all chain stores, as, in fact were the grocery stores in Dennisport: A & P, First National, and, I think, a Nation Wide. They were NOT supermarkets. They all ran more or less like Mr. Baylis' village store. There were clerks behind counters, and especially in the groceries, many goods were shipped in bulk, shipped in large containers, and selected amounts bagged or wrapped by the clerk; there was lots of personal service. You could discuss with your clerk the condition of the lettuce, how long the eggs had been in the store, and were they local, and whether the melons were properly mellow. Often you gave your prepared list to the clerk, and he bustled around filling your order while you attended to other business.

The meat man would bring a large hunk of meat from the cooler, and you discussed which part he should cut off for you. When lamb was selected, the butcher took it out back and tied it into a neat, bone-free roastable roll - the piece you looked at and asked for, not just something taken from a precut-prepacked-plastic-covered-don't-look-at-the-back-that's-where-the-FAT-is selection hidden in a foggy glass case. We liked to shop on Saturday evening, because, for one thing, that was the night when Father was most liable to have some money, what with collecting for his week's work. Also, stores closed on Sundays so if there were bananas which seemed a bit too ripe to stay in good saleable condition until Monday, the manager at the First National would sell them to Dad for a pittance - often a bushel basket full. ("Bring the basket back when you come this way, will you, Freeman?") We feasted on the dead ripe fruit, and Mother promptly started cooking; corn starch pudding with sliced bananas was my favorite, or a custard and banana pie, a couple of the kids were sold on peanut butter and banana sandwiches, (Link used to slather his with mayonnaise, yuck!) There would be banana bread, sometimes banana fritters and slices with your cereal on Sunday morning.

There was a shoe store in Harwich Center where a clerk carefully measured your feet, helped you into BOTH shoes, with a long-handled shoehorn and made you walk around on a soft rug, assuring you of a proper fit. I got my high cuts there, the ones with the JACK KNIFE pocket on the side. They were the only thing that made my corduroy knickers bearable. There was also a boring place in Harwich Port called Buttners where we kids went only under duress. This was where Mother bought our underwear, dry goods, sox, handkerchiefs and such. They also sold cloth, buttons and thread that mother needed for her efforts to keep us clothed. Notions, 'course, if it was just notions you needed, why, there were three 'shoppes' right there on the main street of South Dennis! Besides the Lumberyard and the P.O. / Grocery.

You'd pretty much have to know where they were to find them, hidden as they were in the front rooms of homes, and I shan't allow you to believe they were well stocked, but you could sometimes fill in if your needs were small, and of a common variety. A paper of needles? A box of common pins? Sure! Although I seem to remember that Mother got one batch of needles that had rusted, old stock, I guess. The shops were run by the ladies of the house, going from south to north, Edith Fredson (Thacher), Alice Lewis and the Misses Thacher up the road (Dad's Uncle Peleg's daughters). I rather doubt that any of the three grossed more than $2.50 in a good week, they carried a small and similar stock, and were less than a country mile from farthest to farthest.

Alice Lewis was the most businesslike, (her shop was in the middle, and she seemed to have more of a selection). All three ran to pencils, bobby pins, knitting needles, (but only in the wrong sizes) and yarn (color problems; if you started a project with yarn from one of these front room stores, it's dollars to donuts you couldn't match it, or have to wait for enough of the right yarn to finish. Also, some of the yarn had been around the store so long, there was apt to be some fading), candles, pads of paper, crayons, a few ribbons, and some sewing supplies: notions.

Edith-Fredson had two boys, so she wisely did not carry anything edible, and I don't remember that Alice Lewis did, but the Thacher girls had penny candy! Two problems, they'd had that same candy for a good while, (they were only there and open in the summer) and they didn't like children in the store. Blanche and Louise Thacher were maiden ladies who lived with their mother. I think they were both schoolteachers. When school time came, they draped tablecloths over their tables of stock, and lit a shuck back for their winter home. I bought a couple of bolsters from them one day when I was delivering the paper. They charged a startling 2 cents a piece (Mr. Baylis charged 1 cent) the chocolate looked strange, and they were hard and musty tasting. But outside of that, they weren't too bad. They also had some of those hard sugar sticks, with various flavors, like maple, mint, banana, watermelon, but they all tasted alike, and always seemed to be kind of soft and sticky. I had the good sense not to make it a habit.

One of the Thacher brothers apparently was holder of the patterns on the 'Kewpie' doll, and made much of his living from them. Neither of the two boys married, either. The Thachers and I think Alice Lewis, too, carried some picture post cards, a bit of stationery, even a few little Cape souvenirs: practically gift shops!

There had been for a number of years a general store on the Main Street, about half way between Alice Lewis' shop and the Railroad Track, run by Watson F. Baker (to identify him from Watson B. Baker or 'Wattie B.' who lived across the street). It had closed as a store before I was aware of it, but had big store windows in front, and an entrance porch. The family lived in, I think, Wollaston, and summered at the old store. I played with a boy there, named Watson, and one year (1942) they rented the old store, (nee guesthouse) to the family of a BEAUTIFUL girl! I remember her name was June. I had seen that someone was staying at the house, and thought it was young Watson. Turned out not to be. June sang on a Boston Radio show which used talented kids, and after we had struck up an acquaintanceship, she sang for ME! "Tangerine": she sang it every bit as good as Helen O'Connell did in the movie, "The Fleet's In" and on the hit record. After her family's two weeks rental was up, she went back to Boston and I never saw her again. (The next year, I tried singing, "You'll Never Know" from the Movie "Hello Frisco" to a pretty girl in West Yarmouth ...(Long Bike Ride!), but it didn't have the lasting effect on her that June's song had on me.)

Not to be out done by the neighbors, we had a little home store for a while in an entry room in the "new" house, the one Dad bought from his Mother's other heirs. We did not carry notions (but Nancy did try to start a lending library: a nickel a week for Bobbsie Twins books), just penny candy, and Mom's home made Root Beer. We just told the local kids, and about the only one who traded at our store was Harold Wilkey. He LOVED that root beer. We made solemn vows that we wouldn't eat or drink up the profits, and it was torture on a hot day to watch Harold slurp down a quart bottle of that fine cold root beer when we couldn't grab a bottle for ourselves; the store soon reverted to an entry.

My own early selling experience did not depend entirely on veggies and newspapers. Around 1940 I started on my candy route. It began at the First National, when they had a sale on nickel candy bars six for 25 cents! Figured out you could sell them for 30 cents, and make 20% on the deal. If you sold them, not if you ate them. I used to go where the money was, to the Town Hall, a few candy eaters there, and the Lumber Yard, not too bad! I tried houses, but with indifferent success. However, any group working in the area was sure to be good for a sale, and Harold Wilkey, who had a source of income we'll discuss later, always bought.

My real success began in the summer of '41 when Uncle Sam sent me a giant surge of customers in the form of the U.S. Army! It started in the black of night when huge vehicles rolled quietly through our little main street, and disappeared in the direction of Mayfair. Up and out the next morning, we found the Army hiding in the piney woods along the river, and some even in our front yard and woods, dug in, and involved in heavy-duty maneuvers, which were supposed to be a deep dark secret.

After spotting the camouflaged vehicles and the troops in foxholes, I flew home for my candy basket. It was emptied in no time, and I prevailed on Mom to whoosh me down to the store for more. Dad had been buying some goods from a wholesale firm in Hyannis, where they had big boxes of candy bars, assorted, for way under the Chain Store price. My fortune was made! I wondered from foxhole to foxhole, dealing out candy, and taking in nickels until my supply was gone. Over heard two officers talking, "Here we are, supposed to be a big secret, and even the kids selling candy can find us!" As long as the troops maneuvered in the Dennis area, I replenished my supply, and sold candy to the soldiers (most of whom seemed to be from Texas, and were horrified when I dipped an oyster from the river, opened it with my trusty jack knife, and swallowed it). I suppose this all makes me a pre-war profiteer, but business is business.

THE FAIR

We have an announcement before the last prayer,
The Ladies Benevolent Club now advises,
That Wednesday's the day of the annual fair,
With potholders, aprons and doilies and prizes.
There's dozen of ashtrays they've made out of clams,
And marvelous marmalades, jellies and jams.

The pony rides will not be with us, I fear,
They're canceled, you know at the Deacon's insistence.
The dear little creatures escaped us last year,
And trampled his tulip bed out of existence.
But there is pet judging from turtles to lambs,
And marvelous marmalades, jellies and jams.

We're looking for any white elephant item,
The girls from the thrift shop are bringing old clothes.
We're sure to have paper-backs, ad infinitum,
And dear Mr. Brown's magic act, I suppose.
The bridge club is bringing the beans and the hams,
And marvelous marmalades, jellies and jams.

CHAPTER EIGHTEEN
If You Can't Do The Time -

Seldom a scene of such utter perfection, as the view from the steps of the House of Correction!

It's the truth. The old brick and barbed wire H. of C. looks out from it's hillside over the Barnstable Village, the harbor, Sandy Neck and the Cape Cod Bay beyond. A helluva place to put a jail. I've been up and down those steps a few times, visiting friends, and doing a couple of Christmas shows for the inmates. Seems too bad that they have scrapped it and sent all inmates to the new Jail on the upper Cape. The Barnstable Jail (nee: House of Correction) has a long history. There has been a jail in that area since at least 1690, it moved a couple of times before settling down on the hillside between the two County Court houses facing the Barnstable harbor. The inmates were there awaiting trial, or serving time for such crimes as not supporting the minister, to spying during the Civil War, to murder. The spy, (according to "Cape Cod Confidential" by Even J. Albright) was also General Custer's mistress, one Annie Jones and although sent to Barnstable to serve her sentence, she really spent her time in a rented room in the village. There were no facilities for a woman prisoner in 1864. Mostly, though, the Barnstable jail housed naughty local boys, middle aged misdemeanor-ites, and aging drunks who disturbed the peace. I get the feeling being incarcerated in Barnstable was not usually considered 'hard-time'. In fact, persons who had experienced compulsory stays at the facility often referred to it as "the Country Club". In fact, as far back as 1897, a Legislative Committee on Prisons found that it was "...A prison in name only." (From the *Boston Evening Record*, from research by Even J. Albright). Nobody seemed to get too excited about it.

Item: A regular user of the "club", Benny (not his name), managed to be found obnoxiously drunk and disruptive every winter, and get sent to Barnstable for a short sentence, usually lasting out the remainder of the cold season, when sober Benny was a friendly and sociable soul, and was well liked in and out of the jail. One colder than normal winter Benny didn't show up on the arrest sheets, and consequently was not in his usual spot on the prison roster when the hard chill of January came around. Fearful of his well being, the SHERIFF went personally to Benny's home. Benny 'llowed as how he had been falling down drunk and laid outdoors in a snow drift over night early in the winter. Lost some of his toes to frostbite, so he had been laid up, and didn't get up town drinking this winter. Pretty good now, though, and probably see you next year. The Sheriff said he was glad it hadn't been worse, and they missed him over at the farm.

The Farm was just down the street a piece from the jail. It was tended by inmates, and the produce, both garden and dairy, helped supply the needs of the prisoners. One "regular," Henry, was particularly good with the dairy herd, and when one of the cows became sick. The Sheriff noted Henry was not currently serving time, so he made another visit. Henry thought he could get the cow, a favorite, up and running again, and would the Sheriff give him a lift over to the farm. He would, and Henry stayed at the farm for about a week, nursed the cow back to health, and left with thank you, and I'll see you later.

In a thinly populated and informal area such as the Cape was, justice sometimes tended to be a bit on the personal side. John, who was in trouble, and in jail a good bit of the time, was being sentenced for a small infraction.

"Three Months in the House of Correction," toned the judge.

"Three Months," sneered John, in what he assumed was a voice inaudible to the judge, "That won't give me time to take off my shoes."

"Six Months," snapped the judge, "That should give you time to take your socks off, too!"

Proving, I suppose that Justice may be blind, but is not deaf.

One chronic offender complained that his three month sentence would set him free in

February, which was cold and as work was just about non existent in the deep winter, he would probably be arrested again. The judge 'lowed as how he might just as well stay in until May when it was warmer. He agreed, and the sentence was changed to six months to accommodate him.

Law in general was quite loose when I was a kid, although I remember a man on the north side being arrested for drunken driving with a horse and buggy. A man I later worked with sipped on little bottles as he drove a big sand truck. One day he took an extra sip, and smashed head on into a large oak tree in Harwich. The police, when called, carted him home to his wife and called the truck owner to collect the wreck. No arrest, no tickets, no complaints from any one in town. We had one policeman in town that I remember, and sometimes an auxiliary to help with the summer influx. The main policeman became chief, when they formed a more formal police department, but for some years he toured the town in his own car, siren and red light attached, and very handily kept things under control. He knew everyone in town, and if you got out of line, he knew just which father to speak to. An out late and potentially mischief directed group of teen age boys would dissolve at the mild suggestion that it was time they went home.

The auxiliary policeman was used to direct traffic in West Dennis . . . let folks across the street, you know. Once in a while he would cruise the busy beach. One day, after a tour of the beach, he met up with the "chief" He said he had found an auto which was noted on the stolen car list. The both went back to the beach, to find the driver and car gone.

"Damn," said the assistant, "I told him to stay right here till I got back." He was the same assistant who was set patrolling summer cottages one winter. The following spring the body of a man was discovered near one of the houses. As it had obviously been there all winter, the house checker was asked why he didn't see and report it. His answer was that there were 'No Trespassing' signs on all the seasonal houses, so of course he didn't go anywhere near them...for fear of being arrested. He wasn't bad, though, at letting people cross the street.

A good friend of mine, who later did our taxes, was accountant/treasurer for a local firm, when he allowed love to lure him into an indiscretion on some magnitude. He fell in love with an out of town girl, a plane ride away, and aching to impress her with wining, dining and gifts galore, skillfully siphoned off the cash he needed from the firm whose books he kept. Did it so well, that when conscience forced him to confess his crime, he had to show the investigators where and how he had gotten the money. He was given 6 months, and promised to refund the money. Then came February. He had a fair sized tax business, and the people and firms which he serviced were making worried noises about getting their Income Tax done on time. At their behest, he approached the Warden.

"I can't let you out," he was told, "But I see those people are depending on you, and there is an unused room in the front. Could your clients come here to the Jail to get their work done?"

They could, and would. All through tax season, his clients trotted up to the House of Correction clutching their records, marched in through the locked doors, got their tax work done, and headed back out to freedom, and the nearest mail box.

SEWERAGE

This year's meeting lacked for color,
Fact, I've seldom seen one duller.
Almost every motion passed without a sound.
But t'was faction fightin' faction,
Pure democracy in action,
When the sewerage proposal came around.

They was advocates and doubters,
Plus some throw-the-whole-thing-outers,
And a bunch who hadn't heard of it at all.
Johnson stood up to remind us,
"We can't put this thing behind us!"
And that got a snicker going 'round the hall.

Caleb Smith put forth a motion
They should drop it in the ocean,
But young Johnson quickly pointed out a flaw.
He said Smith was being selfish
As he'd always hated shell fish,
And besides that wasn't quite within the law.

Alvin Kimble told a yarn
'Bout the shanty by the barn,
And allowed we didn't need no fancy gear.
Then, we couldn't make our mind up
Where the stuff had ought to wind up,
So I guess we'll hear it all again next year.

CHAPTER NINETEEN

I Been Workin' On the Railroad

There were four big red letter days on our youthful calendars, Thanksgiving and Christmas, Fourth of July and the DAY SCHOOL LET OUT!! Winter is an uncertain time on the Cape. The vagaries of weather, stuck out in the ocean as we are, limit out door sports. Many winters were bare. Cape Cod has been off and on advertised as a twelve month golf paradise and then deep snows would make it impossible to play even with a red ball. Mother always said that one of the unkindest Christmas gifts for a Cape Cod child was a sled because as sure as you got one, you would wait in vain all through the winter for a slippery slope. We have winters of clear uncovered ground, and others with blizzards equaling a bad week in Minnesota. Even the basic temperature swoops from bone chilling cold to "Sorry, kids, no ice for skating this year."

Spring, on the other hand is pretty dependable. Most years we almost don't have one. Chill and damp follows winter, with a full measure of gray days and gloom. Autumns are usually splendid; cool mornings, and bright sunny days but you just can't make much use of them, when you have to sit around listening to the teachers yak. Leaves summer. The short back end of June, with the greens piling up as the slower trees put on their finery, July in full bloom, and the lovely heat of August that melts tar, browns the lawns and makes the sand almost too hot for bare feet. Luckily, you have been treading around in those bare feet through the summer, and they are so tough it will be a shame to stick them back in the high cuts on the morning of the first bus.

There was so much that had to be done in the summer! Bicycles to cruise the roads with, when you weren't chasing baseballs or evil doers. The river, and lots of ponds to splash in, jump in, and boat on, and miles of pine woods to walk in, sit in, tell stories in and get out of sight of the world. The woods behind both our first and second homes extended about three miles before getting close to the outlying houses of the villages to the east or north of us so we had a veritable forest to wander in. And then there were the Rail Road Tracks. Those two marvelous, mysterious metal rails that split our village in half. One thing, there wasn't any 'wrong' side, we had a good balance of residences on both sides of the track, and our only sense of a dividing line was Mother's directive to stay on this side, so that we could hear her Nova Scotia Cow Bell when it was supper time. (I made the mistake just once of being late and saying I hadn't heard the bell until the third time she rang, oops.) When we got bigger, and more mobile (what with bicycles and longer legs and all) that prohibition faded, and besides, we had moved to the other side of the tracks by then.

Trains didn't get to South Dennis until after the Civil War, and in fact, the boys coming back from the war had to disembark at Yarmouth and hike, or be met by relatives with horse and wagon. By the mid 1870's the tracks were all the way to Provincetown. The Railroad came in for two kinds of 'riding', one the conventional kind, on the seat of your pants, the other in the form of jokes. A local used the train to get his first view of the big city, Boston. There were a good many shops and restaurants inside the South Station, and gawking at them filled all his time between arriving, and the train home. Said the city was big, like he had expected, but he hadn't realized it had a roof over it. A well known northsider who had a pronounced stammer, encountered difficulty asking for a ticket to S-S-S-outh D-D-Dennis, so, "Harwich, dammit, I'll walk back!" A lady, not wanting to miss her station, asked the conductor on the end of the down Cape run if the train stopped in Provincetown. "If it don't, ma'am," he said as he punched her ticket, "There's gonna be one heluva splash!"

Regular passenger service to South Dennis ended just before WWII, but before that you could get on the train right there in the center of our village, and get off Lord knows where. Movies featured

scenes of people detraining in Hollywood, Chicago, New York. A favorite Radio show started with the train pulling into Grand Central Station (Cross roads of a million private lives!!). Just to stand and look at those rails stretching out of sight in the distance, moving closer and closer together as you gazed further up the track (but always turning and out of sight before they met). Even when the passenger service stopped, we would often watch the freight engine back and fill as it moved cars of lumber or coal around on the double track by the lumber yard. We rode the train to Hyannis, a few times and, just Nancy and I, on several excursions to Boston where we were met in South Station by Aunt Rena, our Mother's delightful maiden sister. She DID marry, later to an equally delightful man, but the younger years, when it was just she and us, were shear magic. From the South Station in Boston it was a ride, either to Haymarket square, for a bus, or to the start of the Narrow Gauge Railroad, which I remember left from Rowe's Wharf, carried on a ferry across Boston Harbor, and hence the eight slow miles (with 12 stops) past Revere Beach and the Roller Coasters to Lynn, (Nana said they stopped at every house, and twice at a double house) then a bus the rest of the way to Salem.

One, at least, of my ancestors bought stock in the railroad; I found a dividend voucher, for two dollars, dated 1870. Interestingly, it is signed in lovely flowing script, by the then treasurer, one E. N. Winslow. Winslow was my wife's maiden name. She's from the North Carolina Winslow's, by way of Hartford, Connecticut, but the family tree shows they slipped through to Massachusetts from England on some of the same ships as my Thacher forbearers, and, in fact, an early Thacher married a Rebecca Winslow here on the Cape, in the far past, and two historic homes side by side in Yarmouth; the Thacher house, and the Winslow/Crocker house. I guess Cape Codders just like to keep in it the family.

Riding on the rails, however was only one of the attractions. There was the penny squash, put one on the track, hide until the train passed by and you had a cool flat penny, if you could find it. There were often a few men at the station waiting for the train to bring them this or that from the outside world, and Mr. C. who was a brakeman and went off to work on the trains but lived in the neighborhood put in a lot of time around the station when the train was due, and was always full of stories. When I was around 6 Dad worked for a while at the nearby town office, and would occasionally need to slip mail into the mail bag to make sure it caught the train. One day I ran out between the freight wagon and the track when the train was braking to a stop, and was plucked out of harms way by some helpful grown up... Thanks!!

Walking was big. There were sometimes strange men working on the roadbed, or an inspector in a little gas buggy putting along the track, often a strange empty bottle lying by the tracks to consider, and when the engines were still steam driven, an occasional fire to report, and a genuine fresh water spring to stop and wet your whistle. Harold and I had sunk a small barrel in the spring, so that the water bubbling up from deep in the earth kept itself clean. It was cold and delightful.

There were several ways to walk the tracks. Scuffing dirt along the side of the rail bed, short steps, stepping on each tie, long steps stretching for every other tie, hopping or jumping from one tie to another, walking backward to talk, one foot on a rail, or doing the 'circus' thing, walking on one rail as on a tight rope. (Who can stay on the longest?) Along the way, we had to stop often so Harold could press his ear against the steel to see if there was a train imminent. We pretty much knew the sparse schedule, but there just might be a special. This was especially important as we came to the trestle over the river. It was touchy going across on the bare ties. The fast current was visible down below, and to be caught out there if there SHOULD be a Special could spell instant annihilation! 'Course the whole trestle was less than forty feet across, but you can't be too careful. I had an adventure with Harold on that bridge that I kept quietly to myself. It was winter, duck season, although we didn't have a trace of a hunting license, or any business carrying guns, Harold had two, a .22 rifle, and his father's double barrel 12 gage shotgun. There were ducks, a whole flock of them, swimming up above the bridge. He said he could pick'em off, but you just didn't shoot sitting ducks, only flying ones.

So I was to fire off that shotgun, startle the birds, they would fly up, and ol' sure-shot Harold the sportsman would shoulder his trusty single shot .22, and BANG! Duck for supper. Trouble was, I had never fired a shotgun, had no idea about recoil, and didn't accommodate for the fact that we were up on that railroad bridge with most uncertain footing. I fired, both barrels, the kick

put me flat on the open surface bridge, clutching a tie with one hand, and the nasty old gun with the other. I could look down, if I dared, and see the rapid current lashing against the icy rocks. Harold took the gun, and I got up and off the trestle with dispatch. Last time I ever fired a shotgun.

The birds? Last seen heading north by east, and no member of the flock left behind. Some later, under the hot summer sun, we got so easy with the bridge that it was a jumping off place. Ride the current through, climb up the rocks, and do it again. Back toward the village from the trestle where they had cut through a hill to accommodate the road bed, there were grassy slopes where the heat of August warmed us after a session of skinny dipping there in the river. Frenchy, who was a great story teller and two years older, than I, would regale us his superior knowledge of the facts and fantasies of life. Ghosts, Martians, extrasensory perception and masturbation. You sure could learn more by the Rail Road Tracks on a hot summer day than out of all those stuffy winter days in school.

COMMUNICATIONS GAP

The stove's gone from the country store,

They've boarded up the flue

Can't set and toast and talk no more,

The way we used to do.

The old post office isn't there,

It's moved a mile away.

And folks you meet don't seem to care

To pass the time of day.

The fire station's warm and new,

But it's not worth the walk,

Those fellers have so much to do,

They don't have time to talk.

They've up and closed the lumber yard,

And razed the railroad station,

In all, it's getting mighty hard,

To find a conversation.

CHAPTER TWENTY
You Look Sick, Do You Feel Pale?

Mr. N. from up the street, who tended toward the rotund, complained one day at the Post Office, "Every time I eat a quart of ice cream and a box of chocolates after dinner, I get the guts ache!"

He had a reputation for stuffing it away in good fashion. When Mr. N passed away before his time, Father remarked, solemnly, "Too many hot Suppers!"

Dad had a double handful of expressions aimed at illness, and its consequences, some of which were rather cryptic. Man in Dennisport "hove his stifle". Actually, he hurt a joint in his leg, but people do not have a stifle, that is a special bone in the rear leg of a horse, or dog, not a man. Close enough for Dad. Some one who had lost too much weight, from a sickness, perhaps, to Dad looked "a might peaked", or "as poor as Job Chase's Turkey". Well, I figured the Biblical 'Job' would have been some emaciated after all he had been through, but Job Chase? He did not explain.

He said his father was getting deef as a haddock, and I guess he was, as he got older. He used to say "What?" until Grandmother all but shouted, then said, "Don't raise your voice at me, woman, I hain't deef!" The prize though was when Dad said someone who died must have had the 'Corramorbus'. I came across the answer by accident. Try Cholera Morbus, which is gastroenteritis, or collywobbles, a summer disease we might call a serious case of the trots. A 1907 medical book said to treat it with a mustard plaster on the abdomen, and hot water bottles on the feet. What they prescribed for inside would surely make you think twice before eating any more cucumbers or radishes. Or drinking ice water, either! Don't read much about people dying from it, although they sometimes wished they would. Mustard plasters, I experienced one of those. A real heavy chest congestion from a cold, and some old lady told Mother about a mustard plaster instead of skunk grease or Vicks Vapor Rub. Guess it was not mixed quite right because I got a good burn out of it.

Mother had quite a store of cures, many of which seemed to work quite well. For a cold, the skunk grease or Vicks, slather it all over your chest, and wrap in flannel. For a sore throat, a small glob of the Vicks swallowed, or some slippery Elm. Sodium Bicarbonate, a spoonful in a glass of water worked wonders for a stomach full of indigestible whatever, good for poison ivy, in a tub of water or in poultice form, mixed with molasses as cough syrup, you could whiten your teeth with it, and deodorize the icebox. Lame ankle or an infection? Hot water and Epsom salts. Multiple applications of this pulled my Father back from severe blood poisoning when his cat bit him. Epsom salts could be taken internally for other disorders, but we will not go into that. There was always aspirin around, and iodine in large bottles, (I needed frequent applications) and Cod liver oil to ward off colds. A Dr. Haas said bananas were a good cure for Celiac, a childhood digestive track disease. We never had it, so maybe those Saturday Night banana coups were good medicine.

There were tons of cures out there. The skunk grease mixed with lemon juice was said to do wonders for a sore throat, as was lard and turpentine. Old wives' tales from the past spoke of dandelion greens for an ailing liver, saffron tea for jarnders, peppermint for 'neurelgy,' wintergreen for the 'rhuematiz'; medicines which had come down from Pilgrim days, along with the spelling, while medicine chests at sea carried such items as carbolic acid for stopping infection, laudanum for pain, and hartshorn for heavens knows what.

Mother never had much truck with pattern medicines like 'Fletcher's Castoria', invented by Samuel Pitcher of Hyannis, as a pleasant substitute for Castor Oil. Started as 'Pitcher's Castoria', but Sam sold the pattern to Mr. Fletcher who made a bundle from it. I hope Sam made out all right. I do not remember seeing any Lydia Pinkham Vegetable Compound around our house, either. Lydia made her compound and "Pink Pills for Pale People" on the Lynn-Salem line, and we went past the factory every time we went up to visit Nana. The compound was supposed to help women (with Women's Troubles) feel better. Women swore by it and Lydia had tons of testimonials from all over the country affirming the efficacy of her product. Of course, it may have been the alcohol that Lydia mixed her veggies in, the stuff was 40 proof!

Since 1920, courtesy of Mr. Ayling we have had a hospital on Cape Cod, but our family rarely used it. As children, I can't remember anyone staying over night there, and of the six, Mother only had one birth in hospital. We did use doctors, but as with my arrival, they were often chugging along in their Ford at some distant part of the Cape just when you needed them. One doctor was only here part time, to begin with. He went on cruise ships, and rejoined his practice on the Cape between voyages. A very distinguished man, always formally attired, with stiff collar, a Panama hat, glasses on a chain, as I remember, and sporting a goatee. He was not a young man when his wife died, but in a suitable time after her passing, he shed his formality like an old overcoat. More conventional glasses, sports clothes and a less staid manner, plus some talk of a lady friend. Physician heal thyself?

There were several doctors around from time to time. What with the small population, and all those home remedies, I guess some of them left to look for greener pastures, or a sicklier clientele. One who stayed acquired a reputation for curing pneumonia. No small thing in that day with no antibiotics. Of course, it was said down to the Post Office that pretty much anyone with a good case of bronchitis would suddenly acquire a bad case of Pneumonia when the good doctor stepped in the door, so he could cure another one.

The doctor we settled down with as our family became more numerous, was Dr. Rowley, a fine gentleman from Harwich. In fact, he might have been part of the inspiration that started two of my sisters toward becoming nurses. He helped Mother through her last deliveries, relieving Dad of his officiating duties, sewed or clamped shut various places on my parts which should not have been open, cut out a non-malignant lump on my chest, told me solemnly that my slightly irregular heart beat would not prevent me from chopping wood and patched and prescribed for us all. Dad, I think in his early seventies, decided to have some repairs on some painful conditions he had carried for years, namely, hemorrhoids, and a bad double rupture. The Doctor used local anesthetics, and talked to Dad thru the operation. As he started work on the one of the hernias, he joked, "Freeman. You have a roving appendix, keeps getting in my way."

"Well, take the damn thing out, then," sez Pop.

Dr. Rowley chuckled, and did...

PERSPECTIVE

Sitting, knitting and rocking away,
My, but vacations are certainly fun.
Soon all the girls will be down for tea,
Most of the ladies are older than me,
I'm only eighty-one.

This dear hotel, where I always stay,
I knew the first owner and now his son.
The father died, he was ninety-three.
He was a tidy bit older than me.
I'm only eighty-one.

My Joe, last winter he passed away.
Straight out into the waves he would run!
Joe did so love a dip in the sea.
He was eight years, you know, older than me.
I'm only eighty-one.

A honey-moon couple came in today.
They laugh and they frolic as children do,
And, oh, how loving they seem to be.
They're so much, very much younger than me.
I'm almost eighty-two.

CHAPTER TWENTY-ONE

Ain't We Got Fun

Actually, there was a decidedly diminished amount of amusements around after the fall solstice chased most of the visitors and the summer weather out of the area. For kids, there were still lots of woods to walk in, and some football. I wasn't near as bad at football than as at B.B. Then home to homework, chores, supper, and RADIO! We didn't miss T.V. a bit. In fact, hardly anybody had heard about pictures thru the air unless they maybe saw it in Popular Science Magazine or a comic book. There was some notice about television at the '39 World's Fair, along with news about Frequency Modulation, radio without the static; funny idea! I don't recall much argument about what programs we listened to (some sputtering from Dad when we gulped our vittles to rush back to the set) but within the 5:00 pm to 7:00 pm, the radio was pretty much kiddy land. 'Renfrew Of The Mounties', 'Tarzan of the Apes', 'Buck Rogers in the 25th Century', 'Little Orphan Annie', 'The Lone Ranger' ... My goodness, what excitement!

Some times, particularly during the War, we got shot down in the middle of "I Love A Mystery", leaving Doc or Reggie in a pickle because the owners of the house, our parents, wanted to hear some dumb news report and of course the set went off when Mom called Supper...for a scant few moments while the swallowing was going on, then back to Fantasy Land! But we were off at 7:00 when the Adult shows started. Hey, some of them were pretty darn good, too. There was 'Grand Central Station' (crossroads of a million private lives), the one that started with the train, 'Lux Radio Theatre', where we got to hear Radio versions of lots of the movies we hadn't been able to see. And scads of comedy and variety shows. One not too bright company thought they could put a Ventriloquist on the radio...how silly; the unseen Charlie McCarthy and his voice, Edgar Bergen were a smash hit. So was grown up 'Ziegfield Follies' star Fanny Brice with her funny and endearing Baby Snooks. Sometimes we played a game like Monopoly, or Slap Jack, or Whist while we listened. Dad would seldom get involved in the card games, he was too serious a player, and Mother and we kids were more concerned with the radio show than with winning. The programs went on after we had been condemned to bed, some of the best ones.

The 'Rudy Vallee Show' was a favorite, and I seldom missed it, even though I had been tucked in during the first commercial. You see, not uncommonly in those days, there was little or no insulation in our house, and none between the upstairs and ceiling. I found that by lying beside the bed, with my ear to the floor, I had a regular loud speaker, and the radio down stairs was perfectly audible. So, I heard the 'Rudy Vallee Show'.

That is I did until that ONE NIGHT! Aside from the comedy and music, Vallee often featured a short dramatic sketch, generally with his guest of the week as star. One week his star was Peter Lorie, the skit: 'The Tell Tale Heart', by Edgar Allen Poe. Oh Boy!

If you don't remember, it involves a man, clearly mad, who because he thinks his roommate has the 'Evil Eye', kills him, and buries his body beneath the kitchen floor. Scary enough, right? Hey, that ain't nothing to the scene when Peter thinks the murdered man is coming up through the floor after him! Can you picture lying on a cold floor, alone in a dark upstairs bedroom while Peter Lorie goes bonkers? Well I did what most any chicken hearted eight year might do, I bellowed! Picked my Mother right up out of her chair, and had her flying upstairs in split seconds. It was a relief to be tucked back in bed, and I didn't have to be cautioned against doing any more floor time that night. Trouble was, when Mom flew up the stairs, Dad snapped off the set, and I didn't hear the end! Didn't know how the damn thing came out until years later in dramatic school. For a class, I found and performed the 'Tell Tale Heart'. Got a pretty good mark. Why not, I'd been coached by Peter Lorie.

Dad said his post office had one of the first electric services, and in 1927 he turned on his Electric Radio, with loud speaker, and had quite a crowd around for the N.B.C. broadcast of Lindberg's triumphant return to the U.S. after his across the Ocean flight. Radio mixed the gay and jolly in with the sad, frightening and melancholy, and of course wide coverage to the sad search for the Lindberg baby, and the trial of the kidnapper.

The dreadful crash of the Airship Hindenburg was also carried live by Radio, and the Halloween Special on which Orson Wells scared the pants off New Jersey and shook up most of the rest of the U.S. in 1938. The show, 'War of the Worlds' was so convincing, that when the news of Pearl Harbor was broadcast in December 1941, the stations received many calls from irate disbelieving listeners who said they didn't think it was right to broadcast that Orson Wells stuff again. As kids, that Sunday afternoon announcement was a bummer because it interrupted 'The Shadow' (sponsored by Blue Coal - "Crime doesn't pay, the Shadow knows") but we slowly grew to know that bombers over that previously unheard of Hawaiian navel base had changed our lives.

The first moving pictures in the area, according to Father (silent, of course) were presented at the Masonic hall on Division Street, between West Harwich and Dennisport. The hall still stands, and is now the Harwich Junior Theatre. I don't know what they used for a light source to project them, electricity was not yet available in the area, but I do know the machine was cranked by hand. I and my magic (appearing as 'Benny The Great') did more than one performance for the Eastern Star in that venerable building, and later as a grownup, appeared in a couple of H.J.T. productions, (NO autographs, please). The Modern Theatre in Harwich Port had the first electric power around Harwich by running a private generator, a big noisy affair behind the theatre. The Modern, scene of some rare but wonderful Saturday matinees, a few exciting family even-

ing outings, and my first date (read debacle). It was about grade seven, and her name was Mary. Her hair was long and fair. I asked her, she said yes, so we met at her home in Dennisport, and bicycled, to the theater. I don't remember the movie, I stayed well to the center of my seat, and she stayed in the center of hers, but I knew she was there. It was afterwards that disaster struck. Part way up Killdee Hill, while I was proving I could pump all the way to the top without stopping, my front tire blew! She was sympathetic, and walked along with me while I pushed my lame steed. Then my handsome cousin Freddy came pedaling along. Mary regretfully allowed as how she really should hurry along home and off they went. For me, it was about a five mile lonesome push back home. I didn't die, but it was close.

I knew the story of lots of movies which I never saw. There was 'Lux Presents Hollywood' on the radio and when the folks went, Mom would tell us the story line with breakfast the next A.M. When the Depression cut back on audience, the theatres started to give stuff away. On 'Dish Nights', you could build up to a full set of table settings if you didn't miss a week, and then there was 'Bank Nite', when they gave away actual money. Dad usually saw to it they had enough spare change for the fare, which I think was a big twenty-five cents, but never saw much in the line of cash. One night when he didn't go, a neighbor stopped by the next day and "Doc," (a nickname I never could find the reason for) "Heard they called your name for a prize last night." Dad was sick! He never missed another Bank Nite, and never had his name called again.

The Grandparents went rarely, and sometimes weren't too impressed with this new fangled business. Grandmother, asked about a Shakespearian movie, couldn't readily remember the name, "I think it was 'A Big Fuss Over Nothing'." A tale of a neighbor, asked if he had seen the movie the night before, "No, don't go for them movies. I and the wife just sot to home and listened to the radio like the Good Lord intended!"

WORK

It seems that there's a sight of work
Attached to any season,
But 'fore I go to working hard,
I like to know the reason.

I labor for the daily bread
As hunger is distressing,
But struggling with Nature's whims
Don't, somehow, seem so pressing.

The Wife is of a different bent
And thinks salvation's found
In shortening grass and pushing leaves,
And moving snow around.

I figure when the Lord made trees
He meant for leaves to fall,
And I just can't find nothing wrong
With grass that's growing tall.

Snow? Tromp it down and let it melt,
It won't do any hurt,
And even old spring-cleaning
Just makes way for summer dirt.

There's work to do the whole year through,
But I can live without it.
I'd ruther set here on the porch,
And just not think about it.

CHAPTER TWENTY-TWO
How You Do Talk!

Sister Nancy proudly finished playing a piece of music which, frankly needed work. "Dad, do you know what that song was?"

"Well," said Father, in his usual complimentary way, "It sounds like the tune the old cow died on!"

Stepping out of the door on a cold morning, into a messy snow filled yard, he would look up at the sun, and say, "Well, it's a good day over head, if you're going that way." Or, stepping in from a freezing day, "Kinda 'balmy' out."

I never knew for sure if he heard these things, or made them up, probably a little of both. Like the 'galfunion' which was any tool of which he couldn't quickly recall the name, as in, "Ben, hand me that 'galfunion'," and I had to figure which of an assortment of tools would be of the most help in the present stage of his current occupation. Another beauty was 'titravate', which, under various circumstances might mean add a little more, take just a bit off, move this or that a tiny bit, slop on a good coat of paint, or a variety of other adjustments or repairs as in, "Just titravate that picture about one dog hair to the left, and she'll hang straight." If, by the way, he had saved some paint over the years, and fetched it out to do some touchup, he might find it had separated, skimmed over, that the old paint pail had rusted, or that the paint was otherwise contaminated. If so, it was "bonny clabbered," which might mean curdled milk to some people, but spoiled paint to Dad.

Some times his comments tended to be less than delicate. Once while playing scrub baseball he joshed a Portuguese friend who missed an easy catch, "Cripes, Manny, you couldn't catch a fart in a mitten!" Manny, after some thought answered, "Gawd, Freeman, I don't t'ink nobodys could!"

If the proper name for a person, place or thing temporarily eluded him, he would come up with a new one he felt fit. A woman for whom he often did odd jobs had a name which didn't rise easily to his tongue and hair which did rise in a rather unruly manner. She became 'wild Aggie'. Talking of some person whose cognomen slipped his mind, the person often became 'Flubry Lubry'. "I'm going to take this saw over the north side to have old Flubry Lubry sharpen it."

If I was bending an oar (rare, because he usually rowed), he gave directions to get us right over his favorite scalloping spot (where the big 'channel scallops' lay) and like as not, he would come out with some whimsical nautical slang, like, instead of 'hard a port', "Hard up in the pork barrel". Coming from a seafaring area, and from a family who had gone to sea, I guess that's not so strange. Dad did go on at least one voyage, either on his uncle Pele's ship, the 'Mercedita', or on the 'M. E. Eldridge' his other uncle, Roland Kelly's ship (most likely) but only up the Hudson River. He told me that during that voyage he was set to tying off one of the lines which moored the ship to the dock and proud because he knew how, tied a complicated knot called a bowline instead of the usual slip knot. A bowline (pronounced 'bolin') is used to make a semi permanent loop in a rope (I was proud when I learned to make one in the Boy Scouts) but not as a quick release tie on a mooring line. When the vessel was leaving the dock, the slip knot people slipped their knots, and Dad tried desperately to untie his bowline, which tends to get tighter as the rope is pulled. The safe departure of a ship from a dock is regulated by releasing ropes on order (I.e. "Loose the stern line", or "Cast off the such and such…", and so forth) to allow the ship to float out into the current in an orderly manner. Dad's fancy knot was tying up the works. Luckily, a sailor with a hand ax pushed Dad aside, and chopped of the offending knot before any damage was done. Needless to say, he was demoted from the tie off crew for a while.

Many of the old Cape Codders had a tendency to siphon vowels through their nasal passages, and, as Father said, "Talk flat as a cow flap"-which is somewhat flatter than a buffalo chip, but of the same family, so to speak. Things like cow came out 'cayow', boy was restructured somewhere between 'buoy', and 'bowie' and nothing became 'nawthin'. Nawthin' is a grand word, often used in a double negative. A fisherman asked how well he did during eeling season answered, "All as I did was just barely make back my expenses, and they wasn't nawthin'."

Jerome Howes, a Brewster boy and excellent painter of sea scenes, who has been a friend for years, told of a day when, down in the dumps over a broken love affair, he encountered his uncle, a salty character from Orleans. When told Jerry had girl troubles, the uncle asked the nature of the problem.

"You wouldn't understand," said Jerry.

"Understand?" bristled the uncle, "Boy, I been married three times, had two mistresses, two live-in girl friends, and a Cape Cod housekeeper. There ain't NAWTHIN' I don't know about women!"

Fish don't fare too well in Cape Cod vernacular. A grouchy person is an 'old crab', a departed soul - 'dead as a mackerel', a situation which seems not quite right is 'fishy', an unsociable man is a 'cold fish', loaning money at high interest makes one a 'loan shark', cold hands are 'clammy', a person, who doesn't hear well is 'deef as a haddock', and someone from whom it is difficult to get a straight answer is 'slippery as an eel'. About the only favorable fish expression is 'happy as a clam at high tide'. Peculiar, hain't it.

A boy who acts up is a 'cuss', a boy who doesn't act up might be a 'cute little cuss', one who acted up a lot might be 'that divilish cuss' (Brother Link was affectionately called "that little curly headed cuss") a man who vents his intestinal gas in an occupied car or building is a dirty cuss and heading out on a stormy day you don't approve of the cussed weather especially if the cussed car won't start.

A man, who worked for a landscaping company, was on his knees weeding a flower garden in Harwich when a large car stopped on the road behind him. The lady in the driver's seat 'hoo hooed' to him several times, then: "Excuse me, my man."

Henry (for it was he) rose to his feet after about the third call. He walked slowly to the car, dusting the dirt from his knees, straightening his baseball hat, worn backwards for better visibility while in the kneeling position, "Ma'am?" he queried.

"How much would it cost to have you weed my gardens?" asked the woman.

Henry, not to be accused of usurping his boss' prerogative regarding things financial, wiped perspiration from his forehead, and answered thus. "Ma'am, not knowin' with any degree of certainty, I darsant say, for fear I might err." And with a gracious tip of the head, he returned to his previous position and resumed. There was a good deal of dilly dallying around with names in the old days, both of persons and places. Some of the name part is understandable, with great numbers of surnames being the same in some villages, substitute nick names helped to identify the individual. As with my aunt who had the same first name as her husband's (at that time) unmarried sister, and was identified by the use of her husband's first name (Edith Fredson) so Susie Thacher, who married Seth Baker, of the numerous Baker Clan became known as Susie Seth. Seth and Susie lived in "Baker Town", part of West Dennis, not to be found on maps. There were lots of Bakers lived around there; lots and lots of Bakers (Peter Howes says there were 40 some families of Bakers in the small town of Dennis in 1820, and a deal of them settled there in West Dennis. Fact 'twas said you couldn't swing a bucket over your head in that area without striking a Baker!). The historical house 'Jericho' was a Baker house, (belonged to Miss Emma when I was a kid, and I delivered her the *Standard Times.*' She talked to herself a lot, but always had the 25 cents ready on pay day). The land for the Elementary (Consolidated) School, built there on the edge of Baker Town, was given to the town by Ezra Baker, for whom the school is named.

Other parts of our town and the surrounding areas had unofficial names: 'Searsville', around Swan Pond, and the head of Swan River, 'Battle Town' was the on the other end of Swan River, where it empties into the Sound, 'Punkhorn', along Setucket Road, (named Satucket in Brewster) where Dennis and Brewster join and at one time the area around the Brewster herring run and mill was called Factory Village. There was 'Little Taunton' on the Dennis north side, where a lot of wash-a-shores (from the city of Taunton, up there on the main land) built small summer houses among the sand dunes back in the 20's, I think, and later converted many of the cottages to full time homes. A lot of the families were of Italian decent, and the area was also known as 'Little Italy'.

Along Kelly's Bay, and Follins Pond, near the head of Bass River, is another section with an unofficial name; 'Mayfair'. Even some of the town's citizenry rated nick names: There were the Wellfleet 'bible faces' (there was a religious camp there, and sometimes camp meetings, and revivals), Chatham 'scrabble towners with a brick in their stocking', (don't ask!) and of course the Harwich 'hair leggers'.

Nicknames for people seemed to be a special preoccupation, Dr. Howes from down Cape was always called 'Hum', Judge Hall of

Harwich, as afore mentioned, was 'Judgie'. My dad, and the two Hall boys (Leon and Richard) all called each other 'Doc'. (I asked Dad why, but he didn't seem to remember. He and Norton Nickerson called each other Nate, and Dad didn't seem to know why that started, either). Leon, by the way, was always Leon T. to everyone else in town, and his father, Leon W., the same way the two Watson Bakers (only distant relatives, but lived just across the street from each other in South Dennis) were always Watson F., and Watson B. and Fred Crowell of Harwich was always known as Fred R., but didn't have a middle name which started with 'R'! There was a Henry 'Ding' in Dennisport, Louis Kelly, over to the northside, for some unknown reason was called 'Johnny', and another northsider (again, for no reason I could figure) was called Loki-eye-doodlelum!

Another spur to the nickname business was the liberal spraying around of Old Testament and other awkward cognomens in the early days. Add to the already mentioned Theophilus, Elnathan and Judah such beauties as Alpheus, Obadiah, Ichabod, Darius, Sylvanias, Eurastas, and Nehemiah. For the ladies, Bathsheba, Mehitable, Sophronia, Zimira or perhaps a 'character' name such as Thankful, Mercy, or OOPS, Experience! Plenty of call for making up substitute monikers there.

Plum, short for Plumber, (his real first name, not his occupation) lived in North Harwich, and owned a cabin on the upland near Elbow Pond in Brewster. It was only a few miles from his home, approached by Slough Road, which winds gracefully between several ponds, a twisting hard top country road which young drivers can't resist trying at a good deal above the speed limit. An old dirt wagon road with three tracks, two for the wagon wheels, and the center track where the horse walked, wandered from the hard top up to Plum's camp, a secluded and rustic building, just right for a cook-out, or Sunday afternoon story telling session. Plum was usually a quiet man, who came into his own at these gabfests around the stove, or taking in the sun on the screened porch overlooking the pretty little pond. He recalled adventures from bygone days with sharp clarity, but couldn't remember my brother's name, although Link was a best friend of Plum's son. He referred to him as "That boy from South Dennis", even in later years when Link worked for him. He would set his wife at it, "You woman, call that boy over to South Dennis, and get him over here."

Plum had lived an adventurous youth, including an ill fated wagon trip to Maine where he and a friend attempted to sell their own formula of tick and fly dip to farmers. They called it 'Fly Lick', and even had labels printed up for the big jars they used. "Waren't nawthin' but kerosene and creosote" said Plum. Unable to do much cash business, they made various 'tredes'. "Treded that 'Fly Lick', for potatoes, treded the potatoes for ..." (Turnips, as I remember) and ended up back on the Cape with a lame horse, a worn wagon, and several baskets of mostly rotten apples. "Ken you imagine, them farmers put rotten apples in them baskets, and topped them off with good ones! Down right dishonest!"

In his youth, Plum had a "motor sickle" and at least once, he took a girl for a ride. He coaxed his future wife on to the back seat. Unbeknownst to Plum, a childhood sickness had left her without hair, and she wore a wig. Predictably, while taking a curve at relatively high speed, that wig was gone with the wind. She screamed, Plum brought the motorcycle to a jolting halt, and looked back at his hairless sweetie. "Oh, my Lord" said Plum, "what I have done now!"

Some time before that, as he said, "I was runnin' a girl up to Centerville, and Ed, there, was runnin' some girl in Hyannis, so I used to ride him up there on the back of my motorsickle. Cripes, we'd come home late, you know. We was coming back one night, and Ed yelled in my ear, "Plum, I think I'm gonna get married." "Well," I said, "Ed, you can do that if you're amind to, but, it looks like too long a job for me!"

THE WEEKENDERS

Highways are taking the holiday load,
Four lanes of traffic on two lanes of road.
The heat and the horns and the kids are all taxing,
But weekends in summer are made for relaxing.

Gas fumes and traffic, confusion and dust,
Determined to get to the seashore, or bust.
Oh, what is this sense of compulsion that fills us?
This weekend we're bound to relax if it kills us!

CHAPTER TWENTY-THREE

Get a Horse

There weren't many horse drawn vehicles on the Cape roads when I was a kid. I saw more on a trip to Nana's in Salem than were in service around here. There the city streets and closer buildings made the patient horse more desirable than trucks for the 'stop and start' kind of business of servicing the neighborhoods. The ice man, milkman, mail man, knife and scissor sharpeners, and bread delivery man went up and down the main and back streets of the residential sections as they had done since colonial days. Mother told of how embarrassed she had always been on summer days when her Mother sent her out with a shovel to salvage fresh droppings from one of the passing parade to enhance the growth of their rose bushes.

Over on the north side of Dennis, Mr. 'A' clung to his horse and team even after he had been jailed for DHWI (driving horse while intoxicated - Mr. 'A', not the horse). Alpheus Baker next door had four horses, mostly for riding, but he did keep a fancy carriage in the back of his commodious barn, and it was exciting to see him, usually when he had visitors to entertain, clipping past at a brisk trot. His horses were on two levels, black 'Prince', and white 'Nita' were old, quiet animals on which Nancy and I had an occasional ride. 'Mary' and 'Dick' were brown, young, and frisky. Mr. Baker used to exercise them in his large back pasture riding or trotting them around in a great circle on a line, or occasionally taking a guest for a ride.

The woods were crisscrossed with old sand roads which extended for miles. Some followed ancient byways from colonial days, some just there for access to a pond, cranberry bog well off the main roads, or a wood lot. The 'Ancient Roads' have become something of a problem right up to the present day, in that they are sometimes adjudged to allow legal passage through property some owner wants to build on, or stop the public from walking/driving over. Like maybe through the front yard of a newly subdivided property. Passage on the 'Ancient Way' often cannot be blocked. They all made for free and easy bridle paths in the '30's, as well as strolling areas for kids to walk and talk well out of sight of the Big People. To encounter Mr. Baker and guest, (note, usually one of two young female friends of his wife, who came to visit most every summer from New York City) was an exciting event. Well, 'encounter' is not exactly right, if we heard the muffled hoof sounds up the road and around the bend, it was hide in the bushes time, and we would lie concealed as the two horses walked by squeaking of leather, and marvel at the woman's city accent and bright laughter, contrasted with Mr. Baker's flat Cape tones as they passed and vanished down the trail. Mr. Baker cut a trim figure, always in jodhpurs with leather puttees and sporting a cap or a somewhat western style hat, and with white hair and moustache. Both of the young women were handsome, somewhat exotic, particularly in riding habits, and as viewed from behind an oak bush.

There were other horses in town, of course, but more often on farms, not on the roads. Mostly by my day the horse had given in to the horseless carriage. Linwood's big plow horses of course, when we were very young, came by twice each spring, going from garden plot to garden plot through the village, one trip to plow, a second a few days later to disk harrow the turned sod. It was a real treat for us young'uns to watch those heavy footed work horses walk round and round in Dad's garden plot.

"Stand back," said Linwood, "Or them horses might tromp on yer toes!"

Thoph, of course had an old truck horse when we were small, plowed his own garden, and hired out now and then, before the horse died. The burial, held in a field beside his house was an awesome affair. I never knew for sure if Thoph actually owned that field, but with his cows grazing the front, and his horse buried in the back, he sure enjoyed 'utilization' privileges. Later he boarded a pony for some people. That gave us kids all the more reason to hang around his barn. He never did let us ride the pony, (named 'Peanuts') the little critter kicked a lot, and was apt to bite but was endless fun to watch at feeding time, or when Thoph curried him, dodging hoofs and swearing.

Mr. Lapham had perhaps the last working horse in town. He collected junk. Came around from house to house with, of course, a stop at the dump, buying rags, metal and other resalable items. He always stopped for a 'jaw' with Father, to discuss the happenings around, and discuss at length the value of whatever items Dad had which he might buy. Some conversational dispute about the prices, ending with both he and Dad satisfied that they had each beat the other, and Mr. Lapham would pay up, climb slowly back to his wagon seat, and drive off. Mr. Lapham was tall and rangy and thin, his horse was boney and old, and seemed to hesitate as he put each hoof down, so the rig stayed in sight for a long while after he had left the yard. I can still see it, in mind's eye, so to speak. The old rickety wagon moved ever so slowly until we sometimes got bored and wandered off before his rig disappeared from sight with its four mis-sized wheels wobbling a good foot from side to side as they rolled forward.

Dad was born in '92, and his world was full of horses. Aside from the fact that his father hired out horses and wagons, they were the only mode of private transportation up through the first part of the 20th century. There were also ox carts around in Dad's youth, fine for transporting heavy loads, but mighty slow for traveling. Trouble with horses, aside from not being too bright, and having a jumpy disposition, they still hold it against humans because they have been domesticated. They kick, sometimes bite, and very often have individual unpleasant ways which do not endear them to their masters. Like Junior. Junior had a frustrating habit of, when left alone for a few minutes, stepping over a fence, in a quest for the marvelous green grass on the other side. He managed to do this while still harnessed to the wagon. He couldn't get back over the fence, and straining, as he was against the harness buckles, was impossible to remove from the wagon. Only alternative was, with a deal of effort, to take down the rails of the fence, back Junior up, tie him tightly to a post or whatever, reassemble the fence, and be on your way.

Then there was the balky animal. There can not be anything more frustrating than a 1500 pound beast that refuses to move. A truly dedicated balky horse will resist pulling, pushing, bribery, deception or even beating, and no puny 200 pound human is going to get him off the dime until he's damn good and ready. One such belonged to Grandfather. Dad said his name was Bob, and he was a hard working animal, except when a perverse mood made him decide to stand still. You could plead with him, pretend to walk off and forget him, offer a pail of food, take off his harness, to make him think the work day was over, but to no avail. One evening when Grandfather was ready to head home after a cold day of cutting and loading firewood, Bob refused to move for an extended period.

94

After exhausting all ideas to make him move, and anxious to get home for what would now be a very late supper, Grandfather tied Bob's head close to a tree, and left him there for what turned out to be a cold snowy night. When he was untied in the morning, Bob was willing, in fact anxious, to transport his loaded wagon toward home. On another occasion, Bob totally defied all efforts, so Grandfather tried a method he had heard of which was sure to get the balky animal moving. He carefully build a small pile of twigs, leaves and small branches beneath Ol' Bob's belly and, as the balky animal watched warily out of the corner of his eye, lit the pile on fire. Sure enough, the horse moved! He moved forward 6 feet, stopped, and stood there, as the growing flames set fire to the wagon!

The 'Used Car' dealer during the day of the horse was the horse trader (or 'treder') of tale and legend. Be it not said that any of them were dishonest, but some were prone to be a might sharper on a deal than most of their customers. One such on the north side sold my Grandfather an animal who he said was sound of limb and wind and would do a good day's work. "Only trouble with this horse is he don't look too good." Grandfather who was interested in performance, not beauty contests, bought the horse, harnessed him to his shay, and leading his other horse behind, started across the Cape toward home. The new horse trotted along well and answered promptly to the reins.

Walking him out, a while later, Grandfather let go of the reins, in order to blow his nose. The new horse walked off the road and bumped directly into a tree! Subsequent examination showed the horse to be stone blind! Grandfather came home fuming over getting 'taken' in a trade. Grandmother met the trader in a store a short time later and berated him for selling her husband a blind horse without telling him. "Oh, but I did tell him," replied the trader, "I told him that horse didn't look too good!"

The trader in question had a reputation for making a sharp deal, and having a quick wit unhampered by the fact that he was afflicted with a stuttering problem. A man, to whom he sold a horse, supposedly seven years old, took the nag to a vet for a second opinion. "Horse is 21 years old, if he's a day!" sez the vet.

The new owner in high dudgeon accosted the Trader. "You sold me this horse, and said it was 7 years old. Turns out he's 21!"

"No No, No No," sez the trader, "I t-t-told you he was s-s-s-seven, s-s-s-seven, s-s-s- seven... Now, that's 21, hain't it?"

'Nuff said.

TRADIN'

Come to swappin', Eddie Nick
Was abler than most,
He'd made his style,
And easy smile,
Known up and down the coast.

When trading horses, Eddie was
Completely free of shame,
And if you bought,
You might get caught,
With something old, or lame.

My Grandsire bought a plug one day,
That Eddie said was sound,
"Don't look too good,
But still, it should
Be fine to drive around."

But Grandpa on his way back home,
Was quite surprised to find,
When walking free,
He'd hit a tree,
The animal was blind.

When Grandpa brought the critter back,
His eyes were all a blaze
Loud words he said,
To trader Ed,
Of his dishonest ways

Said Eddie, "Well, I tried to be
As honest as I could,
For it is true,
As I told you
He doesn't LOOK too good."

CHAPTER TWENTY-FOUR

The Men Who Came Around

Mr. Lapham was not the only one who broke up the quiet of Cape Cod '30's afternoons. Rural as we were, there was a market for many traveling services, from Fuller brushes and junk collection to insurance and even a traveling haberdashery.

Our iceman, Alley B. came only in the warm weather. In the winter, perishables kept cold in a box just out side a window, in our round root cellar, or in an unheated little back room near the cellar stairs. We had, as did most homes, an ice box which took a large block of ice in its upper chamber, or chest, and had compartments down below for food stuffs, and a drip pan at the bottom which caught the ice melt, and had to be dumped several times a day. A sign saying ICE, and showing different numbers on the four edges, was set in the window. You set your card in the window with the number of pounds you wanted at the top (i.e. 25lbs, 50lbs etc.) so the ice man could see it as he drove up in his truck: no ice sign, no ice. You can find many examples of the old iceboxes in antique shops. People who think they are cute probably never had to get down on the floor and try to slide out an over filled pan of frigid water and lug it ever so carefully to the door and out, without giving floor and self an ice water bath. No septic systems in those hand-pump houses, just a small drainage area that could over fill easily. Alley B., (Mister Howard to us kids) was always good for a touch, and would chip off pieces of ice for all. Winters, he operated a school bus, which Dad some times drove for him.

Dad also drove for Mr. Nickerson, sometimes when town business called. Mr. N. was a Selectman, for many years, as well as coming around each day in summer in his small truck with the wooden racks in back, to sell things from his farm down along the river. Yep, the very one we used to raid! Mom seldom needed anything in the vegetable line, but Mr. N. also had fruit from other farms, peaches, grapefruit, grapes, oranges and such. We, the felons of the melon patch, tended to make our selves scarce when his truck chugged up the street.

"There's No One With Endurance Like The Man Who Sells Insurance," said the old song, and Mr. Fellows was a star. He drove a car, not a truck, was a very nice man who, in the manner of the times, had to work like the devil to make a day's pay. He went from house to house, not only selling insurance, but also collecting the premiums. Mom and Dad, I think had life insurance policies, which together could not have cost more than 50 cents a week, and Mom had policies for us kids for years, which cost 5 cents each . . . nickel for me, than Nancy, then Olive, and so on down the line. The policies were supposed to cover the cost of burial and Mr. Fellows dutifully stopped at the house each week to collect! He always had time to chat, and he and Mom would sit at the kitchen table while he spread out his thick black account book, and filled in the blanks. Mr. F. was a little stout and perspired a lot in the summer, but dapper with a nice smile, always combed and suited, and a thoroughly friendly gentleman. Later, in my teens, I knew him as Henry, and we both played drums in the State Guard Band - I had the bass. By then he had an office, and did not have to run around collecting for nickel policies.

The Fuller Brush man came a few times a year, and assorted magazine salesmen, (often "working their way through college") trudged by. They probably came from a central located car, several young people with the gift of gab and set sales pitches who spread out through a neighborhood, reassembled at the car, and drove on to another site. 'Liberty', 'Saturday Evening Post', 'Red Book', 'Ladies Home Journal' et al. Whether magazines were ever delivered or not, we never discovered because Mother never bit. Eating was more important than 'pop' slick magazines. We had a milkman, after Thoph, but we did not see much of him, he delivered old style, before dawn, early enough so that on very cold mornings the cream had frozen, expanded, and pushed the cardboard top up and out the bottle, sometimes by inches! No homogenized, no reduced fat. Orders for any change of delivery and payments were left in the returning empties, and the bill slipped under a bottle.

One of the men who came around with whom Mom did a good bit of business (particularly when Dad was working out of town, building stuff for the army) was Joe "Wiggles". His truck carried the slogan, "If It Wiggles, We Got It!" and his fish came directly from the fish piers, far fresher than most of the store-bought variety. Joe would pull a fish out of the ice bins in the back of his truck, let you look it over for flaws such as dull eyes. Dad always checked to make sure a fish had clear, not fogged over eyes, said it was a sure sign of freshness. He also was against fish in a store, opened shellfish, or filleted, and laid out on ice for inspection. Dad said contact with the ice drained the flavor from the fish. Joe, as I remember, kept the fish in a pan, not lying on the ice. Mom was not quite the fish person Dad was. For example, if she bought swordfish, Father often complained that it was 'long line" caught, and had a tendency to be kind if flaccid, but she did her best, and it all tasted good to us. Fish O.K.'d, Joe would filet it right there in the back of the truck, on a table area he some how kept spotless, weigh the finished product, wrap it, and you had fish!

Perhaps the strangest personage who knocked on our door was Mr. B. As I remember, rather skinny, and nondescript, he made and sold vanilla extract. Probably all house wives bought from him. Vanilla was used in cookies, cakes, pies and pudding, and in summer, ice cream made by cranking the ice cream mix in a ice and salt preparation to freeze it. Vanilla extract was made by steeping cured vanilla beans in alcohol. The finished product must be 35 percent alcohol, by law, which figures to be 70 proof, or right up there with cheap vodka. To make a product containing drinkable alcohol during prohibition you had to obtain a federal license, as Lydia Pinkham had to for manufacturing her 'Vegetable Compound', and like the compound, if you took a few good snootsful of vanilla extract, you didn't much care if school kept or not! Suffice to say, it was no business for a drinking man to be in, and in this Mr. B. qualified. He came by every few months, and his condition always made one wonder how he had any 'alkey' left for the steeping. He smelled strongly of vanilla, and I always thought he sipped on the finished product as he tottered from house to house. I think he frightened Mom a little, but he was always quiet and as much of a gentleman as one could be while thoroughly crocked.

Each spring and fall, sometimes more often, on an irregular basis, there came by our house a car stuffed to over flowing with merchandise. Dad would drop whatever and beeline for the car. Out would step a middle-aged man, black hair, chewing a cigar, which was never lit, and sporting such a broad Middle European-Jewish accent that I had to listen closely to understand him. Mr. Prager was with us. His cargo was mostly wearing apparel, but he often came up with surprising items such as a set of pans, or some watches. Shoes were big with Mr. P., and an area in which Dad had functioned in one of his early jobs on the road. Mr. Prager often had Dad's size, and a 'last' of which he approved, although there was always bantering, and bartering, Dad always bought something. Sometimes kid's socks, or undergarments, (Mr. P. spoke a lot about garments.)

"You're interested in a fine garment, look at this fine sweater!" That one often got to Dad, who liked a good coat sweater. "Those shoes, 100% genuine leather cowhide! Check those counters!" (The back part of the shoe by the heel) "Look, no cardboard! You price shoes like those down town! Genuine Tom McCann, Hyannis, Boston, they'll get twice the price!". Every thing was a bargain, but the results were seldom any large sales. After the selling, the men would talk about the hard times, ask about families and go back and forth on the subject of 'That damn Roosevelt' and the New Deal. Then Mr. Prager hit the road, and Dad went back to his garden. Although sometimes Dad and Mr. Prager had a bit of difficulty in understanding each other's words, I think deep down they understood each other. One day Mr. Prager proudly told us he had rented a store just outside of Hyannis, and was going to settle down with his son to help him with the selling, but a few years later, up he drove in another old car, loaded as always. I guess staying in one place just was not his thing. He had the blood of the traveling peddler of old coursing through his veins.

Dad put in a lot of time selling, aside from the shoes, his local endeavors included selling the *Boston Sunday Post*, fresh shucked shellfish (after shucking them), eggs and chicken when he ran the experimental farm for the man from Dupont, and selling the potato chips he and Uncle Ray made out in our back room, the first Cape Cod Chips. Dad loved to sell, and talking to customers sometimes made the 'route' longer than it should have been, with subsequent late suppers which frustrated Mother. Sometimes, before I was 14 and started working at the pharmacy, I would go with Dad on a Saturday. I was supposed to assist him, but he liked to do most of the stops himself, "I have to get Mr. _____ to return my basket," or, "I have to explain to the cook how best to handle these capons..." I did a fair amount of just sitting and waiting. In reality, he just hated to miss a conversation.

We talked a lot between stops, and Dad always had a Mounds Bar or Tasty Yeast in the glove compartment, so the journey was not in vain. One stop in South Yarmouth was the home of Gene Tierney's aunt, Gene Tierney! With the splendid figure, undulating walk and wicked green eyes! I had just seen her racing across the western plains on a galloping horse in 'Leave Her To Heaven', and yearned to spot her around the yard, or gazing out an upstairs window, but it was not to be so! It was, however, on one such trip that Dad steeled himself to the task of giving the male-to-male lecture, which is considered the job of fathers. I even remember the spot. We were driving at a moderate clip down Route 28 in West Dennis, about to turn into Uncle Barney's Road.

"Ben, do you ah know anything about, ah women, and sex, and ah, having children?"

I had, after all walked a lot of wood roads with Hank and Frenchie, "Yes," I said.

"Good," said Dad, and he turned down Uncle Barney's Road, parked and went about his next delivery.

A SEPTEMBER SONG

The summer sports have petered out,
The sun has lost its zing,
But heavy cleaning's done for fall
And it's a while 'till spring.

The brown and empty garden
Somehow fills my heart with cheer,
I need not pull another weed
For over half a year.

A time of long and restful eves,
A chance to take a break.
Oops, wind is knocking down the leaves,
I'd better get the rake.

CHAPTER TWENTY-FIVE

Cruising' Down The River

The ocean is still there, and Bass River. My! The River! It flows from the ocean at Nantucket Sound over half way through the Cape as a border between Dennis and Yarmouth. At the head, it connects to a system of ponds. As kids, we rowed it, paddled it, swam it, dived into it and some winters walked on it. We strolled its banks, made our selves heroes by leaping from its bridges, fighting its currents, and reaching down to its deepest parts, just to touch the bottom, or in a game where we tried to retrieve an old auto tire which had been thrown in for the purpose. Leaping off the bridge was a little daunting at first, there didn't seem to be any older boys around to show us it was possible, and perhaps shame us into 'doing a Brodie' (after Steve Brodie, who they say jumped off the Brooklyn Bridge 140 feet into the East River back in 1886. Rail to water in our case was more like 25 feet). It was scary, standing up there on the railing. So Frenchy and Harold came up with the 'skyhook!' It was a crudely constructed wooden ladder with hooks on the top. We lowered it over the side, hooked it to the rail, and climbed carefully down to the bottom rung, an easy drop into the water. Then, up one rung at a time until at last we were sailing off the rail without a quaver. The fire chief found it, and made us take it down, said it was unsafe, and I guess it was, but by then we were leaping off the top without using the ladder, and how safe was that?

We drank from the clear cold springs at the river's head, built bridges across its inlets, and watched glorious sunsets from the High Bank Road bridge, which crossed between South Dennis and South Yarmouth. We explored it, camped by it, sunned our selves by its edge, grew up beside it and loved it. On top of that, it fed us. There were muddy areas where quahogs (hard shelled clams) could be gathered, dragged up with a long handled rake, or found with your bare toes (this was best, often you could go for a swim, and come home with supper, with practically no effort). The smaller quahogs are, of course, the little necks and cherry stones so good at a raw bar, or with cocktails. The big ones ground up make fine chowder, an excellent pie, (nothing in it but crust, and quahogs) and make a mighty fine dish stuffed.

On firmer bottoms was where oysters lurked, (only to be eaten during months whose name contained an "R"). Soft shell clams (steamers or for frying or for chowder) sought sandy areas, and took some digging when the tide was out, and some sand bars showed. Eel grass beds for scallops (only available from October first until freezing weather called a halt). Chasing after scallops or oysters generally required a rowboat, and Father generally had one, or the use of one. If our skiff was up river, near the bridge, and there were scallops in the Cove, a long row away, why there was always Harry Nickerson's boat to use. Harry had told Father at some time in the shadowy past that he could use his skiff any time. Problem, Dad did not know with any degree of certainty what Harry's boat looked like, or just where he left it. Probably around the cove, somewhere near the landing.

"Why, I expect it is this one right here!"

Then again, if he was after oysters or crabs, or eels in another part of the river, and we had left OUR skiff at the Cove, or it was at home for repairs, there was Harry's boat, conveniently lying near the bridge! Father often had oars and oarlocks in the car, along with his quahog rake and a dip net just in case, so having Harry's boat handy, where ever he wished to fish worked well: mostly. One day as he and I were into a rare spot, and pulling up as fine a crop of scallops as one could wish, a plainly audible "Ahoy!" from the bank caught our attention. Dad waved to the figure on shore, noted his frantic gesturing, and we pulled anchor, and rowed in, to see to his trouble. Before we got to easy talking range, the man began making sounds about Harry Nickerson's boat, only he did not call it Harry Nickerson's boat. He called it (in NO uncertain terms,) "MY Boat!" Dad rowed to the landing, we disembarked, unloaded and let the man take his rightful place amidships. Father explained about his understanding with Harry Nickerson, which I do not think the man believed for a moment, and off he rowed.

"Well," said Father, eyeing another rowboat lying upside down on the bank "Perhaps this is Harry Nickerson's boat over here."

We launched the second craft, and started out, only to find the man in the other boat had dropped anchor in our former spot, and was eagerly pulling up the very fine fat scallops Dad and I had thought of as practically cooked and on our table!

There were tons of mussels, but we didn't eat them, I always thought it was because they are so susceptible to the "Red Tide" episodes, that the Indians feared sickness from them, and so advised the early settlers to leave them off the menu. There were lots of conk, too, which were relished as food in some southern parts of the country, but not up here. Of the scallops, we ate only the 'eye', the big white succulent muscle that connects the two halves of the shell. French chefs say we're throwing away the best part (old folks said 'if a cat ate scallop guts, his tail would fall off'). We do, after all, eat all of the oyster, and the clam (don't eat a clam raw, though, or you'll commence to cough, don't know why). The French ate the mussel, too, and the conk, and did great things with snails, both the water and land kind. Any one who has had mussels steamed, or slurped up a bouillabaisse knows they were right on! From mid summer on through early fall there were also crabs. Big blue clawed creatures that struck back,

if you weren't careful, but contained a white meat far sweeter than lobster. Crabs could be netted, or trapped in a wire or wooden cage baited with, usually, a fish head, and sometimes, when their appetite was aroused, could be caught with a piece of salt pork on a string, and pulled up to grabbing distance, or dropped directly into a bucket. Eels were trappable, or could be speared with a flat broad multi pronged spear that had hooks on its teeth to keep the eel from getting loose. After all, they were as slippery as an.... Well... Flounders were speared, also, after they had settled down on the bottom in the winter. They could also be caught by hand line, from the bridge in the warmer months. In their season, blue fish came up river for the fishermen to catch by line, mostly from the bridges, and, again in its allotted time, the Mighty Bass for which the river was named. There ain't much better eating than fresh bass!

Years back, each spring the river would be full of alewives, swimming up to the ponds above the head of the river to spawn. Up at the head of the river, just as it goes through the 'narrows', and becomes Follins Pond, Dad said there were oyster grants there in his day. The water is by that stage in its tidal flow well mixed with the fresh water from spring fed ponds and streams, and the salt flow from the ocean, and the water is considered somewhat 'brackish'. It was an excellent mix for growing oysters, but they did not have the sharp salt flavor that oysters should have. So, at a certain point in the growth of these fat, healthy but bland bivalves, they were harvested, bagged, and moved down river to a saltier clime near where the ocean spilled pure salt sea water into the river's mouth, and they were left for a while to 'flavor up' the way cattle are fattened before shipping to market.

We used to just drop off our clothes and jump in, up river where the railroad bridge crossed, until some girls caught us one day, and made us stay in the water a long, long time. Not close to the bank, either, the water was too clear there and you could see

Dr. Van Bush's boathouse

clean to the bottom, so to speak. I always thought they knew we bathing in the buff, and came on us not altogether by accident. After that, we kept our garments close. Then, the owner of the one house visible from where we swam complained to the one police man in town about us swimming au natural (though how he could see us from the distance, and through the trees, I never figured out). We were told to keep our skivvies on. So, we went in swimming, reluctantly, in trunks, until we got out to a submerged post. There we moored our garments, under water, and swam the way you were supposed to, 'necked as a jaybird,' donning the trunks before exiting the water. There's more than one way to skinny dip.

During WWII, the lands along the river were those most often used as Military training ground. Between the main South Dennis Village and Mayfair, there were hundreds of acres of scrub pine from the main road across the Cape to the river shore, and the river itself became a testing ground for a new fast landing barge, which rose up in fins as it gained speed. It went about as fast as that twisty old river could handle. It was the invention of (and being tested by) Dr. Van Bush, Father's baseball buddy. He owned a large boathouse on the river, and it was a good place to work on, and test, the craft.

Dr. Bush was head of the Science Research Bureau in Washington, (at one dollar a year) during the war, and had all kinds of inventions to his credit - many of which later helped the later development of the computer, and including one invention he got Dad to try out, a bag to keep wet paint brushes from hardening. Another of his inventions was a salve for poison ivy, which caused a long-term embarrassment to little sister Polly. She came into the house complaining of the itch when Dr. Bush was there, and he rushed right across the street and came back with his newly invented, but untested Ivy Cream, which he and my mother promptly applied to the troubled area. Trouble was that area was the little girl's backsides, and though Dr. B. and Mother were only interested in a cure, Polly was understandably mortified to be up ended, and have this older man with a pipe slathering grease on her hinny. She still remembers the embarrassment, but does not recall if the ivy cure worked.

Whenever Dr. Bush could slip out of hectic wartime D.C. for a minute, he headed down to the Cape, and generally spent what time he could working around his wife's old family home, just across the street from our second home (formerly the Grand's). Often during a project, he would amble across, dressed in an old sweater and drawing on his battered pipe, and consult with Dad. Then they would both go to look at the Dr.'s current dilemma: should he pull all those roses back away from the house, would it be necessary to remove all the clapboards off that corner, and start over, that side of the roof still leaks. On one specific instance, "How do I keep those blamed rats out of the house?" "Cement," said Father, "Stuff all the holes down around that foundation with cement." They started working on the Rat problem together, and during the day, an admiral, a general, several scientists and an assortment of D.C. dignitaries called for Dr. Bush. His answer to all, he was involved in a very important experiment, and could not be disturbed. He and Dad finally got all the rat holes stuffed, and the Dr. went back to the nation's business of War, to earn his dollar.

It's hard to believe, boating down Bass River now, but in the thirty's there were long stretches without a single house, and where people had built, it was just one house, set nearly out of sight among the Cape woods, not colonies of them on land stripped of any trace of natural surroundings. The banks were lined with trees, mostly scrub pine or oak, with some marshes and bogs along the way. Near where Great Grandfather had his bogs was a heavily treed area that was all but cut off from the surrounding high ground by bogs, marshes and an inlet. Dad called it 'Grandpa's Island' and I guess it did belong to George Engs at one time, it was right beside his former bog. There was only one narrow approach, it looked man made, and we used to camp there as Boy Scouts. The Island was where we build our bridge.

There were signs that another bridge had been there in years past, just a piling or two, I suspect it was more substantial than the rough pine tree affair we early teen scouts cut and dragged in to place across the inlet, but you COULD cross our bridge - gingerly (if you were under 150 pounds).

A winter nor'easter destroyed it a few years later, but I note even today, you can see some of the old original bridge piles at low tide. We got several merit badges during our campouts there on the island for tying knots, making fires, and burning eggs, but never in bridge building.

It turned out that the area had been a favored camp for the local Native Americans, many moons before us and scientific searchers have found many shell piles and other evidence. It is good to report that the Town Conservation folk now own the area so that it will never be built on, and is a center for Indian research. Good to know something will stay as it used to be.

Interesting, each late spring, early summer, this former Indian camping ground naturally produces great patches of the delicate American orchid, the lady slipper, also known as the moccasin flower, which are rare, and almost impossible to cultivate in a garden. Each year until his recent death, Dr. Norton Nickerson led a walking tour through the area (of course keeping strictly to the prescribed pathways) to show off these marvelous beauties. Norton knew well the area, as his family had owned it for some years. The family sold the land to the Town at well under its true value. Norton was one of us swimmers who long ago used the river as our private bathing pool. His dad was a boyhood friend of my father, and one of the boys who with Dad did their own 'Huck Finn' thing on a cedar log raft up and down Bass River (I shouldn't be surprised if they skinny dipped and, on occasion, misappropriated a few melons). I think somewhere back, we were related. I hope so.

PARAPHERNALIA

When you're heading for the ocean
Don't forget the sun tan lotion.
Now, this really should concern you,
For the sun can burn you sore.

Bring a hat, or this vacation
You may suffer heat prostration.
Colored glasses too, preparing
For that bright and glaring shore.

Canvas chair, some shoes, a jacket
And a lunch, if you can pack it,
Oh, a novel you should cart, too,
For the sun may start to dim.

Towel, wallet, beach umbrella,
Camera for the local color,
But that dip that you aspired to?
You'll be much too tired to swim.

CHAPTER TWENTY-SIX

I Think That I Shall Never See

Strange, there are more trees on Cape Cod now than there were at the turn of the last century (1899 to 1900). Less beach in many places, as great portions were lost to storms. Less marsh, less open space, less unpolluted water, less clean air, even less fish in our piece of ocean, but more trees. Since the original, pre-settler Europeans first spotted the tall hardwood trees that used to grow on the Cape, our forests have taken a beating: at first, shipped over seas for building English ships and homes, then attacked by the Pilgrim fathers, axe in hand. The 'first comers' found harvesting forest products was one of the few ways they could pay off the large investment business men had made in their trip over from the old country, and the supplies they brought to start their new existence. Much of the best timber was shipped out for spars, masts, and ship hulls made in British ship yards, and clapboards for the sides of English houses. They also cut trees not only for building homes, heating and cooking, but often just to clear the land for farming. It's hard to plow around pine trees. Not that the native Americans were top flight conservationists, they cleared land for gardens the easy way, burned off the trees and bushes.

Wood was burned for making charcoal, (for heating the blacksmith's forge, and smelting the bog iron mined from some of the swampy areas which later became cranberry bogs), to distill salt from sea water (before they discovered how to use solar evaporation), to distill liquor, for manufacturing 'lamp black' (in furnaces called funns) which was used for coloring paint and ink. Other much used products of the forests were turpentine and the pitch, or pine tar used to caulk the seams in boats and ships, and to preserve rope from the salt sea (constantly working with these smelly and sticky materials, sailors gained the nickname of 'tars'.) Even the ash of burned wood became important for making potash, which served a number of purposes, such as making soap, both for general use, and used in quantity in the fulling of wool (to remove the excess fat from the woven cloth) and refined potash, called pearl ash, used in the manufacturing of glass. Interesting, after opening the glass works in Sandwich because of the proximity to all the Cape beach sand, the glass makers found our local sand wouldn't do, and had to import the sand for glass making, but the potash product was fine.

Later when steam power replaced the wind and water driven mills and manufacturing plants, and before oil had come into popular use, the chopping and sawing went into high gear to supply wood for making steam. The coming of the oil burner, and then electricity were too late to save much if any of the native forests. In their place came the scrubs. By the time my gang came along in the late twenty's, with the exception of the tall 'planted' Elms along the roadways and some fancy varieties, 'yard' trees which often were not native, but were brought back by sea captains often from outlandish places, (they varied depending on where the various sea captains had traveled) most of the Cape was covered with little scraggly pitch pines, scrub oaks and bushes. Luckily, we were very short, so it looked like a forest to us. There are, still growing in yards around the Cape, trees from Japan and China, from Europe and the Caribbean Islands as well as small preserved areas of older, natural Cape growth. Down on Cove Road, on the land that Joy and Dr. Wilbur leased from the church, there was a small grove of chestnut trees which used to be numerous on the Cape but have largely succumbed to cutting and blight. They produced real chestnuts, different from horse chestnuts which weren't eatable, but made neat necklaces, and key chains.

Across the street and up a little, were a couple of really big evergreen conifers very tempting to tree climbing kids, but they belonged to our great aunt, Suzie Thacher,

(Uncle Peleg's widow) and all of her yard, was off limits including the trees, and the flat-top board fence in front. She and Grandfather had a falling out because she told him to get his damn coat off her fence. Seems like they had had words before, and seldom had a good word one for the other.

Our front yard trees were two fat and tall silver poplars probably not native to the Cape, but imported from the south. We lost them in the '44 hurricane. One, in falling, clipped off the roof from my upstairs front bedroom...I slept through the night. Funny about the 'silver leaf' trees, they used to be all over the place, but they seemed to disappear after that storm. They were a strange tree, with leaves which were green on the top, silver on the back. Their roots traveled under ground for a long way, and then pop up somewhere new, usually where you would rather they weren't, growing in a small thicket, just like a grove of aspens, all connected. They even sound like aspens, and I guess they are of a family. There were lots of them in the mid-Cape, but that '44 storm seemed to have discouraged them. It was very sad, on the morning after the storm looking at those really impressive giants lying, uprooted and dying on the grass of our front lawn. We also had a yucca lily in the yard, another plant somebody brought in from heavens knows where. They aren't trees, worried not about storms, and seem to live for ever.

If you know where to look, you can find stands of White Pine here and there around in Cape towns. You will recognize them by the way they grow in planted lines reflecting the planning and order of the hand of man, rather than natural selection. Part of the Roosevelt work programs in the 30's included the revival of our forests, national and local. The C.C.C.,

Civilian Conservation Corps, worked in the forests from coast to coast, and Alaska and our various possessions. For meals, lodging and $30.00 per month ($25 of which was sent to relatives), over a quarter million (some estimates say three times that many) young, out of work, unmarried men joined up to plant trees, build fire towers, cut roads, and make roads and camps. For the smaller state and town lands, the W.P.A. supplied money to hire local people to do similar work. Father, as tree warden, was in charge of a work group in the Dennis Town Forest, and spent a couple of years planting several acres of lovely young white pine trees, only to see them cut down in the mid 60's to make way for the Dennis Pines Golf Course. He was heart broken. He took a lot of pride in the fine stand of 30 year old trees, often pointed them out to us on Sunday drives, and to see them trashed for a golf course just didn't seem right. Interesting, some of the old C.C.C. camps still exist as camping areas. The former training camp (Camp Mead in Vermont) is a commercial enterprise, filled with the history of the C.C.C., the 30's and WWII.

About 1940, came the Dutch elm disease. Most of the trees which had formed a nearly complete arch over our summer village streets began to die. Dad had worked repairing some of them back in the mid 30's. The tree crew went around to any injured or partially rotting trees, took down limbs, scraped out bad and rotting wood, and filled the holes with cement. But the plague went on for years, and there are not many of the great trees still around. The people who do such things have come up with some strains of elm resistant to Dutch elm and they are being replanted.

Mostly, though, it was scrubs. We climbed the oaks, and shinnied up the pines, cut branches and saplings to build our 'huts', even constructed a tree hut about ten feet up in one of the most substantial, and chopped some of the taller trees for large projects, like the Boy Scout Bridge. The bigger trees were fun. We took turns shinnying up near the top, and riding the tree down as our friends cut away at the bottom. Most of the scrub wood areas were freely available for kids to do what they would. A fire at the Barnstable County land offices some years back had wiped out most of the deeds, so lots of the wood land didn't know it belonged to anybody, and its value at that time seemed to be only for what wood you might cut for home heating. Nobody seemed to care if you cut wood on their property, either. We always heated with a wood stove, and as I grew bigger, I went up into the woods with Dad, several times each year in the fall and winter to renew our supply. We were always careful to cut selectively, picking dead or dying trees, but we were never questioned as to our right to take wood from any unpopulated wooded area around the village. Dad did most of the chopping, although I "beavered down" a few trees: the sawing was a two man job.

We had a 5 foot saw with handles on each end and once you got into the rhythm, it was kind of a contest to keep up with the

Dennisport

guy on the other end. We kept a piece of bacon rind with us, and used it to lubricate the big saw blade. When we got the wood home in whatever old car Father had at the time, I became the splitter, and the carry-it-in guy. Brother Link joined in when he became big enough. I had a slight heart irregularity at about 13, blacked out a couple of times, took it to the good Dr., and he had me doing exercises for about ten minutes, mostly jumping up and down on a stool while he puttered around, seemed to forget I was there, and talked on the phone. When he had me puffing, he checked with his stethoscope.

"You'll outgrow it," he said,

"Maybe I shouldn't chop wood?" I asked hopefully.

"It'll be good for you," he said.

Man who cuts his own wood, they say, warms his-self twicet.

Back in the 30's I heard Dad and a friend discussing a sale of some acreage out behind our first house. "My Gawd," sez Father, "He paid $2,000, a hundred dollars an acre! Why, it's nothing but woodland!" There are currently about 40 houses on that piece of "woodland", and a friend recently inquired about the price of one advertised for sale: $285,000! My, my, how times has changed!

CAMPING'S OUT

This year we decided to rough it,
To go out and live in a tent.
Oh, the rest we would get,
With the sleeping-bag set,
And what savings on holiday rent!

This year we decided to rough it,
We set out with full camper's kit.
Then one night after dark,
An unfortunate spark,
Floated out of our barbecue pit.

Yes, this year we decidedly roughed it.
The outcome was far from a lark.
We're indebted, so far,
For the tent and the car,
And six acres of national park.

CHAPTER TWENTY-SEVEN

Just Folks

Often, when I feel compelled to mention some of the people I grew up amongst, the Wife, brought up on the eastern edge of Middle America, West Hartford, Connecticut, pops a mystified look, and asks if there were any folks in town who were NOT 'Characters'. Well, I must say, in trying to sort through the people of our village, and its general environs, my thoughts first settle on some of the folk who stand out for individualized behavior and manners. For example: Mercy, an elderly single woman, with wild black hair, who always wore sweaters, yes, even in summer had her stockings, or, rather socks rolled down like donuts around her ankles, and floppy bedroom slippers, indoors and out. She had been an English teacher, I think, and was always correcting our way of speaking. A well worn path across one corner of her property was by far the shortest route from our house to the post office, (shortest for Harold and Frenchy, also). She didn't really object to us using the path, rather, she used our occasional laps of memory to enlist us as indentured servants. We would think we were sliding by as slick as grease, when:

"Oh, Ben, you and Harold come here for just a minute, Now, could you carry off these branches (or pull these weeds for me, or cut this little patch of grass, here's the mower, it is not very sharp, so you'll have to go over it a few times), and then come in, I'll have a surprise!"

The surprise, for an hour's work or more, was cookies, but:

"Now, you taste these, and tell me what I forgot to put in them!"

Well, it was the sugar she forgot. We didn't tell her, and luckily she never offered a second, so we would slither out, inwardly fuming at having walked that path in the first place. She nailed Harold once the same way with oatmeal cookies, sans oatmeal.

It was she who came storming up to our front door accusing our dog of killing her chickens. Dad said he'd do his best to cure the dog of such bad habits, and in the prescribed manner for such problems, he tied a dead hen around the dog's neck (Mercy had brought one as Exhibit 'A' for the prosecution). The dog wore the hen in a most embarrassed manner, for near a week. Then he managed to work it free, and went over and killed another of her hens.

The fire department rushed up her long hedge lined driveway one morning, in response to a neighbor's call about seeing smoke and flames. Mercy had tried to burn some leaves, and the grass had caught fire. As the fire chief came into view, he swears she was standing there spitting on the flames in a vain attempt to subdue them.

Casey was an African American of an unusually dark hue. On Cape Cod, most dark complexioned people were the numerous Azorean and Cape Verdean citizens, of skin shades varying from Caucasian through café olé, but not the deep black as with Casey. He was a huge man, or so he seemed to us, with an accent which made his English difficult to understand, and as small children, we were afraid of him, but he was a very gentle man even in his cups. His strength was prodigious. He could pick up the back end of a model "A" Ford, and hold it while someone changed the wheel. He worked at the lumberyard, and loaded trucks with coal, using an oversized shovel, and doing the work of two men, all the while smiling, and holding his corncob pipe between his teeth, but lighting it rarely. He loved a joke, if it was simple enough for his limited English, and never seemed to be other than a happy person. When a freight car of hay was parked on the siding, and as our school bus stop was there at the hay shed, we saw him at work quite often. There was a moveable plank walkway from the hay shed out to the mouth of the freight car, and two-wheel hand trucks to carry the hay bales, which weighed anywhere from 120 to

160 pounds each, but when Casey first tried pushing a hand truck, a wheel caught, slipped over the side, and caused the whole rig with a heavy bale on it to tip off the plank walkway on to the ground. Trying to stop it, Casey twisted a muscle, and decided he could do better by hand. From then on, he would hoist one bale to his shoulder, and lift another under his arm, and walk with a full stride down the walkway and into the shed, where he would pile the hay, which usually filled the large room to the ceiling, and stride back for another load.

Casey owned a small cranberry bog about a mile and a half from his home, and unfazed by his day of backbreaking work, walked down to the bog on weekends and each evening after work, and weeded, sanded, picked, cleaned ditches and did what other work might be necessary. He was accompanied on his bog journeys by his wife, Matilda. I never heard her speak in English. She had very bad feet, they were large and bothered her when she walked, so Casey carried her to the bog on his shoulders and put her by the bog edge, where she sat and smoked her clay T.D. pipe until darkness halted the work, then Casey would lift her to his shoulder again, and walk the mile and a half home.

Remember, we're dealing here with a town of five villages, containing in total, 1200 people. EVERY body knew what every one else was doing, they only read the paper to see who got caught. It was common knowledge whose daughter was going to the Farnum Dance School, and who was having trouble with the mortgage (most everyone, from time to time). It was part of the conversation at the Post Office, the idol chatter between volunteer firemen as they cleaned up the truck after a grass fire, among the ladies at church circle meetings, at the Knights of Pythias weekly whist games; who was drinking too much, what couples were fighting, who was out of work.

All local happenings were grist for the mill. The P.O. group heard how many barrels of cranberries old Howes harvested, what mileage their car made on a trip, the foolhardy conduct of a neighbor and whether that new boy in town was a loafer; the knitters and darners dissected an absent friend, counted the months between marriages and first births and condemned that dreadful situation with the _____ family in Dennisport, with appropriately interjected "Land a Goshen!," "I declare!", and " 'tis true, 'tis true, every word you say is true!" Yah, it was gossip, but it was also the life blood of a small community trying to get through troubled times, and needing to understand who they were.

We knew our neighbors, and chuckled at the tales told while waiting for the mail to be sorted, like the two older boys who were window peeking, and swore they heard Eben H. yell to his wife, "Hoist your calico, Lorrie, here I come", and the story of Obid (who's wife was a homely woman with a fine singing voice) who, in moments of passion would call out, "For God sake, Mary, sing!".

A particularly nosy lady who habitually went right into the yards of her neighbors to peek in the windows was surprised when the new occupants of a house popped open the door and invited her in for tea. She went, and without embarrassment grilled them for an hour about their lives.

A Young Blood confessed at the fire station (a former school house, where we later had Boy Scout meetings) that perhaps he had deceived a young teacher on their first date. They were riding in his buggy, when she gently inquired if he was a man of means. He stood up in the buggy, swept his arms wide in an arc which embraced some acres of woodland, and stated, "Ma'am, Over there to the south there is nothing I can see that I don't own!" He confessed that unbeknownst to her, he had his eyes closed at the time.

Ed P. was a handy man. One of those people who do odd jobs, and generally relieve householders of many arduous (and sometimes unpleasant) projects that need doing. Came to getting rid of a dead tree, call Ed, he'd cut it up, take it home, and augment his pay by having that much free wood to burn for winter heat. Crawl up into a dirty, cobwebby attic, and haul the contents off to the dump or to his house. Bound to find some metal or rags or such that he could sell to Stanley Lapham, or useable items to trade, sell or keep. Ed didn't work very fast, or charge very much, but he usually managed to make up in 'take-homes' what he lacked in salary. People in the village were used to seeing Ed with his pushcart/barrow going from job to job; a few tools in the barrow in the morning, heavens knows what as he headed home. They were not really prepared however, for the sight he presented after he tore down an old privy. After piling his cart high with the keeper boards, Ed found he had no room for the three-hole seat. Not to worry. With his head through an end hole, collar fashion, and the rest of the seat board with the other two holes dangling down like a giant necktie, Ed marched his loaded pushcart thru town, and home. Note: Ed's house had a dirt floor, and after the '44 hurricane, told of his fright as the winds literally lifted and tipped the place so that Ed, sitting in the kitchen could see out beneath the edge. Then set it gently back down. "Moy Gawd," said Ed as he later told about it, "I thought moy time had come!"

The man down the street, Mr. J. (a truly gentle person, an excellent workman, and a well liked person) was married to a wife who was a nosey gossip, and mean. Mean to friends and neighbors, and mean to Mr. J. It was almost village wide relief that noted her passing, and a feeling that the good Mr. J. could at last call his soul his own. He soon found himself a Cape Cod housekeeper, one that not only cooked, but comforted. In spite of the presumption of not quite legally formalized co-habitation, the lady was welcomed locally, and in fact became a member, and then leader of the sewing circle, before it was discovered that this woman was an even worse harridan than the late Mrs. J. She and Mr. J. eventually married and he seemed happy to again be Mr. Milquetoast, target of her sharp tongue till death did them part.

We had a county official who used to take a daily dip in the river in clement weather au natural and after, clad only in his gray fedora, stand thoughtfully on the shore, smoking a cigar and drying off, oblivious to the fact that he was in full view of passers by. Otherwise, he seemed a perfectly nice man, if rather wordy, and he was re-elected to the county office several times. He was a portly man, a bachelor, with a large nose, and slightly resembled the then popular comic strip character, Major Hoople. He fit right in, as a fellow townsman, and I don't think he was ever defeated in his quest for public office.

As Mother used to say, "Everyone's strange except me and thee, and sometimes, dear, even you are a little odd!"

DEVELOPMENT

I don't suppose it spoiled the view,
Which never was too fine,
Most people look at least as good,
As that old scraggy pine.
But all those houses that they built,
They just don't seem to fit,
All hunkered in there, cheek to jowl,
So close you couldn't spit.

Those roads were only wagon ruts,
When I was playing age,
And we'd pretend 'twas way out West,
And call the bushes sage.
We made a hut where two roads crossed,
(We called 'em Injun trails)
And scared the britches off ourselves,
By telling gory tales.

I guess they farmed there, years ago,
There's stone walls, and the roads.
Cut off the trees, and moved the stumps
By sledge and wagon loads,
There's even leavings of a well,
A short way off the track,
And when they left, why Nature
Just commenced to put things back.

I know that things has got to change,
I've heard the "Progress" speech,
But if nobody stopped them,
There'd be houses on the beach.
For folks to have a place to live,
Seemed fair enough to me.
But we might be better suited,
If they'd just leave some things be.

CHAPTER TWENTY-EIGHT
My Dog Fala Hates War

(Attributed to F.D.R. in a 1940's 'fire side chat' "I hate war, Eleanor hates war, and my dog Fala hates war!")

War was hanging over us in 1940 and early '41 by way of radio broadcasts, news paper headlines, and movie newsreels, but I don't think many people believed we would be involved in it. We were after all some thousands of miles from the fighting, and none of the warring nations could reach us, we thought. Mr. Roosevelt said he, his wife and dog all hated war, and that was good enough for me, and for most. Then in December came the Hawaiian attack. I was 13.

I wore several hats during the war, first the Smokey the bear hat of a 1930's boy scout, (we became 'victims' of fake bombings for air-raid disaster practice), collectors of recyclable materials (balls of Tinfoil, waste metals, newspaper) and received instruction in first aid and enemy plane spotting, my civilian guise as a candy selling war profiteer, the folded paper hat of a soda jerk (no hair in the milkshakes, please!), an underage State Guard bandsman (they were short of drummers), a fearless rifle swinging anti-looter guard after the '44 hurricane, (reassigned from the band for the occasion, and given a heavy old Springfield rifle and bayonet, but NO bullets, and quaking in my boots) and toward the end of high school, a cook's apron, and a bell hop's little jacket. After the shooting war was over, but before peace was finally arranged, I became 18, and enlisted, early enough so my time in Japan made me eligible as a vet, and potential member of the V.F.W. Later, with a not so willing return to the army during the Korean conflict, courtesy of the Reluctant Reserve Corps, I fought the Battles of Hopkinsville, KY and Nashville, Tenn. for an additional year, making me a vet of two wars, with never a shot fired in anger - by me or, thank heavens, at me. I marched a lot, jumped out of a few planes, received corporal's stripes, had my helmet grazed by friendly fire by an inept automatic rifleman in my own squad during a live amo field exercise, sprained an ankle in a track meet, learned to thoroughly dislike the Army, and came home.

It was decided early in the war that Cape Cod, jutting out into the Atlantic as it does, might offer landing beaches for potential invaders. The Coast Guard took over a rather ritzy summer colony on the north side, and patrolled the beach at night with dogs. All street lamps were turned off, and lights on motor cars had to be painted so just the bottom half emitted light. As you came from the south side toward East Dennis and the north (Cape Cod Bay) beach, at the top of the hill, on what is now Route 134, and on the Main road over from South Dennis to Dennis there were painted lines on the road, past which you had to put your head lights out entirely. The field stone tower on Scargo Hill and other high points were given over to plane spotters, with charts of the silhouettes of enemy planes, and radio or telephone contact set up for quick communication with the Powers that be. Black Out drills were held to practice closing off all house and other lights so as not to present a beacon for enemy planes. Special curtains were put in windows, and locally appointed wardens patrolled, and knocked on doors if light was visible from a house.

Daytime exercises practiced crowd control and other emergency procedures, and first aid techniques. The Scouts were victims. Each of us was tagged as to what injuries we had sustained, and stationed at a supposed disaster site. Volunteer First Aid people with station wagons, and small panel trucks were notified where to find victims, and raced to the scene, read the symptoms tag and treated the patient accordingly, then loaded them on stretchers and transported them to an aid station. After an exercise on an icy cold and windy day, we were having head count and a critique back at the fire station, huddling by the big iron wood stove, when it was noted we were one scout short. Checking the list, showed that one of our members had not been picked up by the team assigned to his area. The Scout Master rushed out to the rescue, and brought back a thoroughly chilled, still tagged scout. He was O.K. except for a touch of frost bite from lying on the ground by the rail road track for the entire exercise. Asked why he didn't move around to help himself stay warm, he noted he couldn't get up because his tag said he had a broken leg.

We suffered none of the terrors of war on our home soil, but did send off many of our young men. Lots of houses in town had a blue star flag in the window, and some of the unfortunate, a gold star. War on the home front was occasionally inconvenient with meatless days, rationing, a weekly limit of 3 gallons of gas for non-essential vehicles, and some shortages in the stores, but the physical evidence was only the blackout shades stacked by the window, and signs; "Use less sugar, stir like hell, we don't mind the noise", "A slip of the lip can sink a ship," big, stern, old Uncle Sam pointing a finger, and saying "I Want You!", Rockwell pictures of the 'Four Freedoms' (recently trashed by Attorney General Ashcroft), and "When you shop, don't forget to bring along your fat can". Young children hardly noticed, older people worried and teen age boys yearned to join up and kill the enemy. I joined up, sort of; the conductor of our school band, too old for active service, was asked to lead a State Guard Band, and selected another drummer and myself to help supply the beat. Our ages were fudged, and we were duly sworn in, and uniformed. There were weekly practices, concerts, and we were on hand for any marching occasion which chanced to come up.

Then came the 1944 hurricane! We were mobilized. Carl Nickerson, the other drummer, had a car with some gas in it, so he picked me up. We were issued the obsolete rifles with bayonets, and stationed in Dennisport, near the shore where the hurricane had shattered dozens of summer camps and cabins. Our job: contain all looting! It was almost as scary as the time the boy scouts had been called to search the shores and rivers for the body of a little boy who had been drowned. We circled those shattered piles of what had been vacation cabins for two days and nights, and had "mess" in the field. I guess my biggest thrill was when Larry Lovequist, an Officer who later became my auto insurance man, asked if I could drive. Yes, I could! So, he popped me into his car and drove to his house to get his motor cycle. He drove it back, leaving me to bring his coupe to Dennisport.

Driving back through and around the partly blocked and littered roads in his unfamiliar car, with a steering wheel mounted gear shift (never had seen one), made me feel pretty important. The nights felt like Halloween in a graveyard, but we didn't see any looters. I guess everybody was so taken up with straightening out what the storm had done to their own yards; they didn't have time to visit any other wreckage. It was a mess, not just the camps and houses, but most of the main streets, with poles down, electric wires all over. Many roofs off even some of the more substantial buildings and most of the great elms which the Dutch elm problem hadn't gotten to yet were ripped up or broken off. The wind reached over 100 MPH, a stiff breeze even for the Cape which with so many sides to the Ocean, receives more than her share of strong blows.

Our front lawn, and many others on the residential streets, had been graced with really large and handsome silver poplar trees. The wind took them all down (one of them took off the edge of the roof over my upstairs bedroom, but when I sleep, I sleep; didn't hear a thing). The storm apparently somehow slowed or stopped the growth of 'silver leaf' trees around the area. They grow in groves, similar to aspen, and keep sending up new shoots, which are a bother if they are on your lawn, but the big trees were very decorative. I haven't seen them around much since then.

WWii Ration stamps and points.

We saw our first Jeeps in, I think, 1941 from the second story window of Ezra Baker School. It was during Mr. Mclin's class and he was so excited he let us all stand by the windows, and watch. They came in a long line, it seemed like hundreds, but was probably about 50. They resembled a line of army-brown ants, winding up the rise in front of the school, and then vanishing, one by one, off toward Dennisport. Four armed men to a vehicle, with whining motors and the uniformed soldiers, grave and business like. We were awed. I noticed, regretfully, that they were headed down Cape, not in the direction of our South Dennis woods, so were not potential candy customers. Anyway, a year or so after that I gave up my business, and started jerking sodas, and, when the pharmacist was busy, selling cigarettes, aspirin, Bromo Seltzer and some strange items from the back shelf wrapped in Plain Brown Paper Bags. I gave it my all for two summers, and weekends through the winter, and then went to work for the Light House Inn. What with summer work there, in kitchen, dining room, and then front desk, I kept busy till the war wound down, school ran out and I became eighteen and was able to join up.

The truly sad part of the war was of course the neighborhood guys who didn't come back, including a fine and serious young man who had been our Sunday school teacher until he enlisted, Jakey Wilbur. He helped our male class plod through stuffy church material, and presented a friendly example of how to be both a good and regular guy at the same time. After class he also taught me to wiggle my ears. My last second-handed contact with him was when his mother came into the drug store to buy some 'heat tabs', little pellets that she sent over to him which could be burned in a tiny folding stove to heat a bit of water for tea. It was cold in the fox holes, she said.

CAPE COD GRAY

The sun came out two weeks ago,
And set there for an hour or so,
But then by ten she'd gone away,
Left more familiar Cape Cod Gray.

I'd like to see a bumper crop
Of sunshine that just wouldn't stop,
But Cape Cod dwellers just assume,
Our winters will be big on gloom.

CHAPTER TWENTY-NINE

All In The Family

Mother announced one night that half a dozen was plenty. She had been to see the film 'Cheaper By The Dozen', and disagreed. Not that she was not thoroughly enamored of her six, but there is a lot to be said for knowing when enough's enough. We were five for a number of years, before Polly joined on. Father always said she was conceived in the mad rush of excitement of VJ day, and Mother always blushed. I went in the service soon after she was born and when I had a leave, Nancy and I (in uniform) pushed her around Hyannis, and folks thought we were a couple. She was a welcome addition to the 'Five Little Thachers', and a bright light for the parents' middle years. (Famous Polly line at family gatherings, "Gee, I missed all the fun!") As the oldest, I was supposed to set an example for the rest to follow, but luckily, they each took their own direction. Every one peeled off on a different course, and now, we all six live on the Cape, within a twenty mile radius, and our progeny over flow a local Inn for a Christmas Breakfast just before the holiday. Must have been something in the sand.

In the later years of his life at family parties, Dad used to look around at the milling mass of multiplying miniatures, shake his head and say, "My God, Ben, be I responsible for all this?" Well he might ask. At the last couple of Fourth of July gatherings (traditional) at brother Link's pond side beach, our family picture strained the capabilities of a sophisticated wide-angle lens, and growing still. Dad was in a debate during his 1910 high school graduation, "Resolved: that young people should leave Cape Cod." He argued the negative. Well, it's obvious from the population figures then that many of his generation took the positive route, they left. That is why by the time Mom started birthing, there were so few citizens roaming the often still unpaved streets. As tots, we romped in the small back yard behind the Lower County Road house, and pushed paths through the lilac grove. Nancy and I, then Olive, (Olive Baker, often called OB, named for the sweet faced elderly lady next door, Alpheus' wife who was a good friend of Mom's) then Link (Raymond Lincoln, the Raymond for Mom's younger brother, and Lincoln had been Dad's father's middle name. Dad called him a little curly headed cuss. The curls did not set too well with his two older straight haired sisters, but all agreed he was cute). Jane (mother wanted it spelled with a Y . . . Jayne, not snooty, just liked to be a little different. Problem was, the Dr. put Jane on the certificate. JAYNE sez she might correct that some day.) came on a little way down the line, and she was the baby until Pauline (Polly) Ann, (called 'Pliney', an after thought, perhaps, but we are all glad she was thought of) made 1946 a famous year.

We all played happily around the dooryard until first grade called us, me, and then Nancy into the school system. Olive and Link went to a newly established Nursery School where they played in a percussion band, and Link proceeded to embarrass the family. A boy in his class was told it was impolite to eat with his elbows on the table. He said his father did that all the time. Link chimed in with the information that HIS father ate with his feet on the table! Luckily, very few people believed him. Probably the low point in Nancy's and my association was the day I hung her doll in the stair well. Cannot remember why, I have always been against the death penalty.

As the two pathfinders for the 'Little Thachers' I remember that we had a rollicking good time together. In snow season, there was a 'just right' hill across the street, with a tiny pond at the foot. It belonged to the Leightons who lived on top of the hill, and they graciously offered the neighborhood kids full user rights to the slippery slope. In warmer seasons, we often went across the sandy Duck Pond Road, to the Blashfield's yard, and played 'mountain' on a pile of yellow sand, or got formal and made a visit to the Blashfields. That was usually good for cookies, and some conversation.

Somehow, between her usual chore and extras such as preserving eggs in water glass (not good for breakfast, but worked in cakes and such) and making our weekly batch of doughnuts, Mother got her license to drive when I was about three. When Dad was working at home, she would

The Whole Gang

put Nan in a basket on the back seat, sit me in front as co-pilot, and proceed to drive around our property. I don't remember, but the story was that I noted the circular pattern of the drive, and annoyed that we did not seem to be getting anywhere, delighted Mother by asking, "What's the matter with this damn car, going round and round?" (Just a little gem of baby humor, there). After she obtained her license, there were trips to the beach during the hot months, which were very satisfactory. Dad sometimes joined us of a Sunday afternoon, but it was most often Mother and us kids. Dad had a knit one-piece bathing suit with straps over the shoulders, full chest coverage, and a hint of a skirt over the short legs. Whenever he went swimming, he would dive in, and stay under water for what seemed like hours, coming to the surface a long way from where we suspected to see him. It was scary, and we 'ood' and 'ahhed', and clapped. He must have gotten some satisfaction from our response, because he started every swim that way.

The way to the beach at West Dennis took us past a large stable on 'Trotting Park Road', where there had been a Race Track for Trotters in days past. Seems the sea captains, wanting some off duty amusement, constructed a track here, as well as another in Harwich, and probably others

here and there on the Cape, raised prize trotters, and competed (and bet) for amusement when ashore. The one in Harwich, which was built around a small fresh water pond, seems to have gotten out of hand, and angered the local wives. Whether at the betting, or the amount of time their men spent at the track, I don't know, but at one point (apparently, while most of their sailors were at sea) they hired a construction crew to scrape out one side of the track and let the sea in! Results are there to be seen, the round Wychmere Harbor at Harwichport. The trotters were gone by my time, and the stables there in West Dennis held rental horses, but it was a thrill to pass a party jodhpured and booted, turning out for a canter. The old racetrack is now a paved circle lined with houses.

We seldom went to the main beach, but more usually to a secluded stretch of sand and dunes to the east. There were generally not more than two or three other parties there, usually with children, also, and I guess Mom liked the solitude. She could sit and read, and keep track of us.

120

Of course, we always wanted to go to the main beach, where the crowds were, and where they had a concession stand, with hot dogs, candy ice cream, and such. The main beach at West Dennis was far smaller than it is today, most of the long strip that is now useable, and backed with an almost mile long road and parking lot extending to the edge of Bass River, was sand dunes and sharp beach grass. There were still one or two 'shucking shacks' and old docks extending out a bit into the sea. Scallop draggers would pull their boats up to the shacks in the old days, and the shellfish were unloaded and swiftly opened there at seaside. They are long gone, and most of the dunes flattened, either by storms, or by town road and recreation crews. Even the scallops are mostly gone. They depended on 'eel grass' which has vanished from most of our coast and rivers.

On an occasional Sunday afternoon when Dad was the driver, and for some reason beach was not an option, we would go for a ride often on back roads that Father remembered from his boyhood. We paused to see if the herring were running, (when the season was near) if there was a good crop of crab apples on great Uncle Steve's trees over in Dennis (and check to see if he was well). Then often over to the river to check on the tide (it was always moving) and sometimes parked at an exciting scenic spot, like Hokum rock. I even remember an afternoon jaunt landing us by the side of the Cape Cod Canal, near one of the great bridges, which were not finished until about 1936. The Canal was always moving, too. (Did you know the water is several feet higher at one end than at the other?) Sometimes an auto malfunction such as a flat tire marred the trip and sometimes, as is the way of such things, whatever we went to see wasn't there any longer, but we ended up getting ice cream, which made it all right.

Going down Route 28, thru West Harwich, we passed a Dance Hall on the left, where for a while the 'Dancing Marathon' was held, and broadcast on the Radio. It was exciting, because just around the next curve was a building with a miniature windmill, Dutch Land Farms, home of some of the finest ice cream In the United States of Cape Cod! This later became a Howard Johnson's (28 delicious flavors) which advertised on the radio quite often. After hearing a few ads, and enjoying a Sunday taste session, Nancy declared that Howard was her boy friend.

Another Ice Cream Mecca was on the north side of the Cape, and one we visited sometimes when the beach plums or high bush blue berries were ready for picking. Crowe Pastures, mainly town property now, thank goodness, had quite a variety of fruit stuffs for making jelly, and pies, and all. There were blue berries (both low bush and the high bush varieties), black and red raspberries, beach plums, and a couple of crab apple trees. When Nana grew somewhat infirm, Dad used to take her to Crowe Pasture and pull the car up beside one of the high blueberry bushes and draw a branch down within her grasp, and she would sit there on the front seat, and pick.

At some point, Dad also got us a glob of the multi-colored clay from a bank down on the beach at the end of Crowe Pasture. I remember we tried to mix it with some kind of oil to make modeling clay, but without much success. Years later, our Uncle Wendell Bassett, an artist and potter, tried some in his kiln, and found it useable, but not too satisfactory. Regardless the goal of the journey, however, a stop at D.H. Sears for their homemade ice cream made the trip a huge success.

Church was a Sunday morning affair, when it was available; the tall-spired South Dennis Congregational was often closed for want of a pastor.

There just were not enough of the faithful in the village to support a full time parson, so the church stood, in a state of disrepair and empty unless we could 'double up' with some other parish, and take their minister on loan, so to speak. Even then, the church was pretty cold in winter, heated only by a huge wood burning stove, which Dad, as deacon, and I, later, stoked. In really deep cold, the stove threw heat about 6 feet in any direction, and many a service was held in the back, near the stove, but far from the altar, organ and choir loft. They were usually mighty short services, too. (Those Puritans with their all day sessions must have been made of steel.)

When it became time for us to go to Sunday school, the church was between ministers and closed, so Nancy and I were carted down to West Dennis Methodist Church, where there was a bigger congregation that could pay a full time parson. We did a good bit of church schooling there, including a summer program (where we made needle holders out of oilcloth and cotton, heart shaped, I seem to recall) and at least one 'concert' during which we both amused the audience, and somewhat embarrassed Mom. Nancy, in one of the old style of little girl dress, hanging loose from the shoulders (maybe a 'Shirley Temple'?) and with a big hair ribbon partially untied, went on stage to say her piece with a handkerchief in her hand. She found it distracting, so she upped her skirt, and stuffed the handkerchief up her bloomer leg (YES, Bloomer). She got a merry laugh for that, and Mother blushed a bit, but at least the bloomers were clean.

I performed, to polite acceptance, but got in trouble when the mistress of ceremonies asked if any one knew something else that they could perform. Up jumped Benny the Boy vocalist. The selection was "The Preacher and the Bear", an old Minstrel show comic dialect song learned at my father's knee (when my mother wasn't listening). The trouble was, with my excellent memory for songs and lyrics, I remembered and performed every last word if it... It's about a minister who is hunting on a Sunday when he should have been preaching, filled with humorous biblical allusions, which certainly brought more smiles to the faces of the faithful than 'Rock Of Ages'. Then at the end, when the Parson cries out "Don't yo' help dat Gawd Damn Bear", I broke up the house, jolted the pastor a bit, and turned my Mother beet red!

When spring arrived, and a beginning minister agreed to the pittance the Congregational Church could afford, we bid good-bye to the Methodists and did our churching in South Dennis. I might add, that in the acceptant manner of the old Cape, the superintendent (and main teacher) of our newly opened Congregational Sunday school was a member of the Pentecostal church. Directly Sunday school was over, left the church to go to services at the Pentecostal church, first in Dennisport, and later at a newly built church in So. Dennis.

YARD SALE

We're off to a yard sale,
And Mother's ecstatic,
She says it's like peeking
Through somebody's attic.
Dad's looking for tools,
Which he always enjoys,
While I shop for skis
Bow and arrows and toys.
Big sister, quite frankly,
Is looking for boys.

My uncle is famous
For getting good deals.
Five bucks for a wagon
Without any wheels.
A slightly cracked vase,
And one marvelous find:
An old coffee grinder,
That wouldn't quite grind.
Plus a watch which may go,
If he gets it to wind.

We're off to a yard sale,
With all of our wealth,
To buy tons of knick-knacks
And books about health.
A battered old chair,
And a crocheting ring,
A caged plush canary
They say used to sing!
Well, you'll find the lot
In our yard sale next spring.

CHAPTER THIRTY

Nor Any Drop To Drink

When that oversized mile high ice cube shoved all the sand, rocks and stuff out here to make the Cape and then left, we were very nearly surrounded by salt water. Then, in 1914 when they opened the Cape Cod Canal between the Cape and the mainland, we became an island. What with all of our coastline, and all the bays, marshes and tidal rivers, the Cape is pretty much at the mercy of the ocean. Just us and the gulls. There is an aquifer of fresh water under the Cape, but even it is bound on all sides by the salt. If we use too much of the fresh water, the salt water may move in to the area we over pumped.

The ocean has a lot to do with our weather. The cold Atlantic slows our approaching spring, and the warmer water in the fall gives a little bit more autumn than the mainland enjoys, topped usually, by a final week or so of magnificent Indian Summer before the frost sets in seriously for the winter. Lots of the storms seem to follow one or the other sides of the Canal, some times more severe on this side, sometimes the other, with often even a difference in temperature. Many a Nor'easter has lashed the Cape for its proverbial three days or more, while leaving Plymouth and environs relatively unscathed, or vice versa. In fact, weather and temperature can vary a good deal between Provincetown, Chatham and Falmouth, or from one side of the Cape to the other. A dank fogbank on the bay side may give way to bright sunshine as you drive toward the south. The seas around the Cape which had for many years supplied salt from evaporation, fish of many varieties for our diet and a water highway for sailors, is also the wrecking ground for hundreds of boats and ships, and the graveyard for thousands of seamen and passengers.

I grew up loving the ocean. From playing on the soft sand as gentle wavelets wash the West Dennis beach on an August afternoon, to walking the same sands, bent and leaning on the wind during the blustering power and snarling surf of a hurricane (not recommended). I have lolled in semitropical (almost too warm) waters, gasped for breath swimming my hardest to escape from the clutches of a rip tide, aimed at taking me out to sea, and clutched desperately to the safety rope on the deck of a ship caught in a typhoon, with waves rising so high around as to seem one with the glowering clouds. It's all the same wonderful ocean, our friendly enemy which can at a whim please us, feed us, or kill us. I have always been inordinately fond of fish, swimmers, or shelled variety. Maybe the salt is in my blood (I understand salt water makes up a good part of our body).

When I was very small I used to hang around where Dad was opening oysters, quahogs or scallops, and grab about every third one he opened. I did so much of that, that I got sick, developed cankers, they said, thru my whole digestive system, something to do with excessive iodine, I think. When I was well again, I took up my old stand, and was surprised when the handouts were curtailed severely. Dad loved to go for fish. He didn't go 'fishing,' he went FOR fish. There were hand lines and other fishing gear around the barn but I never saw Dad use any of it except the one time we went out on Archie Ellis' boat to the stone island (breakwater) off West Dennis beach for tautog. The Ellis family lived next door to us at our 'new' house up on the main street, and the boat had been a source of wonder to us. It was an old wooden craft, probably 16 feet long, with a tiny cabin and a big, old motor which I think came out of a junked car. It sat in their yard each winter while Mr. Ellis and his son, Clifton worked on it, and this was our first chance to see it in action, and to have a ride in it. It was a long ride, down the length of Bass River and out through the surf to the breakwater, and a long hot day for Cliff and I, both just pre-teeners, but satisfying for Dad, we GOT fish. Had tautog grilled over charcoal that very night, and a whopping fish chowder.

That breakwater by the way was off limits during the War, as the Army Air Force used it for practice bombing. We did go out there once in our Green Dragon canoe, and swam in amongst the rocks. I brought home a

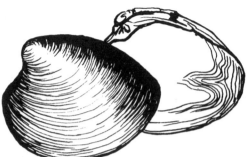

practice bomb casing. We were seen, and caught hell from our scoutmaster/fire chief/civil defense coordinator, but luckily they were not bombing that day. Some of the practice bombs were loaded with a white powder, so the observers could check the accuracy of the bomb run, but some of them had a small explosive charge for realism. I swam out there also, once while I was working at the Light House Inn; got it for that one, too. I miss-calculated the time, and was due on duty in the kitchen. I was with the Chef's son, Peter Roiduolus (Spelling?) and Daddy really gave us what for, in highly emotional Greek.

During the few times a year when the tides were right, (Dad called them 'high course tides') and the water retreated nearly out of sight over the sand flats on the north side, Father was up for a jaunt out on the tidal flats in search of the wily, but oh-so-succulent, sea clam. These were big clams, 6 or 8 inches long, and they always seemed to be on the farthest flat out, and a helluva walk even on the way out with an empty basket. On the way back, if you had dug a 'mess' the basket weighed about eight or nine thousand pounds by the time you got ashore. Dad used to say it was two miles out, and ten miles back. Quite a few people tried to circumvent the long walk by heading out over the sand in old cars, and I guess it worked for some, but there are the remains of several still showing through the flats of those who miscalculated and began their trip back after the water had become too deep.

"Time and tide," they say "waits for no man," but Father never really believed that. If the tide went low at some reasonable hour, fine, but if it chose to be at its low

ebb just a tad before darkness fell, well, so be it. Thing was, when you were out on the last flat, and the water was starting to come back in fast, and darkness was descending, you better stop digging, and hop it back toward shore. Dad used to let us go out with him, sometimes, but sent us back before the pools of water between us and shore started to grow deep, and before it began to be dark.

He would bring up the rear, stopping here and there to put the pressure of his boot near a suspect hole, to see if any clam would squirt, and if so, dig rapidly there to try for some 'toppers', just a clam or two to round off his bucket. Sometimes, he would cast an eye on the darkening sky and say "Ben, better go in and turn those car lights on before it gets too dark, so I'll know which way to the shore." We would, and then sit there in the car, lights blazing, staring out over the rapidly flooding bars, fretting that he wouldn't find his way back through the gathering gloom. It was always very dark by the time we saw him plodding up the beach. Once Mother had the clams ground, she baked them into a sea clam pie, so sweet you could feel it right up to the roots of your hair!

Dad pulled that after dark bit down on the river, too. He was so late for supper one cold night that Mother worried enough to send me, equipped with a flash light to walk the scant half mile to the High Bank Bridge, where she thought he had gone to spear flatfish. "He can't possibly be getting fish in the dark," she said.

He was. He had parked his old car on a down hill slant, so the lights shone out across the water (a vulnerable position if his sometimes chancy brakes gave out) and was just visible in the beams, a shadowy figure, standing up in his skiff, gloveless, stabbing his long spear into the frigid water, set on not getting 'skunked', determined to bring home a mess of flounder if it took until midnight. I sat in the car for a bit while he finished up. He couldn't just quit but he seldom got 'skunked'.

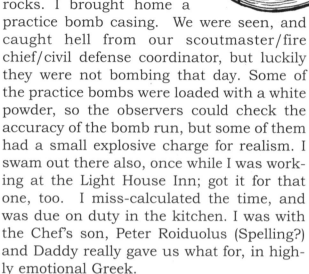

Fin' fish Mother usually got in the store, or from Joe 'Wiggles', but Dad would often go directly to the source. He hit the wharf at the end of Herring River just as 'Than' Wixon's boat came in from tending his weir which was visible straight out to sea from the river's mouth. A weir is a trap made of nets supported by long poles stuck into the ocean's floor. The nets are arranged so that they direct fish into the inner part of a maze, and the confused fish can't find the way out. There are still several along the coast. Every day the owner and his crew go to the weir and scoop out the fish, and land them at the wharf to be boxed and sold. Dad liked to get there just before the fish landed, and bought his

choice right at boat side. Depending on the season, it might be mackerel, haddock, pollack or a small cod, sometimes, in the spring, with the roe inside. Dad would have the fish home, 'slivered' (filleted) and Mom would have it floured and in the spider before it stopped flipping. By the way, Mr. Wixon later became a selectman, and our middle school is named for him, as a tribute to his efforts during the planning and building.

I never heard it about Mr. Wixon's weir, but some of the others were a convenient place for off shore prohibition boats to deposit cases of liquor to be picked up and brought ashore with the fish by the fishermen as they tended the traps. Some catch!

SEA-CLAM PIE

The clam flats only see the light,
When tides go dang near out of sight,
The sand bars set there, high and dry.
I commence to think about sea-clam pie.

It's grab the boots and clamin' hoe,
Right down to Cape Cod Bay you go,
Out on that dry sea-bed you roam,
(It's two miles out, but ten miles home).

It's easy walkin', the basket's light,
My, what a feed you'll have tonight!
With the taste of the ocean, sharp and clean,
A notch or three above French cuisine.

The last bar out, where the big ones hide,
You start in diggin' to beat the tide,
And wonder how anything good as that,
Can grow down under a tidal flat.

You dig a "mess" then you head for shore,
That basket weighin' a ton or more,
The boots like anchors around your feet,
You dream of that pie, all rich and sweet.

The water's comin' across the bar.
You didn't figure you'd walked so far,
You're breathing deep and it's hard to smile,
It's thigh high water the last half mile.

You'll soon forget how your muscles ached,
When the clams are ground and the pie is baked.
The center's moist, and the crust is dry,
They's NAWTHIN better than sea-clam pie!

CHAPTER THIRTY-ONE

Herring In The Crick

If you go down Route 6A, thru Brewster, middle to end of April, you might note a herd, (oops) flock of gulls landed in the marsh or flying back and forth around Stoney Brook in Brewster. They are herring gulls, and they are waiting for the annual arrival of the flocks, (oops) schools of alewives, (herring). The little fish are answering a call of nature too demanding to ignore; to return to their birthpond to lay their eggs and they crowd the small tidal stream on their yearly up hill swim. Yep, up hill! See, many of the ponds on the Cape are set a ways inland, and above sea level and that is where the alewives spawn... Streams, creeks or rivers which connect the ponds to the sea are tidal for much of their length, but as the saltwater flows in to meet the higher, fresh water from the ponds, there is brackish (mixed salt and fresh) water, and then fresh, as the water from the spring-fed ponds takes over. From there on, the fish have to struggle against the out pouring water, and strain to make their way up stream. Aiding their journey are miniature waterfalls, created by stones and rocks in the streambed. They slow the flow of water, and allow the fish to flip flop, higher and higher, up the small streams trickling down between the rocks and resting their tired fishy selves in the small pools behind each miniature cascade until they make it to the pond where they were born (sort of an alewife old-home week). As some of these small falls have degraded over the years, they have been replaced with man-made multi-level 'fish ladders' to assist the critters in their seasonal journey, and also to construct areas where it was easier to catch more herring. Seining rights to certain parts of the streams were sold by the towns to anglers, and they set net traps in the stream, and scooped the fish up by the truckload to sell for bait and cat food.

We caught them mainly for the eggs. Herring roes are delicious, but Dad always salted some or had a few of the whole fish smoked which Mother baked, somewhat under duress. They really smelled up the kitchen. It was a challenge working for the eatable fish, free from mass of tiny bones, but worth it. Like all farmers in these parts since the Indians taught the first settlers, Dad buried some herring under hills of corn at planting: great fertilizer. The herring were far more numerous in the past, but something in our waters disturbed the pattern. Some say it was the early, not well-regulated and not entirely understood insecticides used just after the War on the cranberry bogs, which use the pond water in some seasons, and return it to the ponds in others. Anyway, the herring still run every spring, and many of the old runs have been rebuilt. In most of the Cape's rivers, the herring swim to the head of the river, and then continue along smaller streams. Herring River in Harwich, for example, has a rather high bank where it ends. An elaborate 'fish ladder' allows the fish to climb several feet to gain the stream leading all the way up to the Pleasant Lakes district in the middle of the Cape. A concrete ladder and sluiceway leads the fish through the 'killing grounds' where most of the catching takes place. By the way, one of the nicknames for 'Harwichers' is 'herring choker'. During the minstrel show times, someone came up with this parody on the Irish song:

"Where the River Shannon Flows"...

Two Harwich Boys were talking,
'Bout the time when they should die,
"In Harwich here", said Billy, dear,
"Is where I want to lie,"
"Oh bury me in Harwich, Where the
Herring river flows,
With a scallop shell below me, and a qua-
hog on my nose,
When the Devil comes a lookin' for me
place of Last Repose,
He will never think of lookin' where the
Herring River flows."

Sure got a laugh down there to Liberty Hall!

Years when Dad knew the fish contractor, who bought the seining rights, we were often given free rein to fill our basket from the big dredge net between truckloads, and be headed home in minutes. Other times, there was some scampering about to find where the fish were most plentiful, usually in the Brewster run, or at the Harwich Run, over to North Harwich Beach. (Inside joke of my

Fish ladder at Brewster herring run

father's generation, there was no beach in North Harwich. Now, they have one, on a nice little sand bottom pond called Sand Pond.) Some years when the supply of fish was not too great, the 'Powers That Be' would decree herring for only town residents. As the Dennis runs were usually less bountiful, this condition called for some strategy. A bit to the north of the Harwich run, down one of Father's pet dirt roads, was an access to the herring stream not as well known, nor as easy to fish. There were high banks to either side, and no man made 'ladder' to channel the swimmers to a narrow area where they could be caught with ease. Taking herring there meant hanging out over the water, holding a tree with one hand for balance, dipping in the water with your net in the other, and slinging your catch into a basket set a way from the edge. Herring often became caught in the mesh of the net, and everything was suspended as you removed them, resumed your awkward position, and commenced again. In all, a hard way to fill your bushel basket. It was also rather less than legal. All fishing was supposed to be done at the Fish Ladder, under supervision of the Warden, and with your proof of town citizenship available. Dad, being NOT a Harwich person, should not have been fishing that stream, and the need for identification was moot, as every body in either town knew who came from where. My Grand Mother, Nana, was with him, but as she was a rather large person, decided to watch the activities from the car.

When Dad had filled his basket, he slipped the net handle through the wire handles, lifted the very heavy load of fish, and started the climb back up the hill to the car. He had just reached the top, near grabbing distance from the car, when a small truck came down the dirt road. Immediately the thought crossed his mind 'WARDEN'! Not wanting to be caught with the evidence in hand, he reversed direction, headed rapidly down hill to the stream, and amid loud yells from the driver of the truck, proceeded to dump the basket of painfully acquired fish back into the water. Only then did the man's words register, not "You're under arrest!", but "For God Sake, Freeman, DON'T throw them back, if you don't want them I DO!" Too late, Dad recognized a friend with intentions similar his own, a mess of illegal herring.

A two-man cooperative got both baskets filled, and both fish poachers underway with out additional incident, except for Nana's gales of laughter remembering Dad's skinny butt trucking that Basket of fish down over the bank, and his friend chasing after, waving arms in the air, and yelling. A little humiliation however did not mar the pure eating pleasure of the roe feast that night, with just a few left over to re-warm for the next day's breakfast.

Fish wardens were often as not the villains of the story; however, our local was apt to be more of a guide than a constable. He knew where all the shellfish hid, and would often aim you toward good fishing grounds. One day down at the cove, near where the Big scallops grew, he came up to Dad: "Freeman, fellar just tried to get twicet his limit, and I made him put 'em back. If you was to go over there, just in line with that tree, and out a ways, you'd find a whole pile, otta fill up your basket. You got four, five kids, better you should have them." Now, that's a warden! Had nothing to do with the fact that some years back, Father had perhaps slipped him a pint.

STOPPING BY A HERRING RUN ON A RESTRICTED EVENING

Whose stream this is, I do not know,
The town controls the fishing, though,
And Sunday they will not condone,
An interruption of the flow.

Standing there upon a stone,
I scarce contain an inward groan,
To watch those alewives pass, and yet,
I leave the tempting fish alone.

My little dog begins to fret,
He wishes I would bring the net,
And catch those fishes, flashing fleet,
(He barks at every one I get).

The roe is succulent and sweet,
But there's a policeman in the street,
So I must buy, if I would eat,
So I must buy, if I would eat.

CHAPTER THIRTY-TWO

Food For Thought, And Vice Versa

Glancing back over these ramblings, I find I have been perhaps too liberal with the commas, too loose with grammar, and almost obsessive on the subject of food. On the handling of language and punctuation, I plead nolo contendere, but on the food issue, I must prosecute my case with vigor. In spite of the three-meal custom (same as it is now), food figured as a much larger issue back then. The cost loomed much larger as a part of the average man's take-home pay: there was almost none of today's 'discretionary income', near every cent brought home went for necessities. If you start knocking off the big budget items we have around the house today: TV, washer/dryers, multiple bath rooms, expensive cars, vacations, restaurant meals, outings and other ways we spend money now in the 21st century, it becomes clear that Ye Old 'daily bread' used a big slice of the weekly buck.

So, you got the food home, and you cooked it for supper and sat down to eat? Well not quite. Very little in them days was stove ready, few prepared foods, no TV Dinners, in fact, no TV. First, preparations. Most foods tended to be rather labor intensive. Beans? Wash well, and soak over night, THEN, drain 'em, pot 'em, pork em, oven cook 'em - an all day affair. Peas needed long distance soaking, too, and you started fish chowder by soaking some of the salt out of the boxed codfish. Bread had to be mixed and rolled the night before, then left in a warm place so the yeast could work, baked the next day. In cold weather, hot cereal. No 30-second oatmeal, real crushed oats, and boil it, in a double boiler till it bubbled.

Occasionally during the winter Mom would boil up some 'Wheatina' or 'Ralston' (from checkerboard square - I didn't much like the 'Ralston' as well as oatmeal, but I always ate it, otherwise I would feel like a traitor to the sponsor of 'Tom Mix'). Even margarine, (called oleomargarine) required work. It was sold dead white, with a color packet that had to be kneaded into the greasy loaf, couldn't be sold yellow, for fear it would be passed off as butter (I think the dairy industry had something to do with that). No packaged piecrust, start with flour, shortening and water, mix and roll. Early on, the shortening was lard, then came 'Crisco'! It and other vegetable shortenings had been around for a long while, but I don't remember Mother using them until the War put animal fats on the Vital Materials list. Dad always used Lard for his potato chips. Potatoes washed by hand, sliced by hand, fried in open cast iron pots, drained over brown paper, to get rid of the grease, salted and bagged or canned by hand. Mother's brother, Ray, lived at the house and worked with Father on the Potato Chip business. Kid fashion, I innocently threw a monkey wrench in to the works for a while by giving the two men my MUMPS! Just an uncomfortable sickness, like a bad cold with swollen glands for a little guy, the two adult males suffered. Mother said one of the problems they had was trying to eat hearty vittles with their tender jaws and raw throats. She said I was the only one sensible enough to stick with fluids and such while they moaned their way through their usual big meals, chewing in agony. Luckily mumps is of reasonably short duration, and the Chip Biz moved on.

It was around 1934. They moved two gas flats into our back room there on Upper County Road, and went about it. Tank gas, there were no underground pipes. When they had enough made, Dad went and peddled them. I used to ride with him sometimes in the summer, down around the Camp Grounds in Dennisport, and to several little stores, which all seemed happy to get our merchandise, and ordered more.

In the fall, Dad managed to persuade a couple of the local schools to use our chips, and there in began a problem. The regular supplier of chips to the schools in question (a big and well-known brand) took exception to losing the accounts. After all, there were hundreds of sales a week involved. A cursory look at where the chips came from was all they needed to put the kibosh on the whole business. County Health officials closed us down. It did not matter that the report was strictly a business move by the competition, facts is facts: that kind of food preparation was supposed to take place in an inspected and approved kitchen, and one BIG flaw in our system was a lack of hot running water. That old hand pump in the next room just would not do! The officials 'lowded as how the food was handled well, and was clean all right, but regulations was regulations. Dad and Ray couldn't begin to find the money to bring everything up to code, and put in water, so that was that. It sure was fun while it lasted. Some of the neighborhood kids used to come around, and if we were lucky, we would be given a paper bag full of broken chips to munch out on. I spent years looking for a chip as good as they used to make, finally found Cape Cod Potato Chips, made just up the road. I'm addicted, fine flavored chip, but I have to let them know that they were not the first chip made commercially on the Cape; Thacher's were.

Nothing was easy. No frozen foods, and few cans. Vegetables, grow them, put them in jars, keep them in the root cellar until use. By the War years, we had refrigeration, but when we had our pigs and cow butchered

most of the meat went to a rented freezer cage in the Harwich Red River Ice Plant (the one that put the local pond ice cutters pretty much out of business). In the cold weather, Dad hung some meat in the barn, saved 10-mile trips down to the freezer compartment.

Even prunes had to be cleaned, soaked for several hours, stewed, and the stones removed before eating. Dad was a big advocate of prunes, besides believing that they helped him adjust his systemic functions, he genuinely liked them. Stewed for breakfast, before his oatmeal, or shredded wheat, or as Prune Whip for dessert. We did have boxed cereal, Post Toasties, Wheaties (Breakfast of Champions) and Mom left her system regulating to her favorite, Heinz Rice Flakes. All were good for box tops, and box top premiums made any cereal taste better. I even ate Dad's shredded wheat 'Straw Bales', sometimes, because they had cards between the layers with interesting information on them. The box tops, of course, opened up another world! Plaster Tarzan of the Apes figures that you could color with watercolors, pictures of Tom Mix and his great horse Tony, telescopes, hike-o-meters, code rings, the now famous Orphan Annie and Sandy Ovaltine mugs, and a Genuine Detective Kit with Finger printing powder, Detective Identification cards, a manual on how to solve crimes and a five pointed star detective badge! It took several box tops, and some times a hard-to-get dime on the side, but I managed to send for several of the wonderful items, including the Detective kit. That kit came in handy during our search for John Dillinger. It told lots about the habits of criminals, and how to solve crimes. Without it, we couldn't have even come close to trapping that dangerous crime figure. With it, we did no better, but we learned many, many things.

I suppose I was about eight when I first pinned on my Detective Badge, pocketed the manual, and accompanied my father to the Post Office. The men waiting for mail to be sorted included Mr. Leon Hall, owner of the lumberyard. He was a friendly sort, and asked about the genuine gold star adorning my shirt.

"I am a detective," I told him.

"Oh, and what does a detective do?"

Catch bad guys of course, everybody knew that. Mr. Hall was seriously interested.

"And if someone was being bad here in the store, would you catch them?"

Yep, just like Father catches Herring!

THACHER'S

CAPE MADE

Potato Chips

Made by
F. G. Thacher

South Dennis - Cape Cod, Mass-
Net Weight 3 1-2 oz.

Some minutes later, I was notified by one of the men that Mr. Hall had slipped a can of tuna fish in his pocket! I was compelled to arrest him. He promised to put it back and be good, and all seemed to think that was a good idea.

Mr. Hall said I had done a good job, and got me a chocolate and peanut butter bolster from the penny candy case--which he paid for. Way things were, if I'd made the 'collar', I don't quite know what I could do with my criminal. As I remember, at that time we didn't have a police force in town, or even a police man, so for a while, I was The Law, you might, say: Dennis's own 'Lone Ranger'.

The next thing I sent for was an autographed photo in a silver frame of Tom Mix and his horse. That I kept up in my room, and no one knew.

SUSHI

No mater how,
The Chef has toiled,
I'd sooner have my tuna,
Broiled

CHAPTER THIRTY-THREE
Deck The Halls

Christmas always makes me think of cedar swamps. We had several near around the village. There was the one across from the Post Office where Mr. Bayles dredged out the skating area, another across from the Fire Station, which stretched almost back to our house, ending close to Jr. Leighton's tiny pond, and extending eastward, toward Dennisport. The swamp follows down what is now Route 134, filling most of the area on both sides of the road (in fact the road was built on trucked in material, dumped into the wet marsh-like area, splitting the swamp in two). The swamp areas surround the 'Fresh Pond' conservation area, where there are walking trails around the pond, and extend, hit or miss, down near to the back side of Ezra Baker School. These swamps are not now great white cedar swamps with trees which could make masts for a sailing vessel, but perhaps they were, before they were harvested: there are occasional stumps which are the leavings of rather large trees. The new growth of cedar, like the Cape's oak and pine, tended to be scrubby, growing out of hummocks surrounded by muddy water. We kids had many thrilling jungle adventures in amongst the hummocks, leaping from one tiny island to another (or occasionally jumping almost from one to another) skating around on the various little streams in the winter, or, in spring, when the water was high, poling cedar log rafts down some of the wider mini-rivers. There were lots of brier and 'pucker brush', but we hacked and chopped ourselves small clearings, and had a jolly time, coming home muddy and torn.

Christmas, though ... Christmas suddenly turned our Amazon playground into a Christmas tree farm, and more! To my knowledge, Dad never bought a tree when we were kids. At first, we thought the trees just appeared out of the back of his car, then as I grew bigger, it was, "Ben, let's go get your Mother a tree." and down to the swamp we would go. As the other young'uns got taller it became a well attended yearly trek, with Dad constantly in the lead, and us guys helping each other across wet spots, if the ice wasn't firm. One year we took Sammy (the big old billy goat my Uncle Wendell gave me - the one I brought home in the back of Dad's car). Taking the goat to the swamp was a bad idea, he refused to step on any ice patches, and stayed on each hummock, blatting until we came back for him and pulled him along by shear brute force. He stayed home from swamp expeditions after that.

Dad had very definite ideas about the tree he wanted. It had to be growing separate from others so he could see the shape, not too tall, and well filled out with a reasonable trunk below the bottom branches so that it would fit our stand, a metal contraption which was supposed to slip on to the foot of the tree, and be securely fastened with a screw on each of its four legs. NEVER worked well, Dad fought with it every Christmas, but you don't throw something away just because it is hard to make it operate properly, you just work (and cuss) harder. By the time we got home, it would be late, the short trip somehow always turned into a long journey, and the tree was always a tad too tall, and had to be cut off to fit in the house. Mother would have the floor, where the tree would stand, covered with pads of newspaper, and the boxes of decorations down from the attic, and the stand fight would begin. Dad always won, but it was close.

The tree was not all we brought home from the swamp. The girls were under standing orders to bring back Standing Johnny and Creeping Jenny, two fern-like evergreens, for wreath making, and seasonal decorations around the house. I think most of the families had swamp trees for Christmas, although some searchers strayed out of the wild, and into private yards. My friend Hank was accosted by an irate land owner just after he had cut down a perfect little tree in the man's near back yard. Hank understandably neglected to take the tree with him when he departed, at flank speed. From that time hence, we would on occasion meet him shopping the swamp as we did.

We always had a string of colored lights on the tree, the old type which all went out if one bulb went bad, and many ornaments handed down through the years, but ingenuity played a part in the decorations. Strung cranberries, and popcorn were draped  through the branches, and Mother always got the girls making strings of paper loops (cut from the colorful Sunday Comics).

In spite of my unquenchable desire for "stuff" (presents), the yearly trip to see Santa was not high on my Christmas thrill list. It was embarrassing. Not just the "Ho Ho Ho, sit on my knee, and tell me, were you a good little boy" stuff, which was bad enough, but we always saw him in Harwich Port, at Buttners! The underwear store, where they had dress patterns, safety pins, diapers (no diaper service then) notions, material, kids undies and sox, and not a damn toy in the place! Yuck! For one thing, meeting him in that fun-less practical shop surely meant our Christmas stockings would contain things like sox, handkerchiefs and pencils, with less room for comic books, tangerines, walnuts and small toys, and that at least some of the wrapped gifts beneath the tree would be union suits. For the parents, it was not such a bad deal, a kick for the little kids without needing two hands for each to keep them out of the merchandise while you grabbed off some necessary items.

The Hyannis 5 and 10's were my meat. You could slide in to one of those after another, clutching your dimes and quarters tightly, and searching amongst the open counters and shelves filled with goodies, not only for ideas of what to buy for your family members, but what you-might-get-yourself on the Big 'C' day!! No plastic packaging in them days, boys, that stuff laid out there for the looking, and in spite of parental supervision, you got to touch this and that. Check the wheels on this car, and look through that spyglass, and look at the light through a marble and feel the real feathers on the Indian headdress, and the weight of that Tom Mix six-shooter, and gaze over the barrel of a double barreled 'pop' shotgun, and spin the rowels on a Hopalong Cassidy spur, and peek in a movie machine, which had no film in it and if Mother had gone on ahead, almost nobody said DON'T TOUCH!! Of course the respite was short, then:

"Leave that alone, now, you're to shop for presents for your Father and brother and sisters." - and the bubble burst, but, for just a few minutes - we felt like Owners of the Five and Dime!

When we got up toward our adolescence, (never heard of 'teen agers' until much later) there was Caroling. The Four Square League (a mostly fun and character building group from church) accompanied by a couple of parents, with lots of walking and a cappella (often off key) singing. One year we borrowed a tiny antique organ from church, and a small truck someone's father owned, but the organ was less in tune than our voices, and both the instrument's air pump and the player's fingers suffered badly from cold joints, so that was passed over from then on. There was a lot of work to it, with the village spaced out as it was, long hikes down dark roads often for one house. In the city, where neighborhoods tend to be more compact, it would have been easier, but fun it was none the less. Sister Nancy (a piano student and having some idea of keys), along with Olive (who had a lovely singing voice), usually led our efforts. We tried to be sure to get all the older people and our own homes, and always kept track of warming up stops where the people set out a good table for the Carolers, with sweets and mulled cider (one such, a good walk from any near neighbor was down on Cove Road, a cold way to go, but always splendid 'vitals').

C' eve always had readings around a fire in the living room stove. We heard, of course, the usual Christmas Story, plus the special Christmas programming on the radio, not to miss the perennial, Dickens 'A Christmas Carol', with Lionel Barrymore as mean old Scrooge, and a story Mother was fond of reading, 'A Bird's Christmas Carol', by Kate Wiggin. It was the story of a poor family, the Ruggles, who lived down an alley behind a wealthy family and of the Christmas when the whole gang of Ruggles children (called 'Ruggles-in-the-rear' by the rich folk) were invited by the sick child (Carol Bird) in the big house to come for Christmas dinner. While our group, I believe, never thought of ourselves as poor, we did identify with the antics of the somewhat ragtag Ruggles children as their widowed mother dressed them as best she could, and rehearsed them in the social manners they would need for the outing. As the family had more heads than hats, it was decided no one would wear one, and special attention was given to supplying a reason to give for their uncovered heads. When asked if they wished to store their hats and coats at the party, they were to answer that it was "Such a pleasant evening, and such a short walk," that they had not brought hats. Instead, 'mid the confusion, the older children, spokesmen for the group (in spite of practicing their speech on the way up the alley) inadvertently stated that it was pleasant, and close, but that they in fact didn't have enough hats to go around anyway, so "We thought we'd leave our hats to home..." story ends with Carol dying, quietly, happy to have had a marvelous Christmas (exactly as she had wished) and the Ruggles, as poor folk do, trudged on.

Our Christmas dinner in those early years was usually roast chicken (Dad always raised some roosters with the laying hens) with veggies from Dad's garden by way of Mother's canning, and with a wonderful oyster stuffing. The gifts were not numerous, but they were wonderful, even the year I received two cars, one battery driven, the other wind up, which Dad and Uncle Ray took out on the street and raced until they were no longer self-propelled, and the siren on the red fire chief's car had quit. Dad and Ray really got it from Mother... "Two grown men...child's toys..!" Hey, I was at an age (about 4) when I had no patience with springs and other forms of automatic propulsion any way and wanted to push things at my own speed (mumbling "Brroom, brroom" all the while). Broken or not they were new, gaily painted, and I had a fine time with them. Just another merry, merry Cape Cod Christmas.

FOG

When Fog socks in around the Cape,
The air gets mighty wet,
Here's a tale or two to show,
How soggy things can get.

A feller bathed down by the lake,
But never took a plunge,
Just squeezed the water from the air,
The way you would a sponge.

A man who had to move his skiff,
Just picked a foggy day,
And rowed it right up to his house,
A half a mile away.

One girl whose well went dry recalled
A trick her father taught her,
She'd swing a bucket over head,
And catch a pail of water.

The Cape Cod children love the fog,
And on a soggy night,
They roll the durn stuff up in balls,
And have a water fight.

I'd tell of skating on the air,
Or plowing it like snow,
But lest I "fog" the issue,
Just one more, and then I'll go.

One day a young man washed ashore,
Upon a drift wood log,
He'd walked a furlong out to sea,
Just stepping on the fog!

CHAPTER THIRTY-FOUR
Dear Old Golden Rule Days

At about six years, my life style was rudely interrupted by compulsory attendance at first grade. There was no pre-school or kindergarten for Nancy or me, but for Olive on down there was a nursery school: that is where little brother Link cast aspersions on my father's table manners. The first grade teacher for all of our clan, and even later (my son Robert even started in her room) was Mrs. Susie McHenry. Mrs. McHenry was an oddity due to her time in grade, and the fact that she was a Mrs., the only married teacher we had. Few lady teachers lasted the whole year, we got used to having to learn a new name about two weeks after Christmas as they leaped into the matrimonial pool, and there seemed to be an unwritten law about married women teaching. We all took away the same things, and can still sing the little songs from grade one. ('Mrs. Jones had a brand new automobile', and 'We work while we work, and we play while we play'- The Hits just kept right on coming!) I was reasonably good at reading, dismal at math and penmanship, but pretty fair at 'Red Rover, Red Rover' so school went on apace.

There were two Charles's in first grade, and the other one had an alphabetically earlier last name, so Mrs. Mc. asked what I was called at home. I became Benjamin. Thank goodness, she wouldn't go with 'Benny Bus', or 'sweetie pie'. I saw Mrs. McHenry in my forties; I was newly bearded, and hadn't seen her in years. She was in a store, quite elderly, and in a wheel chair, pushed by one of her legion of friends. She had a bandage over one eye. I said "Hello, Mrs. McHenry", and she snapped, "No use hiding behind those whiskers, Benjamin, you look better without them!"

Mr. Roosevelt's programs were felt at the school, with fresh fruit, cheese and two cents a small bottle of milk from government subsidized farms to perk up the noon meal, art programs, and even a W.P.A. traveling circus on our playground. Hoop rollers, dog acts, slack wire walkers and clowns - all employed due to F.D.R. and the New Deal.

We sang in school from day one, but it was fourth grade before we were able to start instrumental music at school. Nancy already 'took'. She had piano lessons at home. Her teacher, who came to the house (during the warm months) for fifty cents a lesson, was Myra Snow, an older, maiden lady from the north side of town. She had a presence and requested a quiet atmosphere, so we other kids made our selves scarce while the lesson was in progress. Sometimes there were duets (...To the Piano, let us go, and play duets for an hour or so...) Miss Snow drove her rounds in a model "A" Ford, which she put up on blocks at the first sign of winter (then you had to come to her). She also played organ for the East Dennis church where she sometimes wandered from the program, and at least once during the seemingly endless passing of the collection plate, Myra (from playing various religious themes and cords) slipped gently from 'Old Rugged Cross', into 'Home On The Range'.

Olive took some voice lessons, later, from an older musical gentleman in West Dennis, who I think was retired from an upper school level teaching position. ('Where can the swallow be go oh oh oh oh oh oh oh oh oh ohohohing' round tones, and oval tones!!) The rest, I think received their musical, and instrumental grounding in school. Olive played violin and mellophone (for the marching band), Link trumpet and Souza-phone, Jayne clarinet, Polly who came along a good bit later, played the glockenspiel, a kind of short, sideways xylophone on a stick.

In my early day I yearned to play the xylophone. Don't know what fired my imagination; perhaps I saw some movie with a Mexican band. I communicated my desire to Adolph (probably Adolpho, originally) Quersey, the Music Man. Mr. Q. was a stocky Italian gentleman with a noticeable preference for garlicky foods and a heavily accented and moist manner of speaking. On his advice that I needed to learn to drum first, to learn tempos, and use of sticks/mallets, I became a drummer, played all the way thru high school. Looking back, I'm sure there wasn't anything like a xylophone with in fifty square miles of Ezra Baker School, and wouldn't be, until many years hence when Polly marched with the Glockenspiel. In the mean time, drums were my instrument, and later got me into the State Guard Band, due to its leader, our own Mr. Quersey.

Mr. Q. taught and directed all the instrumental music at all the Dennis and Yarmouth schools. Unless you took private lessons, (and he also taught privately after school) you learned to drum, fiddle or toot from him and, in due course, fit into one of his musical aggregations. Somehow he managed to present a couple of concerts a year, and tunes for the graduation ceremonies. He seemed to have a special feeling for "Pomp And Circumstances", and complained forcibly, but without effect when our principal, Mr. Mclin, decided, in honor of the war, to have us march in to 'The Caisson Song', 'Halls Of Montezuma', and "Wild Blue Yonder' for our eighth grade graduation. Come to think of it, my class didn't have a class trip, either, due to the war. We got gypped out of a ride to Washington, or some other historic area, where we could have learned all sorts of dumb stuff and have no end of fun making the chaperones nervous and dropping water filled balloons from a hotel's upper stories.

Mr. William Mclin taught us, some, as well as being the Main Man, and wandered the halls keeping the school, all eight grades, under close supervision. I remember when he welcomed us to chorus, I think in grade three, and he said he loved music, but had one request, that we not sing 'Oh Where Have You Been, Billy Boy'.

By gum, we thought that was a corker. Aside from pointing out the Jeeps to us and telling us of their utility as fast transport for the forties kind of warfare, vs. the horse drawn vehicles of WWI, 'Billy Boy' (OOPS..) was a treasure trove of interesting material, which sometimes snapped up class time in a far more fun time than plodding through the book of written history. For example, t'was he who taught us the Presidents poem, as a means of remembering the succession from G.W. to F.D.R. (started, "George Washington, the choice of all, by Adams was succeeded, and then came Thomas Jefferson, who bought the land we needed..." I still remember lots of pieces it, but there are gaps).

It was also Mr. Mclin who told us of Lake Chargoggagoggmanchaugagoggchaubunagungamaug which according to him, was a verbal contract between two Indian tribes in the area, and meant, 'You fish on your side, I'll fish on mine, and nobody fish in the middle'. Unimaginative European immigrants call it Webster Lake.

After taking a class above us to tour a local wire factory, converted (as most everything was) to war work, Mr. M. was asked to quit principaling, and come to work at the factory as an efficiency expert. When he said he knew nothing about the industry, he was told that would be his value to them. They had been doing the same kind of work, the same way for years, and his questions about their methods during the tour, had already caused them to re-think a couple of processes. He thanked them, but stayed on at the school.

Mr. M. ruled in a time of acceptable corporal punishment, delivered rarely, but with deliberation with a length of hard, black rubber hose kept in a top right hand drawer of his

desk, and used more often as a threat than in fact. The hose, in use, was slapped hard across the punishee's hand, firmly held in position by Mr. M (mano a mano, so to speak) until, as rumor had it, one boy withdrew his hand suddenly, and Mr. Mclin got a bit of his own. There after, the tale went, the culprit's hand was held steady by a firm grip around the wrist. One of the bigger boys, about two years overdue to leave eighth grade, took one blow and popped the executioner in the snoot. That was the last of him around school, and I tend to remember it was also the last of the hose. Later, after Jake Wilber had gone off to war, Mr. Mclin became our Sunday school teacher for a spell.

We left Ezra Baker, in a military frame of mind, and landed in John Simpkins to a definite dearth of male teachers. Mr. Lambert, an elderly teacher from France, retired and living in the U.S., volunteered to teach French and Spanish. He started us with Spanish, and for some days couldn't recall which page we ended on and so started over everyday. Because of starting Spanish first, and having the same teacher, we all began to speak French with a Spanish accent to his dismay. He had been a professor of Math in Europe, and obviously loved the subject. With some slight persuading we spent many periods hearing stories, and watching math tricks on the black board, until the bell rang for the end of class. Needless to say, I ended the year sketchy at best in Spanish, and worse than that in French. Mr. Lambert had a hearing aid, not like today's tiny in-ear units, but one connected by a wire to a fair sized box which pinned to the coat. Our class clown used to raise a hand, start asking ques-

tions normally, then keep his lips moving, but without making any sound. He persuaded the teacher that his hearing aid was performing badly, and caused poor Mr. Lambert to open his aid box, check batteries and change wires. As the student would at this point resort to audible sound, the emergency passed. He was a nice and gentle man, and it would be nice to be able to go back and apologize.

Another lack, due to the war, was a shortage of gym teachers. Ours was a retired State Policeman, with perhaps a dubious background in Team sports, but a pretty good grounding in gymnastics. Worked to my benefit, as I (not over weight, as I later became) was good enough at mat work and on the horizontal bar to be asked by Coach Tulis to take on a class of grade school boys, and teach them some of the rudiments of tiger leaps, and rolls, and other flat mat gymnastics. I could leap over a large number of kneeling bodies, and round off in a good tuck and roll, but my one claim to fame in the athletic arena was a series of 'muscle grinders' I performed at an indoor track meet. It involved grasping the bar between back and bent arms, and spinning your body around the steel bar, over and over. As I remember, I managed 100 revolutions, as the audience counted in unison! Well, we all have to have one moment, even if it's just muscle grinders.

Our senior prom was held on the night of the second Joe Lewis vs. Billy Conn fight, and of course, many of the boys spent a good bit of the evening listening on the radio while the girls danced with each other (what else is new) to such songs as 'To Each His Own', 'Laura', and 'The Gypsy', as Joe clobbered Billy again. Tickets to the fight were $100 which was a good hunk of cash, what with new cars going for about $1500, gas 16 cents a gallon and a loaf of bread for a dime. Interesting, Billy Conn, although the loser, managed to save enough from the fight purse and subsequent movie rights to live a very comfortable, in fact, somewhat opulent life style for the rest of his days.

Stayed healthy, too. Much later, at age 72, Billy punched out a gunman who tried to hold up a convenience store where the former 'Pittsburgh Kid' was shopping. The 'Brown Bomber', champion Joe Lewis, followed his fighting days pretty much grubbing for a living. Winners don't always win.

THE GYPSIES

Sometimes for years they seem to rest,
Those tiny fuzzy starving pests,
Then they appear just over night,
To lunch on every leaf in sight.

They burst out of a billion eggs,
Small hairy appetites with legs
While men spend countless time and dollars,
Treating trees with sprays and collars.

I wonder if the oak and pine,
Think Nature may be out of line,
To turn loose on their brand-new greens,
These starving mini munch-machines.

Or do trees even deign to note,
Who dines upon their new spring coat,
But bear their leaves and drop their seed,
Nor little note what pests they feed.

CHAPTER THIRTY-FIVE

Reveille Revels

Waking up on a school morning was mostly a matter of sound, first. Until we had settled into the new house with the kerosene cook stove in the kitchen, both heating and cooking were dependent on building a fire. Had to take the top plates (cooking surface) off the fire box, put in scrunched up paper, lay kindling on it, carefully position the first of the split logs so that they had the best chance of igniting, light off the paper, re-assemble the stove top, wait until you were sure the logs had begun to burn, then put out the spider, scramble the eggs, call the kids, and commence. Or, if you were having fried bread, well, you get the idea. There was an interesting heat regulator on the cook stove; you moved the pan around on top until you found the properly heated area, which could change any time in the cooking process. Dad usually started the living room stove. He hinted, in his complimentary manner, that Mother, like all women, knew little about how to lay a good fire, ignoring the fact that she did it every day in the kitchen.

About the first feel of a new winter day was the cold rock which your feet found at the bottom of the bed when you stretched. You had of course kicked the flannel wrap off the icy soap stone, brick or sad iron which felt so warm and cozy when you were drifting off, and the heat had dissipated. After the fashion of most homes in town, neither of ours was insulated, which made the first move from under the comforter an uncomfortable experience. Along about storm window time in the fall, Dad piled leaves and pine needles against the foundations, usually covered them with roofing tar paper, and staked here and there to hold this improvised layer of weather proofing close to the building. It helped keep the wind from snarling through the cracks between the old brick work and kept the floor warmer. Mother always did her newspaper thing under any rugs, which also helped, but in Dad's ancestral home, when we moved in, a mean wind sometimes actually lifted the rug up on the living floor. Even with storm windows, which were second hand, and fit just more or less, a winter blizzard would sometimes deposit a small amount of snow on the bed in my north east corner upstairs room, and an especially frigid night sometimes iced the contents of the pot under the bed.

Winter kid garb in the thirties started with a cold weather version of the one piece Union Suit, equipped with somewhat extended legs and arms, but with the same button up rear door facilities. Up through all of early grade school it was shorts in the summer, and corduroy knickers for the winter, with long socks which never stayed up, and that accursed whistling as you walked. How I yearned for long pants!

Dressed, fed, and out the door, lunch box in hand, bus pickup in front of the house, at first, then later at Liberty Hall just up the street. Dad sometimes drove the bus, a square yellow thing (we called it the 'Cheese box') which may have carried twenty kids on its bench-like seats. The route belonged to our ice man, Mr. Howard, and was, as with most happenings in town, sort of a family affair. We always knew our drivers, and they knew us and our parents. The bus could be a tiny bit ripe on occasion, as several of the boys ran trap lines, and serviced them before school. The main 'catch' was skunks. The skins (dressed out and partially tanned) were shipped off to the fur coat industry. More white fur on the pelt, better the price, as I remember from talking with the woodsmen. They contacted the buyers via a magazine ad, and bought the traps, pelt stretching frames, and what ever they needed to semi-cure the skins and ship them, so the dealers made out well. Even before the skunk population got clobbered, the Company was making money. I never found out if the Mighty Hunters made more than their expenses, or not.

The guys all trapped in generally the same area and skunks weren't THAT plentiful. When the morning chore was done carefully, only a vague aroma accompanied the boys as they trooped onto the bus, but one morning, Harold and Frenchie, trappers both, arrived running, a tad late for the bus, but as the driver saw them, he waited. Mr. Ellis, the driver then, a wonderfully gentle and patient man, popped the door open and in rushed the intrepid pair, bearing with them, like a foul cloud, evidence of a direct hit by one of their victims. As they rushed for a rear seat, Mr. Ellis, startled by the sudden enveloping odor swung around in his seat, and in a most apologetic tone said,

"Oh, my God, boys! I'm sorry, but you just have to get off this bus, I can't possibly deliver you to school smelling like that!"

The two dutifully trudged down the aisle, and off the bus, leaving behind kids holding their noses, and the bus pulled away. Just a few weeks ago (seventy years after the great odor affair) I mentioned the day to Harold.

"Oh," He said, with a smile, "That wasn't an accident, me and Frenchy wanted a day off, so we acquired that smell accidentally on purpose!"

A day off was pretty special. You got up whining a bit, and feeling somewhat under the weather, and Mother did her magic thing on your forehead, "I think you have a little fever, guess you better stay put today."

Wow, you felt better already, but you would never admit it. Home meant lolling there between the sheets, and hearing the younger kids getting ready to leave. Mother, at the door, "Be careful, now, Olive don't lose that mitten, Come right home from the bus."

Power, and guilt. You knew you weren't THAT sick, and you should have been heading off, and perhaps there was a book report due, and you told a friend you'd see him at recess, and the bus would be by any minute, and it was Tuesday, and every Tuesday there was...and...BUT, the sheets were cool, and the blankets were warm, and there was a glass of water or milk for

the asking, and soon, soon, the radio would be turned on, and after the news and stuff, there were the soap operas!! The on going stories of 'Our Gal Sunday' (can a girl from a mining camp find happiness as the wife of Britain's wealthiest and most handsome Lord), 'Just Plain Bill' (Barber of Hartford, or Hartville), 'The Romance of Helen Trent' (Can a girl find happiness at 35, or even beyond), 'Stella Dallas', 'Mirt and Marge', 'Old Ma Perkins', if Harold ever knew I was listening to this stuff, he would kick me out of the neighborhood!! No, he would throw up, and then kick me out of the neighborhood!

I got a few extra days off because I had a tendency to bruise my body a lot. I never had any bones break, but they often seemed to bend enough to allow hard objects strike my softer parts. Circuses were dangerous, I always came home convinced that I could do what the performers did, usually with painful results.

Attempting to drop from a knee grip and catch a trapeze in my hands resulted in a snapped and painful neck injury. An effort to reproduce a stunt on the flying rings, put both my shoulders on the fritz for a good spell. I fell off of Frannie Sullivan's big ex-cavalry horse while temporarily standing on his bare back while he trotted (a well muscled young man did that in the Clyde Beatty Circus), I even barked my shins trying to spin a hoop as they did so skillfully in the WPA circus at the school (in lieu of a proper hoop, I tried with a heavy old iron wagon wheel rim). I tore a muscle in my back, tore the cartilage in one knee, tried out a home made slide which hadn't been thoroughly inspected for nails, and did a whole bunch of things which made my ankles swell. A good visible swelling could usually cop a day or two on the couch. And the Soaps.

About the time the programs started, a properly whiney request could get you a seat out in the kitchen, wrapped in a blanket, near the stove and perhaps, (especially if it was a cold/fever type thing) a hot lemon drink. Mother would have her ironing board out (remember when people wanted their clothing pressed?) she would have a pile to iron, perhaps just rescued from the clothes line out side, and still frozen.

Even underwear got the hot iron treatment, helped to finish drying it so it could be folded and put away in a newspaper lined drawer in one of the dressers. The smell of the clean, freshly ironed cloth, the crackling of the wood fire, and the story of 'Young Dr. Malone', or 'Young Widder Brown', and all those other folks, jest kicked the pants out of that ol' cold, and even seemed to reduce swelling, and usually you could make it to the bus on Wednesday, ready to stride forth in the world like 'David Harum' or 'Mary Noble' (backstage wife) with her always close to cheating Star husband. Sorry, Hank, Frenchie, I don't know what you guys did on a semi-sick day, but I got re-charged, and I loved it!

BYE, FALL

You know that Winter isn't far,
When, past the Hunter's Moon,
The children start to leave ajar,
The doors they slammed in June.

CHAPTER THIRTY-SIX

The Rest Of The Season, A Season Of Rest

Fact is it did used to get somewhat quiet around here in the winter when we were kids. All the sun seekers headed for solid ground around Labor Day and, except for some salesmen, cottage owners installing storm shutters, and an occasional writer seeking solitude, few mainlanders stepped east of the Canal till schools closed in June. Us web footed rubes and clam diggers had the Narrow Lands to ourselves. A popular old timer, in a rest home, was asked in an interview if he knew why his mother and father had so many children (I think it was 15), what with the hard times. He answered, "Well, there wasn't much to do around the Cape here in the winter." Let me tell you, boy, they was a damn site more goin' on than what you'd think for!

Oh, the summer businesses closed, and that meant lots of eating places, guest houses, inns, seasonal stores and seaside cottages. The beaches were empty as the weather turned from warm and sunny through first frost, Indian summer, and into serious winter. The sands were empty, and the bathhouses became chilly storehouses for warm memories and an occasional forgotten bathing suit. The whole of the Hyannis west end, with its summer only movie house, and specialty shops took on the appearance of a ghost town. Many of the shop owners headed for Florida, to get their Miami or Key West stores ready for the snowbirds. There was one Hyannis nightclub, the Panama Club, open there during the war, but it catered mostly to G.I.'s from Camp Edwards who were visitors, but not really voluntary guests on Ol' Cape Cod. (By the way, there to entertain the troops was Marie Doherty, later Marie Marcus, well named the First Lady Of Jazz who later honored us by living and playing her piano here on the Cape, and becoming as close to a 'native' as a 'wash-a-shore' can be.)

There was also a rather infamous nightspot, which was very active earlier during the "dry" years: the Casa Madrid, stucco, Spanish style building in the woods in West Yarmouth. The Club (or perhaps "Speak Easy" is a more apt description) was known for many sins. It was the establishment from which the then Mayor of Boston, and later Governor of the Grand State of Massachusetts, The Honorable James M. Curley fled through a back window as State Troopers and Federal Officers crashed in the front door. Had something to do with illegal drinking, and gambling, or so 'tis said. Of course, as afore mentioned, there were the bootleggers who functioned year round, but many of them were of the home-grown variety rather than outlanders. You have to do something when the fishing's lean.

There was a wrestling arena in West Yarmouth at Mill Hill. It was open air, so limited to fair weather use. I think Uncle Ray and Dad went there a couple of times, but it was never considered a fit place for the likes of us. It was said that some of the grunting and groaning which came from the ring was far in excess of the injuries taking place, and that 'cackle berries', small packets of chicken blood hidden in the mouth, were more responsible for the gory appearance of the combatants than the fearful blows they exchanged. Across the street, was the Rainbow Ball Room. As the Rainbow had somewhat of a repetition for catering to a 'fast' crowd, we never went there, either. It eventually became a roller skating arena. Bandleader Ernie Baker, whose band played for the dancing, ran the Rainbow as I remember it. Ernie was somewhat of a local celebrity; he was a slim man, and wore sharp clothes and a soft brimmed hat. At one time, he had a souped up Model "A" Ford with which he used to challenge larger supposedly faster autos, and leave them, much to their drivers chagrin, eating his dust. The Rainbow was one of the few large halls around, and hosted such things as an occasional sportsman show, or 4H exhibit. It was one of the earliest establishments to boast Electric Lights, which were at that time often uncertain. Dad told of two locals settin' on a fence watching the dance hall, with the great illuminated rainbow arched over its roof, when a power failure darkened the scene.

"Wonder what happened to Ernie's e-lectric," murmured one.

"Don't know," proclaimed the other, "But I expect there might be some sedyment in them wires!"

Harwich Center possessed what must have been the Cape's grandest commercial building in their 'Exchange Hall'. Built as a grain exchange, comfortably near the Rail Road Station, in the 1800's the 'New' Exchange Hall had street level shops and Town Offices, a grand theatre with gas lights, balcony, private box seats, steam heat, hot water and indoor sanitary facilities! Above the theater was a skating rink with a hard maple floor, topped by an observation walkway, then a floor where sets where designed and finally a cupola complete with a spyglass! They had all sorts of affairs in the theatre. I remember going to see a popular radio show performance, a western band called Jerry and Sky ("Keep on the Sunny side, always on the Sunny side"). The Exchange Hall also was home to the Harwich Junior Theatre, with whom I was privileged to play a couple of minor roles (remember the Fire Eater in *Pinocchio*...ME!). Of course, they were electrified by that time...

As Fall slipped on to the Cape scene, the Gypsy camp on Route 28 in South Yarmouth took in their lines hung with baskets, packed their caravans, and vanished over night. Even the religious fellowship cottage colonies that are here and there on the Cape decided to do God's work back at main land locations until the sun returned. By November, it was pretty much just us and the seagulls. Church groups pulled in their out door fair tables, and commenced their winter round of meetings, sewing circle for the ladies, 'Four Square League' for the adolescents (a meeting, then 'Kick the Can' out

Watercolor by Milton Welt

behind the parsonage). Here and there, a local men's club started up, but did not usually last long. The Grange, the Redmen, and other established groups got down to their winter projects, Knights of Pithias started up their whist parties, and everybody started to murmur about stage plays, or minstrel shows, church suppers, and Christmas fairs. And of course, School. Weekday mornings, the Big Yellow Bus rolled up, and with the new grade, and new activities, why, they wasn't hardly time to spit! Lesson, clubs, sports and class plays, and picking up musical instruments which had lain dormant for the hot months, and scouts, and 4-H projects (I raised hens). There just were not enough hours in the day!

The movies began their give away programs, dishes one night, cash another, sometimes a bingo type game where they called out numbers, which you punched out of a card, if you had them. My Uncle Wendell was a projectionist there in Harwich, and usually had a few free passes, so the folks went often. Evenings, after chores, home work and supper, the wonderful Radio, (new programs starting, old familiar ones returning) and books.

There were libraries in all the villages, except Dennisport, and they shared one with West Harwich. Ours in South Dennis was a tiny little thing, run for most of my school years by Ethel Hall, one of the off-Cape Teachers who succumbed to the charm of a Cape man. She had been an English Teacher, and was our director for the Four Square League dramatic presentations. She was a lovely woman, and a great friend to the kids. Small though it was, the library had access to other libraries in the vicinity, and long before the present 'Clams' system could usually get a book when requested. I once asked for a popular and somewhat racy novel. Mrs. Hall rang up Mother.

"Go ahead," said Mother, "If he understands it, it won't hurt him, if he doesn't understand, he will get bored, and not finish it."

There was also a wide 'swap' setup in effect, long before Mary Hood Hagler (a wonderfully civic-minded wash-a-shore, formerly of Alaska) started the current book exchange at the Disposal Area (DUMP) in the1970s. Dad used to come home from a day's work with a whole arm full of books and pulp magazines, and take away with him bags full of things he had read. He was an inveterate reader, when he had time, I don't believe he ever missed a word of the daily or *Sunday Post*, from headlines to back page ads.

I don't think Father got any further west than Chicago, but like most boys of his era, he probably cut his teeth on cowboy 'penny dreadfuls'. Stories of the old west, as seen by writers who might, or might not have traveled west of the Mississippi abounded in the cheap reading material available for boys. Tales of the lives and deaths of bad hombres like Billy The Kid, Jessie James, Wyatt Earp, and old 'Hanging Judge' Roy Bean, 'the only law west of the Pecos' (stories often fancied up by Eastern dudes with fast and agile pens) were rolled off the presses in an endless supply - right up through my childhood. Fact, we chased after Billy the Kid some, when we were not after the Chicago and Detroit mobsters.

These stories made up in excitement what they may have lacked in authenticity, and lots of people, like Father and Franklin D. Roosevelt, lapped them up, and made wealthy men of the more popular writers. Zane Grey, perhaps the best known, was a dentist from Ohio and later Max Brand, real name Fred Faust, who did most of his writing while living in Italy (output: about 530 books, over 100 of them 'Horse Operas').

Of the Brand books, perhaps the best known was 'Destry Rides Again', which was made into a movie three times (the first time staring Tom Mix) and years later formed the basis for a Broadway musical with Andy Griffith. Some of the writers did know what they were talking about, like one with the interesting non-cowboy cognomen of Louis L'Amour from North Dakota, who wrote prolifically, and really had 'punched' a few cows (also called 'skinning cattle').

Dad adored the Wild West, on paper, and always had several of the newsstand western magazines beside his chair. As there seemed to be a lot of local men of the same 'Walter Middy' persuasion, there was a good deal of trading activity around, which allowed him to buy few, but read many. After the paper, he retreated into his pulp magazines, right through the radio shows, from supper, till bedtime. Cowboys were popular, and the Barnstable Fair in the thirties always presented a Wild West Show and Rodeo as part of their contribution: they staged Indian attacks, stagecoach holdup, trick riding, a buffalo hunt and sharp shooting. Dad and Uncle Ray usually managed to get me over to a performance; met my first buffalo there (of course from a distance). One year the fair and the measles landed at the same time, and I had to stay home in bed as the elder males went to see the cowboys. Uncle Ray brought me back a cowboy hat, which was unfortunately about the same sickly red hue as my infected face.

Years later, when TV finally found a place in the house, the tube was filled with westerns, 'Wagon Train,' 'Bonanza', 'Judge Roy Bean', and Dad often put his book down. Dad would have made an unlikely cowboy, he had a hearty dislike for the care and feeding of horses, hangover from his childhood duties, had only one cow, (the one he couldn't shoot) and he was a farmer, a sodbuster.

Early movies were heavy into the Western theme, and he and Mother often went to see a Hopalong Cassidy film, as long as it came on a 'Bank Night'. Mom would tell us the story the next day, and before we saw Hoppy and his sidekicks (sometimes "Gabby" Hayes, sometimes the three Mesquiteers), we felt we knew them.

Mother seemed to appreciate the cowboy movies, but her reading appetite went elsewhere. Lots of her reading time was taken up with tales for tots, and whether read from a book, or a re-hash from a movie of the night before, it was pleasant to just sit and listen, even long after we had learned to read for ourselves. Her own reading favorites were wide, the serial stories in the *Saturday Evening Post* and *Colliers*, like the tales of Alexander Botts, and the Earthworm Tractor Co., Hiram Holliday, a shy copywriter who saved his company a fortune by inserting a comma in the right place in a legal document. As a reward, the company sent him on a European excursion, where he had many chances to be a shy hero. And Horatio Hornblower, seafarer. This Horatio was a hero ON the bridge, not, as in the poem defending one. Mom liked novels, (she got 'busted' in grammar school for reading one on the sly inside of her lesson book). She devoured Mary Roberts Reinhart, Earl Stanley Gardner's Perry Mason, and more serious reading, but usually grabbed the shorter material, or *Reader's Digest* condensed versions to squeeze in to what little time she had between wiping noses and cooking supper.

I caught the reading bug early. I sailed thru the kiddy books, and even did a forth grade book report on 20 books. Then, Sax Rhomar's evil 'Fu Manchu' (many men smoke, but fu men chew, Ha Ha), and forward into Sam Spade, Philip Marlowe, and later Mike Hammer, with a reasonable dose of real literature on the side. Cowboys, science fiction, funny books, I pretty much had a book in my face or at least in my pocket all the time. I read in class, as my mother had done with a novel inside my school book. I found I could angle my book so that the street light outside my bedroom window made the words discernable, if you squinted, so I read in bed at night, up until the war time black-out cut that source of illumination. I read at my job at the pharmacy in slack times, often when I should have been stocking the freezer, or performing other essentials around the store. There was so little traffic, that I even read to and from work, (about five miles) while riding my bicycle. Once a gentle rain stopped me under a big elm tree and our postmaster/ scoutmaster (in the one and only car that passed) spotted me sitting on my bike, waiting for a break in the shower, and reading by the flashes of summer lightning (he didn't let me forget it for years). I even carried a book and, in the evening, a candle on necessary trips to the small building behind the house.

Well, O.K., so maybe it wasn't 'gang busters' around here between fall and spring, but perhaps the Cape, lazy old Cape needed some time for the PEOPLE and physical assets to pull themselves back together. It looked like a long, cold winter, in the fall, watching the sun recede a bit more each day, but by the time the town crews pulled the raft out at West Dennis beach and dragged the river buoys up for painting, strung the snow fence in the dunes behind the beach, to help keep the beach sand from wandering across the marsh in the strong winter winds, and put by salted sand to spread on the icy main roads (spread by a couple of men with shovels, walking behind the truck), it was purty nigh time to commence puttin' them back. Take down the fence sweep up the sand (same men, with heavy push brooms). Quick! Here comes summer!

As a character in one of Dad's Western movies exclaimed, "Tempus sure do fugit!"

CRAFTS

The people of Cape Cod have learned how to merge,
The long winter nights with the creative urge.
As fall disappears and the weather gets drafty,
Behind shuttered windows are folks, getting "crafty".

Gone winter courses that taught self-improvement,
Gone bridge and checkers or joining a "movement",
No time for yoga or consciousness-raising,
Too busy carving and casting and glazing.

Doctor and fisherman, housewife and plumber,
Ready their wares for the fairs of the summer.
Folks with degrees out of Harvard or Vassar,
Making a decoy or antimacassar*.

Painting on seashells or hand-dipping candles,
Even ignoring the neighborhood scandals,
With peanuts from Planters or chocolates from Schraffts,
They're parked in the parlor, creating their crafts.

* Crocheted doilies used on the back of chairs to protect them from hair (macassar) oil.

CHAPTER THIRTY-SEVEN
It Might As Well Be Spring

Loved Halloween with the mild destruction, such as the unscheduled ringing of the church bells, upended privies, chalked streets and fences, and an old horse drawn hearse usually found in the morning left on Ed Nickerson's, lawn, or one year on top of his house. We joyfully ate our way through the roast rooster and oyster stuffing at Thanksgiving, gave in merrily to the greed of Christmas, but the holidays heading toward Spring had a special draw. I do not remember much about New Years, only that the year was mysteriously changing its numerical form (it would be March before I could remember to change the year date on my math papers). But from Valentine's Day on, the idea that SPRING was sneaking up on the dirty snow piles grew stronger with every major or minor celebration. Holidays then were pretty much 'do it yourself' kind of affairs. The billet-doux exchanged were of the homegrown, past 'em up variety, and there was little except tiny candy hearts and jelly beans for sale in the stores...or, if there was, we didn't know about it. One or several evening sessions with cutting out images (hopefully apropos) from catalogues and magazines, mixing flour and water paste and sticking them to doilies or crooked cut out red paper hearts (crayon colored) was about the size of it. In early grades, you brought a valentine for every other student in your class - even the kids you hated - but a few years up the line, the true meaning of V. Day seeped in, and you leveled off to giving greetings only to friends, parents and (surreptitiously) to HER!

After Valentine's Day you had to wait for Easter, at the last of March, or first part of April (the most disappointing month of all, as someone said). Good Friday was kind of spooky and gloomy, but the Sunday, in spite of the often cold and damp weather, was a true harbinger of the warmer seasons to come. Easter, of course was full of religious promises as well, with pageants and concerts. Outstanding memory, a youngster whose speech, "Easter, Easter, Everywhere.." left him at the midway point, and he stood, center stage on the church-front platform, and proclaimed, "Easter, Easter, Easter, Easter" (face red between the freckles, fists clenched, body tense, puffed up near to the exploding point with the strain, tension mounting - the audience leaning forward almost desperate to help the lad on with his performance) "Easter, Easter, Easter...." Several more "Easters," then, triumphantly) "EVERYWHERE!" and an audible sigh from the assembled relatives and friends.

Mother's Day, meant going with Dad to get a flat of pansies, which Mother expected, but always seemed pleasantly surprised to receive. Memorial Day, was when the Adults went to the graveyard to leave flowers, and check to see that Edwin Bray had mowed the family plot. There was also a parade to, and solemn services at, one or more of the town memorial plaques, usually in Dennisport at a Veterans Park, but seems I remember one such at the small park near Baker Town. We weren't sure what these were all about, but the American Legion, Boy Scouts and Veterans of Foreign Wars marched, and fired off rifles with a satisfying bang, some distant bugle played a strange tune called 'taps' and there was a lot of talk by older men wearing whole or partial uniforms. Later, during WWII, our State Guard Band supplied the marching music, and the bugler. June brought sunshine, and Fourth of July brought SUMMER and a day at the beach or a picnic around a large table (made from the base of an old square piano) by a hand built stone grill in the grove behind the house. One year Dad and Uncle Paul brought down a 22 pound lobster, cooked by the fish market, it was out of this world, but a tad difficult to open because of the heavy shell; the back end of a hatchet freely swung solved that. No big fireworks displays in the 30's, but until the war put an end to manufacturing of such, fathers and uncles and big brothers bought and ignited cherry bombs, lady crackers, two inch salutes and pin-wheels. Skyrockets were set off standing up in milk bottles, and hopefully blasted off into the sky before they exploded, and Roman Candles, hand held, popped colored fireballs into the air. Trouble with those Candles, sometimes the last fireball would come out through the bottom of the tube, wreaking havoc on the holder, and surrounding spectators. Firecrackers could be troublesome, too, when wise guys threw them near people, or didn't let go of them quick enough after lighting. Eddie Crowell had a two-inch salute explode in his hand one year, and he did not have a pleasant time with it. As I remember, they were throwing the lit crackers into a tin garbage can - really amplified the noise.

For the younger ones, there were sparklers, hand thrown torpedoes, pungent smelling punk sticks (all the kids agreed they were made of camel dung), and snakes (little pills that evolved into a long snakelike ash when lighted). Some years there would be a small community effort. The fathers cooperated on purchasing and lighting off some bigger items, but no ways near today's displays. In South Dennis these took place behind the Town offices, in a sand lot (we called the 'desert') which I think resulted from mixing tar, and other roadwork. This area, by the way, was where Dad found the ill-fated Indian Arrow heads which I later lost in our search for bad guys.

Then, of course, there were the parades. Not usually able, for one reason or another, to get to Hyannis or elsewhere that was having a real parade, bands, marchers and all that, we had our own! We could usually get upwards of 10 kids - what with some of the summer folks. Bicycles were draped with crepe paper, and everyone got garbed up in bits and pieces of what ever struck us as military, and we carried flags.

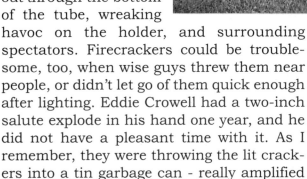

Jayne and Link with Sam.

Center piece for several years, until he died of some unknown problem, was Sammy the Goat, (named Uncle Sam, because he had a goatee like the old red, white and blue feller who was pointing from the posters that said, "I want YOU!!" Uncle Sam (the goat) was black and white and very strong. By dismantling one of Link's orange crate and baby carriage wheel cars (later, an old cart made of stronger stuff) and reassembling it, I made a small wagon which he would pull if you led him. The shafts were handles of a hand pushed garden cultivator, the harness bits of old leather I found in the barn, held together with wire. It was kind of a wobbly affair, but it would hold two kids, and did not seem to slow that strong goat down a bit. He would follow me anywhere, especially when he knew I had some sweet grain or apple pieces or a bit of tobacco in my pocket.

Sam, as afore noted, came to me from my Uncle Wendell, by way of Dad's car (back seat out for carrying more stuff, firewood, refuse for the dump, eggs, goats...etc.). He was a Toggenburg, a neutered male. I don't know where Uncle Wendell got the goat, or why he wanted rid of him, but I felt I got lucky. Sam and I saw eye-to-eye right from the beginning. I would grab his horns, and institute a pushing contest, or if he got feeling rambunctious, he would push me, or butt me. When little sister Jayne came up to him, and grabbed his substantial horns, he pushed, but never butted her. Others, however, would on occasion feel his power in a more immediate manner. Any dog that got too close got it good and once when my knee was between him and a dog, I got it, good! People who he did not feel easy with should NOT get too personal with him, on pain of a good powerful whack. One of Sam's favorite activities was climbing up on top of things, steps, large rocks, picnic tables, or his house.

Probably his Swiss mountain heritage showing through. If I blatted, imitating a goat sound, he would blat back, even greeting me when I got off the school bus, near a quarter mile away. I took him for walks on a lead, and sometimes just let him come along with no rope. He would generally stick close. Left alone, he would often work his way out of his collar, and range freely about the yard, but never tried to run away. His tastes ran to many most unlikely items, dried leaves, tobacco (a favorite, Dad used to hold a cigarette loosely in his lips, and Sam would stand on his hind legs, and gently take it, until one day he came up unexpectedly, and grabbed a lit one - after that he was more circumspect, but never lost his taste for tobacco). He adored bark and killed several young trees by eating all around their trunks. Labels from cans were good, if he managed to get at the refuse.Of course, Dad's hen food was popular and I even saw him munch out on poison ivy! One fond memory, among many, on a rainy day, when he had done his usual Houdini act, and left his tether in the field for the shelter of the old barn, I stepped out of the house, to see a double sheet of newspaper, apparently hanging in mid air, at the opening of the big barn door. The edges of the paper moved in toward the center, and revealed behind it, chewing away merrily from the middle outward, the placid, happy goat.

Mom wasn't always that happy with Sam. His voracious appetite drew no line on the laundry hanging out to dry, and he chewed holes in several garments from time to time before she could chase him away. Also, he butted her. Little Jayne he pushed, but Mother must have looked like she could fight back, so her, he butted. One snowy morning, when Father had the flu and the

South Dennis Children Enlist Goat's Aid in Driving Crisis *1942*

SOUTH DENNIS, Jan. 12—Churchgoers in South Dennis were treated to the sight of a goat pulling a cart full of children from the Freeman Thacher home to the Congregational Church Sunday.

Benjamin, eldest of Mr. Thacher's five children, explained that the innovation in South Dennis transportation facilities was his idea of a simple solution of the walk-or-stay-home edict of Leon Henderson.

"Uncle Sam—that's the name of our goat . . .," Benjamin explained. "Likes almost anything but gasoline. He's not exactly what you'd call a hay burner, but gasoline just never suited him right."

Uncle Sam is a black and white beauty of a goat, complete with a nice set of whiskers and horns that were made for children to decorate. His distate for gasoline has never interfered, observers report, with his penchant for rubber tires, coffee grounds, old harrows or tin cans.

Since all of these articles are on on one ration list or another, life of late has been a series of frustrations for Sam. The pleasure driving edict was the first ray of sunshine he had had in some time. After all, a non-working car meant potential foader.

The Thacher children, Benjamin, Nancy Ann, Lincoln, Olive and Jane, sensed Sam's feelings and decided that gloatings should be tempered with cooperation in an emergency. They rigged a cart, made a set of harness, and hitched Sam to the shaft.

It's about a mile from the Thacher home to church, part of it uphill. An ordinary goat might have decided that five children and a cart were too much to bear of a Sunday morning, but not Sam. Pulling that cart was his way of making the best of things. Making the axle turn was his way of helping to trim the axis.

rest of us were just climbing back to wellness, Mother and I were shoveling the car free for a needed errand, when Sam, again free, snuck up from behind her, and butted her in the nether regions. She landed face down in a snowdrift. Sorry, Mom, but it looked so damn funny, I couldn't stop laughing. Sam seemed to get the joke, and hovered, so she could not get up. Note: there were some harsh words issued from that sweet mouth of hers at the Goat, and at the damn laughing jackanapes too paralyzed with mirth to help her up. What with Mother's abiding good humor, we got it ironed out, but ol' Sam met with stiffer restrictions for a while. On some sunny Sundays, I harnessed Sam to the cart, and took the littler kids to church. Un-harnessed, and tied, Sam grazed on holy grounds quite contentedly till Sunday school was thru, and then, was put back to work for the return trip. Going toward home, was as much work for me as for the goat. He knew directions well enough to realize there was a peaceful pasture waiting, and tended to want to make the voyage at a trot. Holding him back was a job. One day when I was not keeping track, little brother Link, having noted the slow trip out, and the rapid return, felt he should try an expedition on his own, or rather, with Jayne, but without big brother holding the halter. He harnessed up alright, and after a slow, uneventful outgoing walk, about a half mile from the house, Link leading, Jayne riding, little brother turned the goat around, heading for home, and jumped on the cart. Sam reacted. He shortly had the cart bouncing along Old Bass River Road at a good clip, and, safely, due to the scarcity of other traffic, careened into Main Street, and with a violent left turn, just a tad before the opening of the driveway, smashed thru the old fence in front of Dad's corn patch.

The wagon almost made it, the front wheels did, and Link, holding desperately to the reins, rode the rest of the way into the yard sort of belly bumpers, wiping out corn stalks as he went. The back half of the little wagon stopped dead at the fence, and sat there, with a frightened, bawling little Jayne sitting in the wreckage. Luckily nobody hurt, cart a total loss, but there were many more wheels at the dump. Sam left us for some unknown reason, I came home and found him dead. It was probably something he ate, but heavens knows what. We held a solemn funeral, and as sister Jayne reminded me, friend Jimmy Merchant (the guy who was sprinkled with glass shards at my magic show) stood on a stump and gave a eulogy as we lowered Ol' Sam into a grave dug near the edge of the woods at the back of Dad's corn field.

During WWII, the spring influx of visitors started to swell. With little gas, transportation generally at a premium and foreign travel prohibited, the Cape, less than a day's journey from about half the population of the country seemed like a good alternative to previous peacetime vacation spots.

Sam the Goat Ranges Over Wide Area in South Dennis

Benjamin Thacher and his pet goat Sam are widely known in the mid-Cape area. Although the animal is only 11 months old it is tame and intelligent enough to follow its master about like a dog. The pair are pictured above.

Many people liked what they saw, came back repeatedly, pushing up the construction of motels and restaurants even more after the war, and in later years picked our sand spit in the ocean as a retirement spot. With the arrival of these new visitors, and permanent residents came merchants and service people, restaurateurs and builders, ready to move in and call Cape Cod home. The new business people preferred year round establishments to the old ten-week summer only affairs, and there went our quiet winters. The only relief from crowded conditions now is the Snow Bird exodus of retirees to Florida and points to avoid the New England cold.

So, I miss Cape Cod - the quiet August afternoons on a nearly deserted beach, a population small enough for most people to know each other, and gently blossoming springs along quiet roads where a man could safely conduct a herd of cows, or a boy could lead a goat cart full of children. As Grandmother Thacher might have said, "Oh My, My, What Work, What Work!!"

VERNAL RASH-O-NAL

In winter I can walk around,
Not noticing what's on the ground,
In spring I walk that very place,
And wind up with a swollen face.

I can't recall, from year to year,
Where poison ivy will appear,
So, consequently, spring on spring,
I'm scratching, like a maddened thing.

Does Mother Nature have it in,
For people with allergic skin,
Or is this part of God's own plan,
To check on our attention span?

CHAPTER THIRTY-EIGHT

Feeling Good

I guess it's about all this reaching back for pieces of yesterday, but I can almost feel it: the air so clean you can catch a waft of smoke from fires in way distant woods. A few were set each year by future blueberry pickers, clandestinely burning off sections of brush (on land which they did not own) to accelerate the berry crop. A couple of times a month there were faint wafts of smoke from the dump, a mile or more out of town, when Thoph disposed of the loose paper waste on some calm day. There was also the incident of an otherwise very nice and quiet young man who set off a few grass fires, perhaps for the adventure of extinguishing them or, things being what they were financially, perhaps for the $2.00 he would receive as a call fireman. He very soon voluntarily joined the Army, without any permanent record I remember, but with a severe tongue lashing from the fire chief, who was also his fellow scout master. Those rare touches of smoke, the moist salty tang that came with an onshore wind and the natural, not unpleasant farm smells from Thoph's barn up the road were just about all the odors that ever interfered with fresh Cape air quality back then.

The summer-softened tar on the new roads was chewable, and as nobody ever seemed to get sick from it, we had an inexhaustible supply of rather tasteless, but interesting free gum. That new tar could be mighty tough on feet in really hot weather; we tended to be neglectful regarding shoes in the warm months, and tough as our feet became, things like hot tar and the broken clam and oyster shells (used on many driveways, and still on some of the roads) gave cause for some fancy stepping. A good dusty sand road made the best walking, you could kick the hotter surface dirt aside and cool your feet in the chill moist sand below. Next best foot aid was a well-kept lawn, if you could find one on your line of march. Most tended to be rough stubble left by the scythe, but here and there a homeowner had seeded, and mowed (strictly by hand-propelled spool bladed mower, of course) and the smooth soft coolness was marvelous. Press your singed tootsies down into the green, and wallow in it. A good and available alternative to burned feet would have been to wear your sneakers (Mother was always reminding, "Don't forget your shoes, if you leave the yard") but small people always know better.

The storage cellar below the trapdoor in Dad's oyster shucking shed (just a hole dug in the yellow sand below the floor, really) was a dank, always cool area, wide open for investigation during the off-seasons. If you didn't fret the darkness, or the dampness, it was perfect for hide and seek. It was also cool in the underground huts, and a fine place to sit in the dark and spin yarns. Frenchie was a master storyteller, and somehow seemed to have access to all manner of ghost and alien tales. Harold knew a lot of things about the end of the world: one late afternoon when the setting sun made the sky particularly red, he stood up on our hen house and told us that THIS was it, but it wasn't. I also had a jury-rigged tree hut at the house on Upper County Road, out behind Father's garden in a fairly big scrub pine with boards nailed to the trunk for a ladder: access limited to about one and a half kids, so few stories told there, but it was good for some idle dreaming.

Approaching trains were audible way before they whistled at the granite marker with big W on it, about a quarter mile from the station and though I don't remember any airplanes passing over before the war, the Army planes from Camp Edwards, with their whirling propellers, made themselves known miles before they lumbered across our section of quiet sky. On a summer evening, you were aware of 'possums and raccoons crying like human babies in the swamps, and the chickens fussing on their backyard roosts because, perhaps, a dog had passed by. As darkness started to dim the landscape, we could clearly hear mothers, calling their kinder back from farther away from home than they were supposed to be.

Our drinking water was pumped straight from the ground by hand, and later by electric pumps, straight up from the water level below our homes, not from a town run water source and it was naturally cold, sweet and unpolluted, as were the several springs down along the river. (Norton Nickerson, after he went away to school, took samples to the state for testing; the reports were excellent, but we drinkers knew that already.) 'Buster', as we called him, sent river water samples to be tested, also, from the area where we swam, by the railroad bridge. At that time, the water tested out as a fine balance of salt, and fresh, but with the steady tidal flow, as pure as when Leif Erickson rowed up this river with his long boats. Lately, areas of the river are often closed to shell fishing due to human pollution.

At night, the low wattage street lamps made weak islands of yellow light along some of the main roads, with little spill into the dark areas between. And when war measures caused them to be blacked out, the Cape became an astronomer's paradise: the only light in the sky - stars and the moon. Heading home from a 4-square league meeting (and a twilight session of 'kick the can'), we often walked as a rag-tag group up the main street, full of talk and laughs, and frisky from our game, very seldom needing to move to the side for an oncoming auto. One strange, surreal night neither the streetlamps nor the old inefficient headlamps of the stray passing truck were enough to illuminate the two men, both Portuguese of dark complexion, wearing colorless work clothes and staggering from bootlegged alcohol. The one who lived had his clothing torn; it was that close. The other lay on our porch, under a blanket that Mother brought out, until the undertakers came for his body. The man who lived through the horror drank coffee in the kitchen while I, and I think Nancy, came out and peeked in awe out through the window at the shape on the porch. We were quickly sent back to bed to lie awake stimulated by the eerie wonder of the night. Then Dad drove the survivor to his home.

In later years, he saved enough money to go back to his ancestral home in Cape Verde, and buy a goat farm. He spent his last years as a rather well to do man by his village standards, who could recount at least one tale from the other Cape (Cod) which neither he nor I would ever forget...

If you were going somewhere on foot, you would never think of turning down an offered ride, dollars to donuts you knew the driver anyway, usually a parent of some acquaintance, or a few lines of conversation ascertained who each of you were, and how near to your destination you could count on the ride taking you. Generally, the driver would drop you off right where you wanted to go, even if it was out of his way. After all, gas was only twenty-five cents, five gallons for a dollar. Dad used to get his five gallons Sunday mornings from Mr. Keander's, a station near the Ezra Baker School on Route 28, well, three gallons when the War rationing took over. Mr. K sold the Sunday paper, and Dad usually bought from him after he stopped delivering the *Boston Post*. It became a Sunday ritual. Keander's station was equipped with the old style hand operated pumps, which made him the only station able to dispense gas after some of the big storms. As I remember, Mr. K. smoked a pipe, and held it in his teeth as he cranked the gear driven pump, I cannot say from memory if he actively smoked it, or just nursed it. He and Dad discussed the fate of the world, but I don't think they came to any workable conclusions about how to move things forward.

Mostly their conversation was less worldly than local. One area in which the Cape towns have not totally changed (but have blown up with the population explosion) is in the form of Town government. Elected selectmen (used to be three, now five), a town clerk (plus, now, a town manager), and a popular town meeting (two or more times a year where the citizens directly address town business, and make decisions by voting) made up our government. Now, of course, there are dozens of auxiliary positions, inspectors, secretaries, department heads, ad infinitum, but even then, before the dozens of bureaucratically dictated departments we have to day, there were 'positions' within the town government to be filled. Some were paid jobs, like the Town Clerk and Treasurer (one job), three Selectmen and Assessors, and Health and Weight (scales and gas pumps) Inspectors (one job, but three people involved), the Superintendent of Roads, and a Tree Warden. OOPS, not to forget the Dump Keeper, and our one Policeman, hired to help the Selectmen, and later named Chief. Dad was Tree Warden for a while, but held several other positions. He was a polls officer until he was rather old, of course a call firefighter, but the other jobs were positions the state said towns must have, and Dad got three of them. Pound Keeper (no pound in town), Fence Viewer (to make sure fences were built on the right side of a boundary line. Never remember any fence disputes, but had there been some such, Father would have been the man to see), and Field Driver, on duty to herd home any stray farm animals (farmers kept pretty close watch on their beasts but occasionally one of Thoph's cows would pull loose from her chain. They were always so docile, such contented cows, that any passing kid could lead the escapee back and reconnect her). These jobs were honorary, and received no honorarium, so Dad was reappointed uncontested, year after year.

Ben Sears, our two-doors down neighbor on Main Street, was Town Clerk/Treasurer for many years. He was a quiet man, and seemed to be totally approved of by the voters. He wasn't what could be called a gossip, but on occasion would regale the 'mail wait-ers'. Seeking to better serve the public, Mr. Sears took the license application books home with him on the weekends, in case some shellfisherman or cottage owner had been unable (or had forgotten) to come in during office hours. He answered a knock at the door one evening to find a local acquaintance

"Ben, sorry to bother, but I got to have a license."

"Sure, Rufe, hunting or fishing?"

"Naw, need a marriage license."

Ben looked past the man and saw the woman in the front seat of his car, and four kids in the back. "Marriage? Why, Rufe, you and Ruth been together for years, and all those kids..."

"I know, I know," sez Rufe, "But old lady's getting fussy, wants to get married."

He was soon on his way, license in hand to look for a parson as accommodating as the Town Clerk. Mrs. Sears was a dear friend of Mother's. Her given name was Mabel Bessie. She had been a Sears before marrying, though a very distant relative (there were near as many Sear families in town as Bakers). We used to fumble with the old saying, "Change the name, but not the letter, marry for worse, but not for better," but it didn't work what with her having the same name single as married. She used to delight us kids by saying she was, "Mabel B. Bessie B. Bumble Bee Sears, and I've only had seventeen birthdays!" As she was obviously somewhere in her sixties, we spent a lot of time figuring how old you really were if you were, as she was, born in a leap year, on February 29th. Funny what things stick in your memory?

The laws and expenses of the Town were then, as now, brought to the floor of the Town Meeting, under the direction of the Moderator, and the procedure governed by 'Robert's Rules of Order'. If approached properly, a lively debate could help the people better understand the proposition under discussion, and so help determine the direction of the vote. But sometimes . . . a winter storm had destroyed a small bridge over a narrow creek, and a proposal was put before the meeting to replace it, at a cost of $1200.00 dollars.

With no attention to the prescribed procedure, an irate voter jumped to his feet.

"$1200 dollars? $1200 dollars to bridge that damn little creek? Why, hell, I could piss half way acrost that creek!"

Laughter exploded, but the Moderator with hammer and voice sought to quell this violation of 'Robert's Rules'.

"Mister Smith, you're out of order!"

"You'm damn right I be. If I wasn't, I could piss ALL the way acrost!"

After a limited peace replaced the pandemonium, the article was voted down. I admit that I had some doubt of the authenticity of this tale, but Dad, whose veracity was non-pareil in the matter of folk lore (I think), passed it on to me as gospel, showed me the un-bridged creek: the old road still impassable as of this writing.

AN ASSESSMENT

Sirs, This letter I address
To the fellers who assess,
You have caused me much distress,
(As I mentioned to my spouse).

How you judge things isn't clear,
Can't see how it got so dear,
T'wasn't worth but half last year,
And it's still the same old house.

All the doors let in the air,
Needs a clapboard here and there,
She's in gen'ral disrepair,
As I'd gladly offer proof.

Then, that storm, back Christmas week,
Raised some shingles near the peak,
(There's a pail beneath the leak),
And it's still the same old roof.

Back when I was in my prime,
I'd have fixed her up, in time,
Now, I'm just too old to climb,
So I have to leave things be,

That's confounding, I confess,
It worth more, and I worth less,
May I look for some redress?
Signed, Sincerely, same old me.

CHAPTER THIRTY-NINE

Laff, I Thought My Pants Would Never Dry!

They were working on a swing stage, Father said, a plank suspended by ropes and pulleys from the roof of the old school building there in South Dennis, same school he had attended just a few years before. He and another young man were working at the two ends of the plank, with the boss painter in the middle. The building needed to be scraped, primed, and painted. This meant a long time in one spot, hence the "stage". The man who contracted the job, and hired the two young men to assist was Judah Baker, a master painter who contracted jobs, and hired help. The work was boring, and the day was hot, so with a sly wink to his contemporary at the other end of the stage, Dad began to swing back and forth, slowly at first, and then joined by the other boy, a bit more forcibly, until the plank was careening widely, from side to side. Didn't faze Judah, he tried during the first few swings to lay some paint on the clapboards as they swung by, then gave up and sat there quietly until his two helpers, chagrined because they didn't "get a rise" out of the older man got tired, and quit. As the stage plank settled down, Judah began to lay on paint as though nothing had happened, and his 'helpers' in turn applied their brushes and attention to the job before them.

I knew Judah in his older years as a quiet, gentle, man who was apparently very patient with his young workers. I recently found a sign "Wet Paint" with his name on it… My memory of him was mainly his walking. Even in his advanced years he walked back and forth to Hyannis (a distance of ten miles or so, each way) always wearing high laced sneakers, and cradling a slightly humped back by holding one arm behind him, his hand gripping the other arm. He always seemed to have a cheek full of chewing tobacco. That he lived through the time with Dad and company, and their practical jokes, speaks well for his staying power.

There was lots of that 'funning' going on. From early days in these back waters of small Cape towns (as well as during the long hours at sea), jokes, practical and other wise, stories, yarns, gossip and such became a homegrown manner of coping with a sometimes humdrum existence. At sea, the new man usually got it. He was sent up the mast to keep an eye out for a 'horse' mackerel (there is such a fish, but not with the mane, tail and hooves the 'green' hand was told to expect). He would be sent to the maintenance locker for a pail of striped paint, fifty foot of shore line, or a bucket of steam. On shore, sending a new helper for a dozen fence post holes sometimes worked, such tricks as the undertakers pulled on Thoph, or the Halloween stunt of the over turned privy, or the hearse on top of Nickerson's house. Some jokes backfired. Men working for the road maintenance department nailed a co-worker's lunch box to the floor down to the old fire station. They were some surprised when the owner, a bull of a man and hungry for his lunch, snatched up the box - with the nails and a substantial section of the plank floor.

Back some years before the War (WWII) when fireworks were sold and ignited by just about anyone, The Night Before the Fourth was a big night, topped All Hallows Eve in earlier years, according to sister Nancy's research. There was a good deal of hell raising and the town put on constables to try to keep the ruckus in hand, but in my youth, I remember mostly the fire department volunteers (there weren't any other kind of fire fighters) being on the alert for out of control bonfires or fireworks mishaps, and our one man police force, plus a couple of part time summer patrolmen cruising from village to village. They were trying to keep an eye on the older boys, but the troops were few, and easy to avoid. Mostly it was noise. All the older kids had fire crackers, from strings of the 'lady fingers' to 2-inch salutes, and bigger. If you studied it out, you could make a few crackers sound like a full fledged battle.

Throw a lit cherry bomb into an empty tin garbage can, drop the top back on, and run. WHOPPO! That can cover would fly up into the air with a boom like a cannon, and if it was on a hard surface, it made near as much noise landing and bounding around as it did blowing up. Guaranteed to get someone out of the house to investigate. Still, I don't remember too much 'devilishness' except that some of the boys learned that they could ring the church bell from a distance with a .22 rifle, which caused some concern amongst folk in the immediate vicinity - especially after midnight. I knew who done it, but I still won't tell. There were stories of some garden gates disappearing, supposedly into bonfires, and some more privy tipping (one, we heard contained a gentleman quietly going about his business). By the time I was old enough to join in the fun, it was over. War regulations against night lights (enforced by village civil defense wardens) and a total ban on the use of explosives for fun put a severe crimp in The Night Before The Fourth. It never recovered its full vigor, even post-war, but in other ways, the laffs just kept on comin'.

We young'un had our own pre and early high school bits of 'humor'. Phone a store; ask if they had 'Prince Albert' (a popular pipe tobacco) in a can. On an affirmative answer, your retort was, "Well, let him out, he'll suffocate!!" or "Is your house on Route 28?? Better move it, there's a convoy coming!" Was that funny or what! There were also inane sayings you passed around.

"Well, that's Life…"

"What's Life?"

"A magazine."

"Where do you get it?"

"On a News stand."

"What News Stand?"

"Any News stand."

"How much?"

"15 cents.""I only have a dime…"

"Well, that's Life…!"

And "I'm in business." "What kind of business?" "Corn Flakes business." "How's Business?" "Tell you next week, it's a 'cereal'". There was also 'Confucius Says', and guess what, the ever popular Knock Knock was with us big time, complete with a popular song-tune and lyric! And, by the way, soldiers on leave brought us the ubiquitous drawing of the fingers, nose and two eyes peaking over a fence with the saying "Kilroy Was Here". (A comic phenomena which sparked thousands of cartoons, a recorded popular song, a book by Charles Osgood on WWII humor, became the name of a 1946 movie starring Jackie Cooper, and can still be purchased engraved on Zippo cigarette lighters, on tee shirts, and lapel pins!)

The Outhouse: now, that was a subject that got folks to chortling big time. As the Cape was in general (as with most rural areas, I'm sure) well behind most cities in the running water and indoor sanitation department, visitors in the thirty's probably sent more humorous outhouse postcards than pictures of the Provincetown monument, sail boats and Craigville Beach combined. Cartoon pictures of lined up outdoor privies, looking like skinny old fashioned motels with half-moons carved on the door were legion, and can still be found in second stores nation-wide, many with Cape Cod postmarks. Legends such as "Found excellent accommodations here in _____ (fill in your village)" and "Come and visit, more sitting room here than in our house at home".

Cape Cod was a mite moderate in upgrading its facilities. Two carpenters were constructing a picnic table and benches for some summer people over to the North Side, when one of them felt a call of nature, but could not spot an outhouse there in the yard. He asked the owner about the location of same and was directed into the house, where there was a full equipped bathroom. Back at the job, he surveyed the new picnic area and scratched his head.

"By gum, Obid, these city folk sure do things backward. They want to eat out doors instead of indoors, and what you should be doing outdoors, they do in the house!" Dad always called the privy 'Chic Sale's Castle', after a vaudeville act and book by a comic of the 1920's-30's. Chic wrote, and spoke about a carpenter who specialized in creating those little buildings with the half moon on the door. He said

there was much to consider in the building and placement of the "necessary". For instance, if you build it on the other side of the wood pile from the house so every body could bring back a few sticks of firewood, why, the hired girl might have the wood box by the stove half full by supper time. He also recommended that the door swing in, not out; it should not be built under an apple tree, as the sound of apples falling on the roof could be distracting and commented on how long the Sears Roebuck catalogue should last. Any reader who remembers Carl Moore on Boston Radio in the 1930's may have heard him sing a song based on the advice in this slim and popular little book ("The Specialist"..."My name is Lemuel Putt...").

There was a deal of humor, which I suppose would be described as 'lowbrow' (not that outhouse humor is in any way highbrow,) which had to do with such things as Baked Beans, but I think that this time, I'll leave that alone. Give me a call some time, and I'll tell ye about it.

A HALLOWED CHANGE?

A night still full of spooks and fears,
And tons of treats to divvy,
But note, I haven't heard, in years,
Of one inverted "privy".

Benny The Great

What in tunket got me to thinking along the lines of being in the show business, I'll never know. I surely wasn't 'born in a trunk,' as the old saying goes. Mother said she appeared in some school shows, at least one minstrel show in high school back when they used burned cork to blacken their faces with no thought that it might be offensive. She told the story that after the show, an Afro-American classmate noted that if she would leave the makeup on, he could walk her home after the performance. She later appeared in a village play or two directed by our librarian, but by her own admission had a problem with singing; said she sang neither with the white keys nor with the black keys, but rather in the cracks. In spite of this, she sang to us with some regularity, and my memory finds that her tunes were right on target. Dad had a nice voice, which he used a lot when we were small. He sang softly at home, and loudly - and on key - at church. He had been in lots of local shows, mainly the old minstrel variety, and taught me a double ration of old timey songs from his childhood, and earlier (some of them were even sing-able in mixed company). I knew Gay nineties and twenties tunes galore before I was school age. He also played the harmonica and jews harp before he got his false teeth, but after that claimed he couldn't hold the cussed things right with his damn choppers. 'Chopper' is probably more correct, as he never wore his lower set. (I later used them as a gag production item in my magic act, he never knew they were missing from the bureau drawer. His teeth got in show business, even if he didn't.) He did keep singing after he was re-toothed, but mostly to us kids, or to himself as he farmed or painted away on the side of a house. Link and I, while working with him one day, teased him about being old.

"Dad," sez Link, "Was Abraham Lincoln a nice man?"

"You bedamned," said Father good naturedly, "I wasn't alive when he was President."

We chuckled, and let it drop, but soon Link nudged me, and we both commenced to laugh. Dad had unconsciously begun to sing the old Civil War song, "One Wore the Blue, and the Other Wore the Grey".

Uncle Ray, who lived with us during some of my pre-school years, played at a trumpet, but the best he could manage were a few bugle calls, and at that he never got 'Taps' quite right (he was right there on 'Mess Call'). Ray was Mother's brother, twin of Aunt Rena, who squired us around Salem. He had been too young for WWI, but got into a home guard cavalry outfit there in Salem. He knew and taught me the manual of arms with a pop gun, how to salute and march and played imaginative games of soldier and cowboy, and was for a while something of a big brother. When the depression made jobs impossible in the city, he moved to the Cape, and stayed at the house for quite a while.

Ray sometimes smoked Chesterfields, but more often Lucky Strike cigarettes, which he purchased in flat tin boxes with a green label and a big red circle on the front. They were called flat fifty's, and were cheaper than  packs. When finances got rough, he resorted to rolling his own... not in his hand in the old cowboy style, but with a small device on which you laid a paper, poured on the tobacco, turned a handle, and received a fully formed cigarette at the other end! He would make some up ahead and I was present, if possible, to watch. A show in itself. Uncle Ray later fell in love with a pretty young woman across the Cape, and with money so short, and gas so high (twenty five cents a gallon, or five gallons for a dollar) he walked both ways (about ten miles) to do his courting. With the long walks, the late nights, and days hovered over the fry pots making potato chips, our play time suffered.

I think the first 'live' professional entertainment I saw was a puppet show presented at Liberty Hall, and, I believe, arranged via the WPA fund, which sent performers out to small towns. Such also was my first circus, on the school playground, and a vaudeville show, made up of two performers (man and wife, I expect) who did a bit of everything, juggling, magic, singing, playing various instruments. No critic, I, at about five, but it seems the best part was the incredible speed with which they changed costumes. This again at the little hall on the green just up the street, with Thoph's cows lowing in the background. Shades of Broadway!

It was the puppet performance, 'Jack and the Bean Stalk' that somehow lit my wick. I went home and commenced making some kind of puppets from socks and things. I can't remember the specifics, but I did present performances on the kitchen floor, something to do with a cardboard boxing ring, and featuring for lord knows what reason, the song 'The Blue Bells Of Scotland'. (I guess maybe the folks had an old 78 record of it.) Next foray into the entertainment field was at six, wanting an 'Auto-Magic' picture projecting gun. It was advertised on the radio and would make one a real impresario. It came from Mr. and Mrs. Santa (who really should not have afforded it in those heavily depressed days) and was complete with bulb, foldable screen (with printed stage) 10 printed tickets and six film clips of things like the *Lone Ranger* and *Tarzan*. My siblings were very good about it, and dutifully presented their tickets and watched the dim pictures (about 10 frames to a reel and very little in the way of a story line) over and over again.

The kids were real troupers through the whole ugly mess. They rode on and seemed to enjoy the merry go-round I constructed from an old wagon wheel (our former

across-the-street neighbor, Priscilla reminded me of that just recently). They came to view and marvel at the Museum I constructed from the old awnings Dad rescued from the dump (it featured Aunt Edith's coral from the south seas, a piece of the painted desert and a genuine whalebone cane). Also, for a while, Dad's arrowheads, Grandpa's foreign coins, and, oops, the Civil War musket, bayonet and powder horn were featured exhibits. They seemed properly amazed as I fumbled through each new card trick I attempted, and gleefully wrapped me in clotheslines and old tire chains as I went through my Houdini phase. He died, you know, in 1926, just a couple years before I was born and there is such a thing as re-incarnation…isn't there? They stood by while I tried trick riding on my bicycle or stood precariously on the back of Frannie Sullivan's horse, and attempted to jump through a wide, almost spinning, rope loop. They were sympathetic when I pulled all my various parts trying circus stunts and joined in with vigor when I engaged the younger ones in foot juggling and other acrobatic feats.

When I settled on magic, stalwart Nancy became my assistant. She carried suitcases, handed me props, did much of the sneaky behind the scenes bits, and stood before the glass while I fired my trusty skeet gun in her direction. When I went through my hypnosis stage, she became my subject, while I learned from a grand old vaudeville magician how to induce a trance, and give safe commands as a mesmerist. This period didn't really extend past the learning stage, because just after Nancy heard that while hypnotized, she had, on command, become stiff as a board, and had been suspended between two chairs, one under her head, the other under her feet, and that the next stage would feature her in that position, while I stood on her middle, well, that was it for Hypnosis. Otherwise, Nancy stayed the course, however, handing me secret boxes and carrying paraphernalia on and off the performing area. Must have been a bit boring, because she gave up the silver stage fairly early, pleading busy. Well, she did do more homework than I, practiced incessantly on the piano and even before she became heavily boy conscious, her social calendar seemed to clash with my performance schedule. I talked her into command performances for my full evening shows (two) and several return engagements for shows at the Lighthouse Inn, but for all intents and purposes, I became a lonely solo performer.

Show Business.

My first real taste of fame came when the principal of the grammar school, which I had lately attended for eight years, called and asked me to perform for an assembly. My efforts seemed to be well received, and the principal presented me with his thanks, and a roll of dimes! I was a pro! My tricks to this time were, I suppose, pretty gilley, put together from plans I found in books on Magic (the librarian, Mrs. Hall got me some from another, bigger library) or such as I could find in a magic/joke shop my Aunt Rena found for me in Boston on one of our visits. Then in high school, I was introduced to Sidney Victor Wright. 'Twas he became the teacher of the hypnotic lessons, a very important figure in my performing life and my friend. We were introduced by my favorite teacher of all time, Betty Clough, English and Drama. Sid was arranging a Cape Cod Review of local talent and asked various high school teachers for potential performers. Miss Clough took me to Hyannis, where Sid ran a youth center, taught arts and crafts, and made the introductions. Sid had performed on the vaudeville circuits for years and helped me immensely.

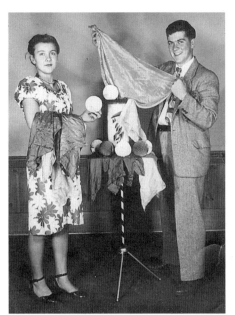

He taught me, got me shows, and helped me build a much better act. A lot of the equipment was from his own old vaudeville days, things he sold me for a trifle. I paid him thirty five dollars for several great boxes of magical props, which should have had a value of several hundred. He spent hours with me to help me learn to use the stuff and improve my abilities to the point where I was able to get paid shows for decidedly more than a roll of dimes. Dad had a fit when I told him I had purchased the equipment, but Mother calmed him, she seemed to understand how much it meant to me. Later, when I began to make money for performing, he relaxed - some.

The first performances I gave with the new act after the Cape Review were for U.S.O. Clubs in Hyannis, Falmouth, and one up Onset way. A man from a local paper saw me and asked if I would play some theatres which his son owned in Maine and New Hampshire. For money! Would I? Some negotiations with my parents, and lil' green-as-grass sixteen year old Benny The Great was on a train, headed for Keezer Falls, Maine. Had tricks, would travel! It was wonderful, I appeared in six different theatres in small towns like Rangely Lakes, Maine and Gorham, New Hampshire (which I later learned had been settled and named by a former Cape man) where the patrons were as unused to live entertainment as I was to being on stage. The owner drove me around, and when we were late for one performance, they stopped the main movie, I did my act, and then the movie was started again. It was strange, to set up behind a movie screen while the short subjects were playing, lighting the rear area with flickering Laurel and Hardy shenanigans.

I stayed in a rooming house, and hurrying to meet my ride to one of the shows, I left my Tux shirt, tie and shoes. When I started to dress behind the screen, I noted the lack, and worried about it to the boss.

"Don't Worry," he said, "They won't notice."

They didn't. I wore the tux jacket and pants, (and plaid cummerbund) with brown casual shoes, a colored shirt and a striped fore-in-hand tie, and the show went famously.

I 'magic-d' my way through high school, doing card tricks at parties, and school functions, and practiced my sleight-of-hand back stage at drama club rehearsals and at such places as a Fall Ball at the Hyannis Yacht Club (my date never asked me again). Boy, I must have been an exciting date, but Show Business is show business. Blackstone, I was not, but I did enjoy entertaining kids, G.I.'s, ladies' clubs and summer visitors.

My one successful Houdin-ish stunt was a rather startling handcuff escape. I did little with it until a performance for the local police, town officials and their guests. The town law had grown by then to a force of several, and relatives and friends padded out the audience. In my investigation of restraints, I had noted that the cuffs used by all the officers were of a type that I was able to escape from in reasonably short order, so I came prepared. After completing a stunt in which I apparently destroyed and then restored the Town Fish Warden's family keepsake pocket watch and plucked a rabbit from a Selectman's wife's purse, I asked the sergeant come up to the front, and "in Full View of the Audience" he snapped the cuffs on my wrists, hands behind me. I thanked him, and as he went back to his seat, I followed him down the aisle, working feverishly to remove the cuffs as I walked. It worked! As he sat down, I was able to hand him his cuffs, as the audience burst into applause! Thrill, thrill for the Magician!! Topper: The sergeant, properly aghast, said, "Good Lord, we just ordered six more pair of those things!"

ALONE, TOGETHER

Oh! How we rush,

To Join the Crush,

With Traffic at its peak,

And strain to reach,

Some Cape Cod Beach,

And sit there, cheek to cheek

My, How Things Has Changed!

I suppose it must be admitted that the Cape hasn't been totally spoiled for everybody's taste. There is after all as I write, a staggering amount of building on what little buildable land there is. In fact, the demand is so high, that perfectly good homes are being purchased, and the buildings torn down to allow larger (often much larger) houses to be built on the same ground. Yearly since just post WWII, people have been flocking to the Cape, not just for a visit, but to buy or build summer, or year round homes. It has become a heavy retirement area, and of course, maintenance workers and businesses have moved in to supply services and goods. The new people, (wash-a-shores) have brought with them from their old homes ideas of how things should be, reinforced with their town meeting votes and taxes. This has had a strong influence on changing the Cape's character. Then, too, the visitors who triple (at least) the population overnight as soon as schools let out in the spring, are with us in ponderous revolving groups far past the old Labor Day end of summer marker. I think someone let the cat out of the bag regarding the beauty of the Cape Cod Autumn.

So, now the old live-and-let-live attitude, which was a large part of the area, has changed. Home building styles and even colors are dictated by historical groups. In many communities washing can not be hung outside on a line; parking of vehicles and boats on your own property is restricted, lobster pots cannot be kept over winter in your dooryard and keeping of farm animals is prohibited. The roads have been re-engineered to accommodate the huge volume of traffic, which comes to a stand still at both canal bridges every summer and fall weekend and often results in miles long stalled lines of cars on the back roads and village centers. Walls of buildings have rendered our beautiful ocean all but invisible, except from the scattered town beaches (which during the summer charge substantial fees for parking during the day, and are are closed, and policed sometimes as early as dusk!) and strip malls and other commercial ventures replace older, gracious shopping areas in the village centers.

Reams have been written about the Cape, from vacation post cards, to works by Henry David Thoreau, Kurt Vonnegut, Norman Mailer and Benjamin Franklin's grandfather. Silvia Plath and Edna St. Vincent Millay are among many who have spoken of the peninsular in verse, and even Helen Keller felt the flavor of the place and wrote about it. The area is, of course, featured in legend and song and lends itself as a location for countless movies. It is the destination for hundreds of bus tours, and featured on travel brochures from coast to coast, and overseas. The sun still sparkles off the ocean waves and the unique salt musty smell of the air after a storm hasn't changed. The white sand which lays in wide strips of beach on the south shore (here and there along the rocky bay side and on the Atlantic side, sometimes as dunes, stretched out below eroded sand cliffs, or as long barrier reefs) is still there, although winter storms sometimes change things drastically. There are still a few spots where you can get the idea of what was once the typical Cape village (now overly gentrified). Maybe it's the essence of freedom that's missing or the times when you could go for months without seeing anyone you didn't know. Or, it may be that stirring up things past puts a golden sheen on times gone by.

One summer evening when I was about fourteen, I rode my bike to Dennisport, where a circus had set up and performed. Evening work at the pharmacy had prevented me from seeing the show, but I thought perhaps I could join in the tear-down procedure as local boys often did as much for the adventure as for the small amount of pay. Too late, most of the props and equipment was already on the big trucks, and the big top, (well, not that big, it was only a one ring show,) was being rolled as I arrived. I was standing there watching the windup of the packing, when out of the corner of my eye, I saw a section of woods at the side of the field move. As

I looked closer, I realized it was the show's elephant, freed from his night's labor at both performing and lifting heavy equipment during the dismantling. He was roaming, unrestricted at the edge of the lot, feeding on clumps of grass, and nuzzling the scrub oaks. Watching its huge shadow-like shape, strolling around freely, outlined in the headlights of the transport vehicles and just a few yards from where I was standing, was strangely satisfying. I stayed and watched it until the keeper approached and coaxed the big docile beast into his traveling van. Today, there is hardly a vacant lot on the Cape to hold a one ring circus, or a ragbag carnival. Even if an open field was available, local restrictions and regulations would no doubt prevent them from setting up. Oh, well, I missed the circus, but I did see the elephant.

Our own dooryard circus quite often had all three rings operational: what with the kids and with Uncle Ray living in for a spell (he used to play cowboys with me while the latest batch of chips were draining on brown paper). Nana got a job caring for an old lady up the street, and moved in for a while, and did some porch time chomping happily on some of Dad's bountiful cucumber crop. She would sit in the old rocker, and Dad would set a bushel basket of cukes near her, and a salt shaker and paring knife. Nana would cut off an end, salt, and eat - skin and all. She loved them. After a small but messy fire in

the kitchen, Powell T., an old friend of Dad's moved into an empty bed in the attic (I think he was at that time having trouble with his wife, because he lived just down the street and around the corner, but for a spell there, he didn't go home). He was a real talented guy, drew us kids lots of cartoons, and showed us how to play the musical saw. He could also eat fire, just like the guys in the sideshow! One show was all we got, though, as with a huge belch of flaming gasoline he smoked up the just-repaired kitchen ceiling, nearly started a second fire, and Mother had a fit. We were promptly shipped off to Nana's home in Salem until things got settled down.

Powell did a second stint at the house (the second house this time) when he helped Dad design and build cabinets for Grandmother's old kitchen. They painted the doors a burnt orange, which didn't please Mother much, but used wood from an old table for the counters, which did please her. She said she was sure she had the only black walnut countertop in the village. Powell was a boat builder, among his other talents, and used his skills to cut and join the doors and counter as well as could be done in that old kitchen, where we kids used to have marble races from one end of the room to the other. It had such a slant that the marbles worked up a good speed on the way across. Babies learning to walk had a difficult time hiking up hill from the low side to the high side.

Nancy and Olive's friends from next door and across the street were very often present after school, Harold and Frenchie would swing by, and of course, whatever pets we had tended to join us in the house whenever possible: dogs, cats, and even Sammy the Goat.

One fall Sunday, just after Halloween, Frannie Sullivan was in the yard, with his two horses, the little kids were spinning around on the wagon wheel merry-go-round. Sammy was unhappily on a chain because he tended to knock the smaller kids down - all in the spirit of fun, but they didn't like it. There seemed to be more than usual commotion, partly because a skunk wandered out of the woods, and was promptly surrounded (at a distance) by various sized children. A girl we knew rode up on her horse, followed, slowly, by her mother in their car. They were moving, and wanted to sell the horse. We took turns trying the horse while our mother, and her mother talked. Several of us, individually, went in to get Father out to have a look. He was hugely disinterested in buying a horse, and would not budge. He must have had the flu, because he was sitting in the living room, reading the Sunday paper (usually an evening project, daylight was for working).

He was so engrossed in the daily ball scores, or something that he didn't hear Richard Hall, the across the street neighbor come through the kitchen and into the dining room. Mr. Hall saw Father sitting in the next room, and:

"Doc, your house is on fire!"

Dad recognized the voice, suspected a joke, and didn't look up from his paper.

"Well, put the damn thing out then Doc, you're the fire chief!" He was.

The sounds of Chief Hall pulling down our flaming curtains and thoroughly stamping out the flames and sparks made Dad drop his paper, but surprise kept him rooted to his chair. A cardboard jack-o-lantern had caught fire. This window was closed, but a breeze in the room had swung the curtain into the flames. It created enough heat so than one of the old glass panes softened and bowed out (we left it like that for years.)

"Much obliged, Doc, "said Father. They talked a while, and the Chief left. Dad finished his paper.

And I've finished my book.

ART AND NATURE

I wrote a poem years ago,
About a man with hair like snow.
Now, mornings when I shave, I see,
The man I wrote about, is me!

I wrote once of an old man's face,
Describing every line, in place.
The self-same wrinkled furrowed brow,
I look at in the mirror now.

How wondrous, that verse and rhyme,
Can all come true with passing time,
And Mother Nature, for her part,
Has learned so well to copy art.

Thacher

This book was designed and typeset by Nancy Viall Shoemaker of West Barnstable Press with the able assistance of Ellery Curran and Jess Creaven. The typefaces used were: Bookman Old Style, designed in 1936 (for the text as used here); Friz Quadrata, designed in 1965 (for chapter titles); and Frutiger, designed in 1976 (for graphic credits).

The graphics on pages 20, 94, and 174 are woodcuts by Thomas Bewick (1752-1828). Pages 126, 127, and 138 feature pen and ink drawings by Jack Viall (the typesetter's father). Milton Welt of Harwich was kind enough to permit reproduction of his watercolor of the Harwich Exchange Building on page 150.